DAILY READINGS FROM
W. E. SANGSTER

DAILY READINGS
FROM
W. E. SANGSTER

Edited by
FRANK CUMBERS

London
EPWORTH PRESS

FIRST PUBLISHED IN 1966
SECOND IMPRESSION 1966
THIRD IMPRESSION 1968

© EPWORTH PRESS 1966

Book Steward
FRANK H. CUMBERS

SBN 7162 0088 0

Printed in Great Britain
by Ebenezer Baylis & Son Ltd.
The Trinity Press, Worcester, and London

FOREWORD

FRIENDS and admirers of W. E. Sangster, for whom Mr Clifford Morris's *A Sangster Anthology** is a treasured possession, will know that I paid affectionate tribute therein to this great Methodist and preacher. The present book is a very willing response to requests which have been reaching Epworth House for a book of daily readings; and that this has necessitated a re-reading of everything that Dr Sangster wrote, has proved, of course, the kind of duty that loses itself in the joy. I have realized that his message is as alive and relevant as ever. His writings touch upon most of the tendencies and concerns with which we are familiar today; the call of 'outreach' is not a South Bank invention as Wesley's writings would prove, let alone Sangster's! (See the reading for September 20: 'The Church Must Invade Society' and many others.)

I have made it my aim to offer a comprehensive selection of his writings, and not merely to gratify my own taste and pleasure—though for practical purposes, the two tasks would be almost synonymous. For some, the sort of emphasis on 'the blood' revealed in the reading for November 2, might prove distasteful; but any who found it so would clearly not know nor remember the awe-ful stress and emphasis conveyed by his voice, and by the gestures of the 'expressive and beautiful hands' of which his son speaks.† Again, there is sometimes a certain naïveté in some passages; but those who did not know our friend must accept our testimony that this was perfectly natural and often very moving. I never heard, but can well imagine, his famous offertory prayer, "From us ... to You ... with love.'

Paul Sangster tells how his father 'revelled' in words.‡ The June 22 reading offers at its beginning an example of the tremendous impression which sheer simplicity can reach. Language was for him truly a supple instrument—but he loved the long resounding multisyllables as well. I cannot find proof that he really did utter the famous sentence 'On this subject I entertain a modicum of dubiety' —but as a Sangsterian rendering of 'I'm not sure' it has something of an authentic ring!

Much of what appears in this book comes from his sermons, and no one who heard him preach will ever forget it. He *believed* in preaching; would that this belief were more vibrant and keen in

* Epworth Press, 1964.
† *Doctor Sangster*, p 273.
‡ Ibid., p 272.

some quarters today! His son quotes a correspondent in the *Church of England Newspaper:**

Ihave no difficulty in understanding where Dr Sangster's power lies. It lies in his passion, is terrible sense of urgency. It lies in the identification of his message with himself. As I sat spellbound, listening to him, I felt an overwhelming impression—'oppression' would be the exact word—of two things (1) that I was listening to a man speaking from another world, to a visitant from some other sphere, and (2) his words were visible as well as audible. They were *things* as well as sounds. It was as though his spare physical frame were dissolving into words.

It is fortunate that so much of his philosophy of and his feeling for preaching has been made permanent in *The Craft of the Sermon* and *The Approach to Preaching*, and that these books are readily available for all who would follow him.

*   *   *

Above all, it has been deeply moving, from the vantage-point of hindsight, to read certain passages in which Will Sangster spoke of the endurance of pain and suffering to the glory of God and to His use in His wise purposes. *Surely no preacher or writer has been more fully called upon to underwrite words which he had uttered or set down in days of health and vigour.* For November 14 we quote such a passage, wherein he turns to his readers with

Will you plead a physical disability, with Paul and Clifford and Helen Keller and Frances Ridley Havergal standing at His side?

Whenever our eyes fall upon those words, we shall want to insert in the roll of that gallant company the name of William Edwin Sangster —to have known whom is to be possessed by a sense of deep privilege; and whom to have 'lost awhile' is to be conscious that life here has lost a zest, an enjoyment, an inspiration which was rich and bracing.

My own hope and wish is that the quiet reading of these passages may give some sense of the personality of this man. His own wish would be rather that his words might point people to the Jesus in Whom he so delighted. These aims and objects are happily not irreconcilable—indeed, in the quiet prayerful atmosphere of early morning calm or of evening peace, they may very well be fused.

FRANK CUMBERS

* Ibid., p 274.

DAILY READINGS FROM
W. E. SANGSTER

I cannot promise you, in the coming year, a new set of circumstances. Indeed, I anticipate, for myself and for you, difficulties and disappointments and obstacles and some pain—for that is life. No year has yet dawned which did not contain them, and, if such a year did come, it might be debilitating to the soul. But, in the name of Him Who sits upon the Throne, I promise you that if you will receive Him into your heart, and if you will submit to His Lordship over you, you can have a new heart, a new life, and therefore, a new birth. I cannot beckon you away from the flinty path upon which some of you walk. I am not commissioned to do so. Those who follow Christ must travel at times 'by stony paths and rugged ways'. But I do promise you, even in grey times, new life in God.

Paul said: 'If any man is in Christ, he is a new creature . . .' Billy Bray declared on the day of his conversion, 'I remember this, that everything looked new to me, the fields, the cattle, the trees. I was like a new man in a new world'. Temple Gairdner went from Trinity College, Oxford, the morning after his surrender to Christ and ordered an illuminated text for his wall: 'Behold, I make all things new'. All things new? This would be great news if it were true. Can He take the monotony away from life? Can He make it fresh and bright and thrilling? Yes. He can do all that. He can give you a new world, with new delights and new comforts, and new hopes and new ends. No! not by changing your external world, but by changing *you*.

Westminster Sermons (vol. ii), pp 32–3, 30

The only time we have is *now*. It is literally true to say that 'now is the acceptable time' in the sense that it is the only time you can possibly accept. It is in the very nature of time to come to you moment by moment. Somebody tried once to scare Will Rogers, the cowboy philosopher, by asking him 'If you had only forty-eight hours to live, how would you spend them?' Will Rogers replied: 'One at a time'.

You can only accept time as it comes. Therefore, in *that* sense, now is the acceptable time. It is the present you have. How are you spending time now? What could happen before this service comes to a close?

. . . Listen! God's forgiveness is now. Now! Isn't that a wonderful announcement to make? Years of sin—forgiven in a moment! Is it possible? Is that a credible statement? Does that make sense in a moral universe?

I do not know whether that makes sense in your idea of a moral universe, but I say that it is the gospel. God's forgiveness is *now*. For Jesus Christ's sake, He meets penitence with pardon, and He meets it *now*.

> *In wonder lost, with trembling joy*
> *We take the pardon of our God;*
> *Pardon for crimes of deepest dye,*
> *A pardon bought with Jesu's blood:*
> *Who is a pardoning God like Thee?*
> *Or who has grace so rich and free?*

Westminster Sermons (vol. ii) pp 23–4

In the World . . .

    Do I speak the truth?

    Am I a man of the strictest honesty?

    Do I pay my debts?

    Do I fake my income tax returns?

    Do I swear?

    Do I tell suggestive stories?

    In my relations with the other sex, am I pure in deed?

                                  word?

                                  thought?

Where I Work . . .

    Am I known as a Christian where I work?

    Is Christ loved or, at least, more respected at my business place because of the way I live? Or have people looked at me to see Him and been disappointed?

    Are some people outside the Church because I am inside?

    If I have concealed my discipleship is it because

I am afraid that my life would not sustain my profession?

    ashamed of Christ?

    just a coward?

> *Ashamed of Jesus? Sooner far*
> *Let evening blush to own a star . . .*
> *And O may this my Glory be,*
> *That Christ is net ashamed of me!*

O God,

it is strange how low one can fall who professes to walk in Thy ways, and how separate a man can keep the different parts of his life.

    I would be *one* person: *Thy* person

    Help me, for Jesus Christ's sake,   Amen.

                                      A Spiritual Check-up

The ancient Hebrew prophets often began their announcements by saying 'Thus saith the Lord'. How did they know? What made them sure? Certainly, many of the things they said were piercing in their spiritual penetration, and amaze us still though twenty-six centuries have passed by.

God speaks in the spirit of man, and those who meditate long on holy things learn how to disentangle the Voice of God from all the other voices which speak inside us. God says 'Be still, and know that I am God', but only those who have tried to make themselves still, and listen, realize what a babel goes on within. Memory, fear, hope . . . all of them talk in turn, and sometimes they all talk together! It's pandemonium let loose. The psychologist could give a neat explanation of every voice one hears.

But (in those whose joy over the years it has been to think on God), another voice awakes on occasion, as quiet as some of the others are strident, and bearing a strange assurance with it. This voice does not argue, or bleat, or natter. It speaks with authority and makes you certain that this isn't you. It is an awesome experience and leaves one in no doubt that God *does* speak in the spirit of man. . . . Those who have the experience are not deluded, and many of them have read enough psychology to be on their guard against the obvious errors. Nor is God a respecter of persons. It isn't only to prophets and saints that He speaks. With enough faith to listen and enough patience to persist, *you* might hear this Voice—personal, penetrating and deeply persuasive.

'But any maniac could claim to hear the Voice of God', the incredulous will say . . . Of course. We know that also. That is why we check the guidance which comes from the Voice within by the likeness of God revealed in Jesus Christ.

The Little Book of Sermons, pp 96–7

In the nature of things, a printed sermon is a poor substitute for the preached word. There is a divine 'mystique' in worship —in the setting of which our preaching is done—which cannot permeate a printing press. The majority of preachers—and I belong to their number—neither read nor recite their sermons. They go steeped in prayer and with their thoughts shaped and marshalled, their illustrations ready, a clear conviction how they will begin and end—but the actual phrasing they command in the moment of its utterance. They know by long and ineffable experience that there is a 'plus of the Spirit' which no human skill can command—something God adds in the hour itself, which is born of His blessing on the prayers of people and preacher alike. It measures, I suppose, the length of a pause. It adds its own overtones and nuances. It leads you to say *some* things, at least, you had not intended, to linger here and speed there. . . . There are, indeed, times when the Holy Spirit seems to 'take over', and the preacher has that sublime experience of being just 'spoken through'.

How can *that* go into print? It just can't. All that I can do from the notes which survive is to set down the theme, and give the substance of what was said, and hope that the condescending Grace of God, which owned the word in its utterance, may be able to make some use of it when it is read.

Westminster Sermons (vol. i), Introduction, pp viii–ix

[*Would not such a word send all worshippers to God's House with deep, affectionate and fervent prayers for the preacher?—Ed.*]

Isn't it a fact that some Christians seem to live at a higher spiritual level than others? There are people who go to church on Sunday, and may even put in a regular religious meeting in the week; but there is nothing about them to distinguish them from people who have no interest in religion at all. It is true that they don't curse or tell bawdy stories, but they don't stand out in any positive way. People could work with them for months and not notice anything special about them. They worry, fret, get irritable, show pride and jealousy, and even lose their temper now and then, just like the people who laugh at religion.

But there are other Christians who shine. They don't *try* to shine: they just shine. It is an event to meet them. When they come into a room, it is like the light being turned on. They seem to have some secret of inner happiness, of poise, of patience, and an inexhaustible capacity for love. They never speak ill of anyone else; they praise people who surpass them and do it with complete sincerity; they seldom talk of themselves and they listen when you are talking to them as though your thoughts were the most interesting thoughts they had ever heard. They are quietly strong and, for the things they believe, one feels that they could be terribly brave. They may not be clever, or 'smart', or 'dominant personalities', but they take hold of you and, in some unselfconscious way, they leave an impression of utter goodness. Without knowing it, they put an ache in you to have this quality of life as well.

Can ordinary people be like that? If that is holiness, it is the loveliest thing in all the world.

Holiness (Pharos Paper) pp 3–4

He wrote no book: He formed no creed: He framed no code. This was His method; we have it in the text 'And He chose twelve, that they might be with Him'. Ah! that is it. That they might be with Him. The religion of Jesus is as wide as life, and as long as life. You get the secret of Jesus only by personal contact with Him. You may read the book, learn the creed and keep the law, and still miss *Him*, because it is a matter of the Spirit. That is why we say the religion of Jesus is caught not taught. It is more a blessed contagion than a science. It is a divine infection that spreads from heart to heart. You can get it only by getting near to Christ Himself, and when you have it you can't keep it: somebody else will get it too. It permeates the whole life: it irradiates the entire being: it peeps out of the eyes and puts a new song upon the lips. I do not deprecate the study of the Book. I stress it. I do not minimize the importance of the creed. I emphasize it. I do not neglect the law. I keep it. But it is neither of book nor creed nor law that I would ask. This is my question—Do you live the life? Is there in you that quality of being that draws to higher things? Does contact with you stir other people to holy thoughts? Could it be said of you as it was said of the Apostles, 'They took knowledge of them that they had been with Jesus'? There is a type of person known to medical science as 'carriers'. They are capable of spreading an infection without being, in a sense, infected themselves. There is no counterpart to these people in the spiritual realm. People cannot catch the religion of Jesus from you unless you have it yourself.

Why Jesus Never Wrote a Book, pp 15–16

I have lived all my life among people who praised 'the open mind'. Tolerance they taught as the great virtue. Any dogmatic insistence on one's beliefs was frowned upon. A little pursing of the lips and a barely perceptible shake of the head, and you were made to understand that it wasn't done. I want to put in a covert plea for the closed mind. An ever-open mind, like an ever-open drain, can become the receptacle of much rubbish. If any real progress is to be made in the life of the individual, or the life of the race, there must be some clear measure of value; some definite body of belief; some fixed standard of behaviour.

The art of navigation depends on the existence of fixed points from which the sailor can take a bearing. Granted those, he can find his way. The trackless ocean does not bewilder him. I am on a voyage across the ocean of life, and I must have fixed points from which to take a bearing. Without those fixed points I shall not voyage: I shall drift and—as like as not—shall drift upon the rocks. On some things I cannot afford to have an open mind. I cannot doubt my chart, my compass, or the stars. My mind is pleasantly open on thousands of other things, but the fixed points are not there for my taste and approval: they are there for my guidance and my respect.

Here are some of the fixed points on the voyage of life. I believe in God. I believe in the love of God. I believe in the trustworthiness of Christ: that He was the Authentic Word of the Father: that He lived, died, and rose again. Mercy I believe in—and judgment. These are not opinions with me. These are convictions. By these I steer . . . Call me dogmatic if you will. But I am on a perilous voyage, and I should be a fool to doubt my chart.

The Little Book of Sermons, pp 72–3

I have a letter before me from a man of seventy-three. He says 'I have tried for years to hear the voice of God. I have never heard it. Is it all illusion?' He does not know how to listen. He seems to expect a human voice. To quote the poet to him and say 'God speaks in silences' won't help him; it sounds silly. What is the answer? How does a man listen in prayer to the living God?

The prophets often said 'Thus saith the Lord'. They claimed to have received special messages from God. How did they receive them? How did they distinguish these messages from thoughts of their own? The saints often claimed that God spoke to them—sometimes in quite precise terms. People of our own acquaintance use similar expressions. Maybe we do ourselves. When we make these claims in the hearing of unbelievers or half-believers. . . . 'What does he mean?' they wonder to themselves. 'How does God speak to him?'

There begins the difficulty. Many voices sound within our mind. People who have never practiced listening in the silence are astonished, when they begin, at the pandemonium of voices inside. At times it sounds like babel. Fear, hope, memory, ambition, all find voice inside us and sometimes they even talk together, and the high skill of this interior listening is to learn how to know the voice of God from all the other voices. . . . It isn't simple. One must be prepared for patience and practice, and resolve never to use the words 'God said to me . . .' or 'I was guided . . .' (or any similar expression) without great care and reserve.

The Pattern of Prayer, pp 20–1

In the Home

What am I like at home?

Do these who know me best, believe in me most?

Am I thoughtful for those who are serving me every day?

Do I criticize the Church and other Christians in front of the children?—heedless or careless that it is nearly the most damning thing I could do for them.

In the morning half-awake, and in the evening over-tired, am I still a Christian, courteous, grateful, good-humoured?

Do I acknowledge God (guests or no guests) with grace before meals; and do I ever call the family to prayer?

Do I think of the home as mine or God's?

Am I as free as I can be with hospitality—not chiefly to those who can ask me back but those who can't—

the boy in lodgings?

the nurse off duty?

the lonely and the poor?

Gracious Father,

I am ashamed to be guilty of discourtesy at home which would be unthinkable elsewhere, and that where I am loved most, I sometimes act worst.

I mean to end all that.

Help me, for Christ's sake.   Amen.

A Spiritual Check-up

Is He able? May *all* come? Can He deal with *every* phase of human need? There are those whose difficulties arise out of their body, the sick, the unemployed, the sex-obsessed. Can He deal with all these? In the days of His flesh, He had a special care for the bodies of men. Did His concern with those things end when a cloud received Him out of their sight? Or does He still heal the sick, feed the hungry, and cast out the demon of uncontrollable passion from the heart of tempted men? There are those whose problem is largely a problem of the mind: the worried man, the futile and frustrated members of society, the people whose minds are haunted by fears, and the bereaved and broken hearted. . . .

When we add the complex spiritual ills of our poor race, the egotisms and the jealousies, the lovelessness and the loneliness, the absence of prayer, the pride, hypocrisy and vanity; when we add also the little sins, which are so large in their entail of evil, the idle gossip, the tainted hint, the self deceit and the limited consecration, we wonder if even Jesus can possibly meet them all. We look at the infinite variety of human need and ask 'Is He able?' . . . From the laden souls of thousands who have turned wistful eyes and weary steps to Jesus, this urgent imperative question bursts, 'Is He able?' and back from the released, redeemed, exultant souls of as many thousand more crashes the triumphant answer,

> . . . . He *is* able,
> He is willing, doubt no more.

He is Able, pp 10–11

The saints believe utterly. Their faith in God's love and wisdom is so deep that it seems to become the basis of all else in their beautiful lives. Anyone reading of their absorbing attention to God, and their complete obedience to Him, might well conclude that neither is wonderful the moment you realize the depth and strength of their faith. Who would not adore and obey a God clearly seen in the lineaments of Jesus Christ, and in whose power and love one had unshaken trust?

But how did they get that trust? It is hard, in the analysis of sanctity, to decide which grace came before which . . . To ponder long on whether faith preceded love, or love preceded faith, overlooks the fact that they grow together in the soul and each aids each. Sanctity is really a single jewel. . . . yet it is clear that the facet of faith was cut early on the rough stone. So much else seems shaped around it. . . . Some tremulous essay in faith must have gone before the earliest affirmation of love, or how else could the love be directed? Some primacy must be given to faith. How did it grow into the unshakeable trust which it becomes in the soul of the saint? It would be mistaken to assume too readily that it came to all the saints in the same way. Some seem to have received it in childhood and never to have doubted at all. With others, it was the fruit of titanic conflicts. . . . But—howsoever it came—they are mighty in faith. They believe! They believe in every particle of their being.

The Pure in Heart, p 210

The purpose of God for man is to make him holy. Not happiness first, and holiness if possible, but holiness first and bliss as a consequence.

But the unreflecting man is not sure that he wants to be holy. He is not certain, to begin with, that he knows what the term means, and he is almost certain that he does not like what he thinks it stands for. To him the word seems musty, and hints at otherworldliness and repression carried to unnatural heights.

... The word eludes precise definition amongst scholars ... but something in the soul of man recognizes and responds to the holy even while he cannot give the concept clear expression. Lacking a neat definition, holiness, none the less, lies at the heart of all devotion.

The best way for a man to approach the study of holiness is not first to seek a definition ... but to gaze steadily and long at those in whom, by general consent, this quality appears, and then to consult his own heart and mind on the reactions which he feels. Let him gaze most of all at Jesus Christ. Let him examine the lives of the saints. Let him think on those obscure disciples he has met on the road of life who seemed always to have the breath of God about them. Let him be unhurried and teachable.

And he will then find that, so far from holiness repelling him, it will fascinate and awe and subdue him. Adoration will stir in his soul. He will wonder at all God can do with human nature and sink to his knees in marvel and surprise. Unutterable longings will awake in him and he will catch himself shaping the question 'Even me?'

The Pure in Heart, p x

I was in a Women's Meeting the other day. It was lovely to hear those good women warm the church and warm their own hearts by singing their choruses. They sang with special fervour one entitled: 'A little talk with Jesus makes it right, all right'.

Would that do as a definition of prayer?

It would in a way, and God forbid that I should seem so technical about prayer that I left folk supposing it was like a doctor's prescription, and would be wrong if even one element was omitted, but truth compels me to affirm that 'a little talk with Jesus' could be very self-centred, very narrow, and (among other omissions) leave no room for listening at all.

Some folk speak as though the only thing required to make prayer holy is to be sure that it is sincere.

But the test is not stern enough. We can be sincere and selfish. . . . Prayer, properly understood, is not just petition or a little talk with Jesus, or the outpouring of selfish sincerities; it has range, and richness, and sweep. . . . A child can use it, but the profoundest saint cannot bottom it. It is, indeed, the highest activity of which mortals are capable. It is learning to know God at first hand. It is the sovereign way to holiness. It is the royal road to assurance.

. . . What would it be worth to you in this atomic age to be utterly *sure* of God? What would it be worth to you when you are beaten by sin and 'weary of passions unsubdued' to feel the conquering power of God mounting within your soul?

Prayer is the way. All progress in religion centres in prayer.

Teach us to Pray, pp 12–14

For people who *do* believe in the Christian God, evangelism is a duty and privilege so plain, so incontrovertible, that all talk of 'relevance' is a half-vulgar intrusion of the utilitarian in a realm where it cannot apply. One could as soon enquire of a son concerning the 'relevance' of his love for his mother, or a lover for the beloved, or a great scientist for his devotion to truth. One could as sensibly enquire of people bound together in Christian marriage of the 'relevance' of their mutual vows. . . . [There are] things which soar above utilitarian tests and are right in themselves and not simply because of ends they serve.

The proclamation of the gospel is such a task. It is right in itself. . . . The preaching of the gospel has never seemed relevant to unbelievers. . . . But it has to be proclaimed! Not apologized for, or watered down, or twisted in the interests of immediate relevance, or half-altered to suit the 'time-spirit' or disguised to get it past an unbeliever's guard. It has to be preached—in all its seeming irrelevance; above the cat-calls and sneers of those who hate or despise it; in the face, also, of the amused contempt of those whose vanity leads them to feel superior to it. 'I, if I be lifted up from the earth' said Christ 'will draw all men unto me'.

Let us lift Him up, therefore!—in the atomic age, as in all others, and leave God to prove His relevance to those who will some day profit by our faith.

Let me Commend, pp 13–14

. . . If I turn from my problems to my *sorrows*, I find it just as dark among those who deride religion, and just as bright about my Lord. I turn to the purveyors of religion without revelation; the people who believe that we can save ourselves, and say 'I am in deep trouble, I have lost a dear one'. Or: 'I have suffered the heaviest reversals in my financial affairs'. Or: 'I have learned the gravest news from the doctor'. Or: 'I have been cruelly dealt with by a man I thought my friend'. I pour out my heart to them, and they say, 'Well, you must cultivate other interests'. Fancy saying that to a man who has lost his wife. . . . Or they say: 'You have just got to put up with it'—which one knew already, but craved for a crumb of comfort in the meanwhile.

Perhaps they answer; 'We have all been through that, and you must take your turn with the rest'. Nor do some of them conceal their conviction that they never made half the fuss about it that you are making. And if I go further and expose to them my very heart; if I say 'I dread the thought of this hydrogen bombing . . .' some of them say 'Cheer up, it may never happen. Besides, some of the bombs may be duds!' And that is all. Little chips of worldly wisdom; a flickering match struck in the dark. They do not know. They have not seen a great light.

So I turn to Jesus. 'Lord', I say, 'I am in trouble—' And before I can go farther, He says 'Come unto me . . . and I will give you rest'. 'Lord' I continue, 'I will keep nothing back. This hydrogen bombing haunts me. Have You no word for me in these dread times?'

And He says 'Work for disarmament but, in the meantime, be not afraid of them which kill the body and after that have no more that they can do'.

Westminster Sermons (vol. ii), pp 6–7

At the Altar

Am I a converted man?

If I cannot recall any great spiritual experience or unusual visitation of God to my life, have I, at least, given myself to Him without any reserve?

Having given myself to Him, have I ever drawn back?

Do I live day by day in conscious dependence on Him and alert to the guidance of Heaven?

Do I find time early in every day for Bible Study?

Unhurried prayer?

Quiet listening to God?

Do I love God's Day?

His Word?

His holy Table?

Do I seek fellowship with other Christians in the week?

A Spiritual Check-up

This book has been written during the period in which I forsook my home to share the life of bombed-out people in a public air-raid shelter. . . . When the last incendiary had been put out and the last group of homeless people received and made welcome, I filled the hours of the vigil which had still to be kept by thinking on perfection. If that seems a little mad to some who read this, I can only reply that it was part of the way in which I kept sane.

. . . There is an experience of God the Holy Spirit, available for all who will seek it with importunity, which imparts spiritual power far above the level enjoyed by the average Christian; which inspires a caring God-like love different in kind and degree from the affections of normal nature; which communicates to the eager soul the penetrating power of holiness. No book can give this experience. It belongs to the secret intercourse of the soul with God. It lies at the very heart of personal religion. Its wide reception would transform the Church and shake the world.

. . . Within the covers of this volume an effort is made to examine part of the teaching of a man* who enjoyed this experience and who passionately sought for more than fifty years to share it with others. Some of his explanations now seem unsatisfactory and even obstructive if overpressed. But my deepest hope is that, jettisoning some of the explanations, I might myself share the experience—and that others might be quickened in the quest for it too. Faith and prayer are the ordained means, and progress may be measured by one's progress in humility. . . . Man's chief problems are with himself. The conquest of Everest, Antarctica, Cancer and Inter-Planetary Travel are all small beside the conquest of pride, greed, selfishness, hate . . .

The Path to Perfection, Prefaces to the 1st and 5th Editions

* John Wesley.

It depends what you mean by 'proof'. 'Proof' is of various kinds. The proof most people prefer is scientific proof . . . but that kind of proof is possible only in a very limited area of life. Mathematical proof is very satisfying in its own sphere. When the calculations confirm themselves in various ways, it leaves a sense of certainty which barely admits of doubt. But, again, that kind of proof is limited to its own world. In maths, all the factors are really 'given'.

Logic has its own kind of proof. . . . But many logical 'proofs' get upset by a serious challenge to the first statements. The major part of life is all outside the possibility of laboratory, mathematical and logical proofs. Honour, justice, loyalty, love (which are among the strongest forces in the universe) can none of them be 'proved' in any of these ways. Nor can you put God into a test-tube. Most life depends upon enormous probabilities. . . . The arguments for the existence of God can't be worked out on a laboratory bench or by logic or maths; yet collectively they amount to an enormous probability, and if—on the probability—people will pray and experiment, they can have a personal certainty which allows them to say 'I know'.

Give God a Chance, p 18

I used to talk often with a young lady whose conversation was constantly interlarded with the phrase. . . . She was young, beautiful, happily married, in most comfortable circumstances, and with a wide circle of loyal friends . . . but she had no children. Two children had been born to her but died at birth, and her doctors did not encourage the hope of another child. She was full of bitterness. She said the experience had made her an atheist, but with strange inconsistency, she hated the God whom she declared did not exist. 'What have I done to deserve this?' she would ask with concentrated bitterness and never pause for a reply. This personal disappointment proved to her beyond a peradventure that there was no God in all the wide world.

I was tender with her sorrow but I could never get her to attend when I turned her phrase in other directions. She was beautiful. What had she done to deserve that? She had the love of a devoted husband. Nicer women had been passed by. She was well-to-do largely by her father's generosity. What had she done to deserve that? Despite her disappointments in maternity, she had wonderful health, friends, a keen mind . . . and for all these things she had done—just nothing. They were gifts which she barely noticed in her spurning accusations of a God who mis-managed His world.

Unhappily, this self-tortured soul is losing the good things she has. Bitterness is poison. It begins to affect her looks. Her husband is unhappy and her friends less devoted. . . . Her cure . . . is to go and attend to that Strange Man upon the Cross. No one ever loved as He loved, served as He served, nor suffered as He suffered. . . . He never says 'What have I done to deserve this?' He says to all tormented souls, 'Come unto Me . . . and I will give you rest'.

The Little Book of Sermons, pp 88–9

We love Him because He first loved us. God started it. . . .
No man can or will ever explain *why* God loves us.

> He hath loved, He hath loved us,
> Because—*He would love**

He chose to—just because He *is* love. He is such a God! Seeing
the love at the heart of the universe, the saint sees the tragedy
which is there also. . . . God loves, as only God *can* love, and
men are heedless of it. Even when men hear of that love, they
do not realize it. The cost to God never becomes clear in their
sin-dulled minds. The cynic† says: 'God will forgive; that is
His business', and it is plain that no one could soil his lips with
such blasphemy who had really seen the five wounds and
watched the dripping blood.

So the world drifts heedless past the Cross . . . and the
world's Saviour cries through His silence: 'Is it nothing to you,
all ye that pass by?'

But . . . the cross is *everything* to [the saint]. He sees as much
as mortal man can see. . . . His mortal eyes peers into the bot-
tomless abyss of the divine love. Who the crucified was, and
why He died, became clear to him when he came to Calvary.
Wonder breaks out at revelation, and rapture swells in the
saint's adoring soul. To his Saviour, he says:

> *'Tis Love! 'tis Love! Thou diedst for me!*
> *I hear Thy whisper in my heart;*
> *The morning breaks, the shadows flee,*
> *Pure, universal Love Thou art;*
> *To me, to all Thy mercies move;*
> *Thy nature and Thy name is Love.*

The Pure in Heart, pp. 241–2

---

* The same 'glorious inconsequence' of this verse is shown in Deut. 7. 7,
upon which Charles Wesley drew.—Ed.
† Heine.

But there is something else I want you to forget beside your gaucheries and your sins. I want you to forget the hurtful things that have been done *against* you. In the Lord's Prayer we say 'Forgive us our trespasses as *we* forgive those who trespass against us'. You need forgiveness yourself. 'With what measure ye mete it shall be measured to you again'. I want you to forget the sins of those who have sinned against you.

Have you been sinned against? Has somebody slandered you? Or done you the deepest injury? Are you nursing the hope of revenge in your heart?

Forget it! For your own sake and God's sake, cast it out of your heart now. However justified your resentment against another person may be, to harbour that resentment is to poison *yourself*. Be rid of that poison!

If it seems easy for me to *say* this, remember that I realize how hard it must be for some of you to *do* it. Indeed, I realize that you can't do it alone. 'This kind cometh not out but by prayer'. Only by the special help of God can you deal with these deep resentments.

But the help is available. Claim the help now! From every bit of the memory of it which is damaging for you to recall, ask God, in His mercy, to make you forget.

Westminster Sermons (vol. i), p 7

. . . If this is holiness, it is the loveliest thing in the world. Ordinary people can be like that—though it will certainly make them extraordinary. It is a gift of God. These winsome souls have not worked it up out of themselves; they received it as a present from heaven. God has no favourites. He is eager to give the gift to anyone who truly wants it, and who proves his keenness by daily putting himself in the way of its reception.

Let me tell you how to go about getting it. . . . Go over your life quietly in His white light and examine with thoroughness any habit or area of life concerning which you have any discomfort of conscience. Whatever you find of sin, surrender to God and claim forgiveness in the name of Christ.

But now fix your mind on the fact that God can do more with sin than cancel it: He can break its power. God can not only *impute* righteousness: He can *impart* it. That is, indeed, His final purpose with us—to make us saints. . . . Hold it in mind that God is both able and willing to make you holy. Murmur to yourself, as Charles Wesley was fond of doing: 'He wills that I should holy be'. Carry a picture in your mind of yourself as God could make you—good, truthful, wise, happy, poised, loving, virile—hold the picture in a yearning heart and remember that nothing but your own unwillingness can prevent it.

Holiness (Pharos Paper), pp 4–6

In the Sanctuary . . .

Do I love to go to God's House?

Do I prepare myself in heart and mind before going?

Is my chief purpose to give or to get?

Do I realize that the adoration of God is the highest activity of which I am capable?

In manner and purpose, in heart and mind; with devotion and the highest sense of privilege, do I give myself to worship?

Am I deeply loyal to the family of God, defending it from attack, never speaking ill of it myself, and ready to bear any part of the scorn the world might pour upon it?

Do I pray fervently for the purpose of God, and for those who minister in holy things, seeking to create when at public worship that very atmosphere in which it is easy for sinners to be converted, and those already in this way of life to love Thee more and more?

A Spiritual Check-up

It was with the Pharisee that our Lord came into conflict from the start. The Sadducee, through His early ministry, barely knew that He was there.

But they did on occasion, and on one occasion in particular. It was when our Lord cleansed the Temple. Jesus arrived at the Temple to find the outer courts used as a cattle and bird market, and as a place for the changing of money. The holy place was being desecrated. Instead of the decent quiet which should attend God's house, there was the hustle and scurrying and smell and cheating of an oriental bazaar. It was all done with the permission of the priests, who had their own 'rake-off' from it. They would have argued, no doubt, that the law required the sacrifices, and that it was a convenience to the people to have the birds and beasts at hand . . . and that facilities must be provided for the visitors to obtain Jewish currency when they came. They turned a blind eye to the fact that the poor were fleeced, and they lived in luxury themselves on their share of the dirty trade.

They could not turn a blind eye, however, to the action of Jesus. The iniquity and the profanity of their Temple market so overcame Him that He picked up some cords and drove the animals and traders out, and turned over the tables of the money-changers. It is one of the most terrible examples in Scripture of the 'Anger of the Lamb'. He was a marked man after that. Even the lofty Sadducees (their pockets being touched) took sinister heed of Him.

They Met at Calvary, pp 26–7

Jesus chose the Apostles to be with Him that they might see the life lived and then live it themselves. And it was the only way. His privacy must be sacrificed to it; His mind continually jarred by their inconsequential chatter concerning position and prestige. But there was no other method, because in its very essence this message was a way of life. The origin of all life is deep and mysterious, and deep and mysterious is the origin of this spiritual life as well. But its fine flower all may see. And its fine flower is a fragrant life.

Let me remind you again of one of those inimitable stories that Jesus told. There was once a man who went on a journey through a narrow mountain pass and suddenly was attacked by robbers who stripped him and flayed him and left him half dead. And a certain priest came that way. A priest! . . . Oh have no fear. All is well with this unhappy man. A priest is coming; a student of the sacred writings, a scholar of the book. And he saw the man . . . looked on him . . . and passed by!!! Then a Levite came. A Levite! . . . Take heart once more. *This* man will not fail. Is he not skilled in all the Levitical law? Is he not master of the code? And *he* saw the man . . . looked on him . . . and passed by!!! Finally came one of no position, no profound learning, no boasted birth; simple of heart and full of the spirit of love . . .

Did you say you know the Book? I am glad. Lay it to heart. Did you say you know the law? I am glad. Live in its light. But tell me, what did you do for that bruised and bleeding traveller you stumbled across on the road of life?

Why Jesus Never Wrote a Book, pp 16–17

I don't think I should ever have known the bitterness of loneliness myself if it were not for my time in the Army. My first Christmas Day in khaki gave every promise of being utter misery. Santa Claus doesn't come round and fill your stocking in the Army. It is the orderly sergeant who comes round—with other ideas in mind!

Breakfast was all gloom; most of the men in the platoon were in a hangover from the night before. Dinner was worse. It was good food spoilt by foul cooking. The officers actually waited on us (!) but they seemed to think that the only thing we wanted came out of barrels. The bawdy stories were worse than ever. I was sick in my soul, and left the mess with the food untasted, to mooch around the streets for the rest of the day. One could at least think about Bethlehem.

And then it happened! As I traipsed about in the drizzle I met a civilian who seemed to recognize me. He stopped—hesitated—spoke. Hadn't he seen me in the Methodist church? What was I doing for the day? Would I care to come home and spend the rest of the time with his family? *Would* I? And home I went! His kind wife made me as welcome as her husband. I romped with the children and sat by the fire. I ate so heartily at tea-time that I felt compelled to offer some halting explanation about having had no dinner, and I marked the birth of Jesus where all was light, and love, and joy.

I thank God for that experience. It taught me to say 'Come in'.

Methodist Magazine, 1947, p 103

What is the Christian Gospel? What precise message is the evangelist commissioned to bring? It is news of God. This news! That God has come to earth in Christ to give new life to everybody who will receive it. What He came to do, the evangelist affirms, He has done, and does still. It is life in all its fulness, abundant and eternal; it is, indeed, the very life of God Himself.

By faith—itself a gift from God—any poor, stained and stunted sinner may be united to the life of God. His old self may die. He can say 'To me to live is Christ'. He can, indeed, so have the life of God as *his* life, that it is not enough to call it the *power* of Christ, or the *help* of Christ, or even *Christ-likeness*. It is Christ Himself, not just saving him from without but actually living with; thinking, feeling willing, in the life of His consenting servant.

It is incredible—but true!

The offer is to persons, and can be accepted, therefore, only by persons, but as persons receive it, it transforms their related life and whole families may glow with the supernal life of God. Communities could be transformed. It could change the world.

Let me Commend, p 29

Is Christ able to succour us when we are worn with sickness; when every known resource of healing, spiritual, mental and medical has failed? Can He keep us brave, if not blithe; at peace, if not in joy? Is He able?

We *know* that He is able. We believe that in the same way as human parents must sometimes allow pain and discipline to press upon their dearly-beloved children, so must the gracious Father in Heaven allow pain and discipline to press upon us, not in any neglectful and unloving spirit, but for some high and holy purpose known to Him. Though He does not will the calamities, He wills the conditions in which these calamities are possible. We believe also, that when we cannot interpret the dark mystery of life, and God seems indifferent to our plea for explanations, it is not because there is no meaning in it, or because He does not know, or does not care. It is just because, as yet, our minds are too small, and we cannot take the explanation in. We have reached that stage in human development when we are able to ask the questions, but are not always able to understand the answers. God expects us to trust His love.

He is Able, p 15

There is need to examine our own hearts. Have we been loyal to our central message? Have we applied it faithfully and fearlessly in the modern world?

. . . have we failed in the proclamation of the faith? Do we still believe that all men need to be saved, or has the secularism of the world so seeped into our churches that it is tacitly accepted among us that to be a decent fellow is all that we can reasonably ask of men? . . . It is not just stupidity from which a man needs to be saved. It is sin. Man is utterly incapable of saving himself—now or at any conceivable time in the future, alone or in the mass.

We have many differences with our chief opponents in the world today, but they all centre in this. They deny the existence of God and believe that man can save himself. We assert the existence of God and deny that unaided man can ever find peace in his own soul, or peace in the world. It is no part of our purpose to disparage the achievements of modern science and technology. We are not of those who deride the machine, or deny the operations of the Holy Spirit outside the organized Church. We bless God for all that the research student has found for the blessing of mankind, and yet we still assert that all men are sinners and need to be saved. God forgive us if, failing to emphasize that, we have encouraged men to think that redemption is by human effort alone, and that there is no great loss to those who do not bow the knee 'unto the Father from whom every family in heaven and earth is named'.

Proceedings of the Eighth Ecumenical Methodist Conference,
1951, pp 73–4

With Fellow-workers for Christ

Can I work with other people? and can other people work with me?

Do I tend to dominate?—or leave the real work to others?

Do I *love* the people I am called to work with; know them intimately and at depth: clear up misunderstandings with them quickly and never criticize them to others?

Have I a secret longing always to be first? or can I truly say that I don't care who is second, third or fourth, so long as Jesus is first?

Do I want God's cause to advance, or is my chief desire that *I* should advance it?

Can I hear my colleagues praised and sincerely enjoy it?

Can I hear others praised for what I have done for God and still be more glad that it was done than grieved to be neglected?

Am I willing to take my wages in Christian service from God alone?

Am I after anything for myself?

A Spiritual Check-up

When men pondered about the love of Jesus, they wondered why He loved as He did. They never found out. They have never found out yet. Charles Wesley thought long on it and said:

> He hath loved, He hath loved us,
> *Because He would love.*

Just that! He *chooses* to.*

God's love is for nothing. So much human love is *for* something. 'Love me and I'll give you . . .' 'Give me and I'll love you . . .' 'Love me and I'll love you . . .' So barter creeps into love.

Sometimes parents (who ought to know better) sink to it. 'Be a good boy and I'll love you'. 'Pass the exam., and I'll love you'. 'Do what I say and I'll love you'. I should be bound for hell—and so would you—if God's love were like that.

God's love is for nothing. Nothing in me gave rise to it and nothing in me can destroy it. I can sin against it, but I cannot sin it away. If I choose hell—and I can—love will dog my feet as I go there. God's love is for nothing.

Let that truth sink into your mind. Say to yourself (however much you may be sunk in sin) 'He loves me. I am poor enough —but precious', but you will never be all He wants you to be until that quality of love is in you also.

In *you* also! Is it possible? After Christ died, a friend remembered a prayer He offered one day to His Father. He prayed 'that the love wherewith You loved Me may be in them' (John 17²⁶).

So it was possible! The love of God *could* be in the hearts of men.

The Greatest of These . . . , p 8

* See p 21 (January 21).

It is taken for granted by some people that it is no good praying unless you 'feel like it'. They believe that the worth of prayer depends upon our emotional keenness at the time.

So far is that from being true that the precise opposite comes nearer the truth. Our prayers are more acceptably offered when we *don't* feel like it than when we do. Nor is it hard to understand why.

When we pray because we feel like it, we are pleasing ourselves. We want to pray and we *do* pray, and our prayer is acceptable to God in the degree that our will is in harmony with Him.

But when we pray *not* feeling like it, we bring God not only the content of our prayer, but a disciplined spirit. We have kept our appointment with Him *against* inclination. We have displeased ourselves in order to please Him, and His pleasure is real indeed.

Feelings can be very sweet, and never to know the rapture of religion would be dreadful, but feelings are too unsubstantial and too variable to be the guide to our praying. Feeling fluctuates with our health, our temperaments, the weather, the news; it fluctuates also with what we eat and whom we met last. . . .! Our commerce with Heaven cannot depend upon things so fortuitous as that.

. . . If, in time past, you have prayed only when you felt like it, pause now and take a vow. Vow to keep your appointment with God whether you feel like it or not. You would not fail to keep an appointment with a fellow mortal because the inclination had ebbed when the hour of meeting had come. Courtesy would carry you there if desire didn't. Can you be less courteous with God?

Teach us to Pray, pp 15–16

Those early Methodist preachers could not have foreseen in any detail the unfolding of the centuries. . . . Of one thing only were they sure. They must preach Christ. . . . They knew less of the 'higher strategy' than any 'desert rat' on the eve of El Alamein knew of the plans of Montgomery, but they had a loyalty and it held them even in the dark. It was God's business to use their faithfulness how He would; to bring streams of social redemptiveness down from the hills of their evangelical pleading . . . and God did it! He freed the slaves, cleaned the prisons, and began the long battle for a living wage with men and women new-born of this evangelical faith. William Wilberforce, and John Howard, and the Tolpuddle Martyrs, all drank of this stream.

Let a man take the most sombre view of world events that he can. Let him—if he wishes—toy with the possibility that atomic war is only fifteen years away.* Let him conceive whole cities made desolate in a moment, and civilization, as we have known it, sponged out. . . . How would he—as a Christian—want to fill those intervening years, and on what task would he care to be engaged when that blinding flash blasted him into eternity? I have thought hard, and I can conceive of no task nearer to my heart's desire than that of following Christ myself, and of commending Him to others. I can imagine no work more worthy of our manhood and womanhood. If fulness of life matters more than length of life; if abundant life and eternal life are only two names of the same thing . . . how better can I be employed than to spread abroad His fame?

Let me Commend, pp 19–21

* 1949.

34

The future is not ours. People are fond of saying, especially to the young: 'You have the future'. Well—can you be sure of it? I hope you have, but—in the language of the bookmaker—could you call it a 'cert'?

There are few mistakes more common and more tragic than to count on the future. Cecil Rhodes planned big things; big things for his own future, and big things for Africa also, and died at forty-nine saying: 'So little done; so much to do'. Keats died at twenty-five; Shelley at thirty; Byron at thirty-six. Friends had prophesied a great future for each of them, but none of them really reached middle-age.

You cannot count with absolute confidence on tomorrow. . . . We are all mortal. There is no ground for morbidity in this; it is just plain horse-sense to look at the conditions on which we hold life here. When you take a job you accept certain conditions of contract; a month's notice either way, or a week's. There is no such contract when you accept life. A moment's notice is all you may receive.

A few years ago, in a restaurant not half a mile from here,* at the annual dinner of a certain association opposed to religion, their chairman for the year was making an after-dinner speech. . . . [He] was lampooning religion and guffawing over the vision the apostle Paul saw on the Damascus road. Presently—all the papers reported it the next morning—in the middle of a blasphemous sentence—he just went pale and sat down. He was dead. 'Heart failure' said the coroner. The notice can be as short as that.

The future is not ours.

Westminster Sermons (vol. ii), pp 22–3

---

* Westminster Central Hall.

[Wesley] believed and taught this; that, in an instant, and by a simple act of faith, perfection was 'wrought in the soul'. It was, indeed, the second of two distinct stages in the Christian experience of Salvation as he conceived it: the first consisted of justification and sanctification; the former being a change in our relations with God, our pardon and reconciliation: the latter a change in ourselves wrought by the Spirit of God. In the first stage, a new heart is given to us, so that we now love God and desire to please Him, and will not *willingly* sin against Him in anything. . . .

The second stage, with which we are now chiefly concerned, is *entire* sanctification, which comes as an immediate gift of God, entirely cleansing the heart from sin and 'slaying the dire root and seed' of it.

Wesley believed that this perfection was plainly taught in the Bible . . . he finds no lack of pertinent references capable of passing the most sensitive expositional test. . . . Wesley contended that no close student of the New Testament could deny that the doctrine had emphatic scriptural warrant. . . .*

A man perfected in the sense for which Wesley contended was still liable to infirmity, ignorance and mistake, but he was not now guilty of sin. His heart being full of love to God, 'every evil temper is destroyed: and every thought, and word, and work springs from, and is conducted to the end by, the pure love of God and our neighbour' . . . Wesley believed also that the possibility was fulfilled in multitudes of his followers. He tested hundreds who claimed this perfect love and approved their claim. He never claimed it himself. . . .

The Path to Perfection, pp 27–31

---

* Wesley quoted, *inter alia*, Matt. 5[48]; John 17[20–23]; 1 Thess. 5[23]; Gal. 2[20]; 1 John 1[7]; 1[9]; 4[17].

Some people think that faith is peculiar to religion and that it is putting blinkers over your eyes.

Faith is not peculiar to religion. It is found all through life. We use faith when we get on a bus. (The driver had 'L's up last week.) We use faith when we go into a restaurant to eat. (People have got food poisoning before now.) We use faith when we send our children to school. (The teachers may put terrible fears into their little minds.) We use a lot of faith when we get wed. (Think of the awful number of divorces!) Faith . . . faith . . . faith! All life is lived by faith. It should not surprise us that we meet the need for faith in religion.

Here is the plain fact. The Bible is quite frank on the point. It says: He who comes to God must believe that He is, and that He is a rewarder of them that seek Him (Hebrews 11[6]). Christ said 'He that does the will, shall know the doctrine' (John 7[17]). It is not 'know and do' (as we should like it) but 'do and know' —as with swimming and so much else in life.

Well . . . why not get into the water? Only experiment can issue in experience. If you really want to be sure, put this thing to the test. Pray. Talk to God, believing that He will hear you. Read the Bible: it has fed the lives of multi-millions through nearly two thousand years and could feed your life too. Put yourself into fellowship with a group of vital Christians.

Give God a Chance, p 26

The Stewardship of Money

How much money do I give to God?

If I have never been systematic in giving, am I not in grievous danger of supposing that I am giving more than I am?

Let it be granted that a Christian may spend part of his money on pleasure; ought I not to give at least as much to God as I spend on my own enjoyment?

But have I?

Let me add it up honestly. Tobacco, the cinema, the theatre, sport, personal adornment, joy-rides, this . . . and that . . .?

And how much have I given to God?

Only that?!

God forgive me!—I have been mean with God.

What about tithing?

Many Christians—even poor ones—give a tenth to God, and give it under guidance to God's work at home and abroad. Should I?

Is it true that a tenth is too much for some and not enough for others?

But never mind about others at this moment. *What about me?*

Everything precious He gave me. I have given Him . . .?

A Spiritual Check-up

It is any time between 1616 and 1654 at Cartagena. A slave-ship is soon to arrive. The port is busy and expectant at the prospect of another rich cargo of black ivory. A good sale means prosperity all round. The ship appears in sight, and, with it, the most appalling stench that can assail the nostrils of man. It comes in firm and solid like a wall . . . and the crowded quay is cleared in a moment as people run from this awful breath of corruption. One man remains at the quay-side—one man and his blanched assistant. Serene of countenance, and aching with love for the suffering, Peter Claver is at his post. Hardly before the ship has tied up, he hurries aboard. Is he human? Does he not see and smell what coarse men cannot stand? Straight for the dying he goes. In every thirst-racked, pain-racked body he sees his dying Lord. He whispers words of love to them. They do not understand his words but they see his blazing eyes. He puts his arms around their . . . bodies and kisses them into eternity. He turns next to those who may yet live. 'A bit of tobacco for this one to chew; it will dull the unbearable pain. A sip of brandy there. He will wash those festering wounds. Put aside the dead for decent burial. . . .'

. . . The kindness of the saints, who can measure? . . . Some political revolutionaries have taken to sneering at the saints on the grounds that their charity buttressed an order so rotten that it would have collapsed of its own wickedness but for their unconscious help. The strength of Claver . . . should not have been spent in mercy on the slave-ships but in protest against the foul iniquity itself. But protest meetings, however indignant, are less costing to those who undertake them than the work which Claver and others . . . undertook. Protesting *can* be cheap. The whole lives of the saints are a costly protest against wickedness.

The Pure in Heart, pp 138–9

39

... What answer shall we give to those calamities that seem involved in the very frame of things, and which cannot honestly be traced to human activity at all—earthquakes, floods, typhoons and volcanic eruptions? That is the darkest part of the way. . . . Let us begin by reminding ourselves of a few elementary principles.

1. We shall not expect to have, at this stage of human development, a complete answer to all our problems . . . it will not surprise us when the answer we seek is sometimes beyond the reach of our immature minds.

2. We shall remember that this life is not the whole of life. If men demand of us proof that every life is the *complete* outworking of some beneficent purpose which can be traced from the cradle to the grave, they are making an unreasonable demand. Too many lives have been cut short in a way which God could never intend. Yet His conquering love will vindicate itself in eternity. Sad as untimely death must be, we need to guard against exaggerating the tragedy. How can it be *ultimately* grievous to exchange the limited life of earth for the richer, fuller life of heaven?

3. Pain is not an *unrelieved* mystery. Its purpose as a guardian of health is plain and precious. If we felt no pain when fire burned and knives cut, the race would long since have perished.

4. Pains cannot be summed. It is customary with people who think at all about such terrible disasters as the earthquake in Tokio in 1923, to be utterly appalled by the effort to assess the sufferings of the 165,700 people who were killed. But . . . the problem is worst in the *one* person who suffered most. . . . There seems some probability that the One who suffered most is the Man who died on a cross 1900 years ago with a thief on either side of Him.

(*continued* p 41)

5. God has set us in this world in a great family life. The sweetest things that have come to us have come unmerited from other people, and we are debtors every hour we live, not only to our own immediate circle, but to the whole race. . . . Having gained so much by our place in this fellowship it should not surprise us (whenever we think of accidents and contagious diseases) that we must also share the penalties as well.

6. Without sentimentalizing, we must remember the gains of suffering. It is pain which provokes the passionate quest for a cure. . . . If a sufferer can feel that, even in an infinitesimal degree, a cure has been brought nearer by the pain he has endured, there is surely much comfort in the thought. Others will suffer less because he suffered more.

It is not less true with the great disasters of the world. They are seldom without their fruit. The loss of the *Titanic*, for example, gave tremendous stimulus to wireless telegraphy, led to the stringent revision of the obsolete regulations regarding emergency boats, moved the track of Atlantic liners further south, and inspired many improvements in life-saving apparatus.

While God, in His infinite love and wisdom, insists on treating us as persons and not puppets, and will not rob us of our freedom even to save us from a woe, He yet makes it possible for the bitter tree to bear a precious fruit, and is willing to work with us to produce something worthy of the price pain has paid.

Providence, pp 5–7

You have heard, I imagine, the oft-told story of the man who expressed the strong opinion that the most beautiful word in the English language was the word 'which'. When his friends dissented from his idea, he said this:

'I was once a drunken sot. All my money went into the pub. Every Saturday I soaked until I was nearly spent up, and then I rolled home and flung the few remaining shillings into my wife's lap. With a spate of obscene language I told her to stop snivelling and to be thankful for what she got. Through all the years I was a slave to drink. I never had a smart rag to my back. I hated myself and most decent people despised me. Then I met God and was gloriously changed. I listened to a preacher's message, responded to his appeal, and a wonderful power came into my life and revolutionized me. I cut the drink entirely. I dropped my filthy talk and gave my wife her proper week's money and began to buy little extras for the home. As the months went by, I gathered a wardrobe.

'One summer evening, six months after I was converted, I said to my wife, "Let us go out for a walk", and she went upstairs to put her coat and hat on. While she was upstairs I called out "Bring my overcoat down with you", and she said "Which?". Which! I could not answer for a moment. I was staggered by the word "which". I had *two*.' The poor odorous rag-bag, who had been the pillar of the pubs, had two overcoats!

Westminster Sermons (vol. ii), pp 34–5

The history of the Sadducees shows the absorbing and, at times, the spiritually debilitating character of public affairs. It is not easy for a man to go into the turmoil and compromise of public life and keep his soul. That a number do so is a thing for marvel and thankfulness, but no man should face this form of Christian service who is not ready also to face the risks involved.

We greatly desire in the Church of Christ that more and more of our sons shall go into public life in all its forms; into municipal life and parliamentary life, into leadership in their trade unions and in their employers' associations. . . . If Christian men and women fail to serve the community in this way, those who oppose the faith will do it with tragic results.

Yet . . . when men *do* go into public life, religious life is in danger of being crowded out. . . . The Church is often neglected and spiritual values lightly esteemed.

One may recognize, also . . . the danger which threatens spiritual leaders: that they may become more concerned with their 'church politics' and ecclesiastical machinery than with the souls of the people. Ambition can intrude into any highly organized Church. . . . It is when ecclesiastics actually assume temporal power that the worst tragedies of all occur. Roman Catholic historians themselves have written of the ghastly iniquities of the Papal States, and no informed Protestant can forget Calvin's major share in burning Michael Servetus. . . . We should remember from this study of the Sadducees that we have a special duty to pray for those in authority over us . . . in Church and State as well. . . . They are bearing great burdens. They could make mistakes with most fearful consequences. . . . Pray for them!

They Met at Calvary, pp 30–1

It is not certain that our greatest achievements belong to our palmy days. It is given to some to do their best in the shadowed way. The Cross of Jesus is more than the triumphal entry. That rough-hewn, blood-soaked, grisly cross knows more of our redemption than all the swinging ritual of His palm-strewn path. And it is given to some men and women to do their most effective work when the prime of life is past and the shadows have begun to lengthen on their homeward way. There was Eli, for instance, the priest of Israel. When Samuel was entrusted to his care he was perhaps a mumbling old man, the best of long life past him and with an eventide of vain regrets. 'My palmy days are long since past', he might have said . . . and then God gave him Samuel. Nothing that Eli ever did was so well-worth the doing as the training and shaping of Samuel. It was a bigger achievement and had a finer influence for good than anything else that had gone before—and it was all done at eventide when the palmy days were well behind. Did you say your palmy days were all behind you? That may be so, but are your days of service and usefulness all behind you too? Look up to God and ask Him 'has He not service even yet?' 'Is there no task I can fulfil?' And let your petitions end in songs and tell Him that your days of service as well as your days of praise will ne'er be past while life or thought or being last, or immortality endures.

Why Jesus Never Wrote a Book, pp 22–3

44

February 14

The Fruit of the Spirit

Does the Holy Spirit dwell in me?
How can I tell?
I can tell by the fruit of His presence (Gal. 5^{22}f).
Love Can I love the people I don't like?
Joy Am I a happy Christian?
Peace Am I poised and serene?
Long-suffering Am I free from self-pity?
Kindness 'I was hungry and you gave me meat . . .'
      Have I excelled in simple kindness?
Goodness My Saviour went about doing good. Do I?
Faithfulness If He slew me, would I still trust Him?
Meekness Am I so crass that I confuse meekness with weak-
      ness?
Temperance Am I temperate in all things?
My Lord Jesus,
   I am shocked to find how engrossed I have been with myself.
I look back over the years and it has been mostly self, self, self.
   I want to die to self: to my opinions and preferences, tastes
and will. I want to die to the world, its approval and blame,
and die even to the approval and blame of my brethren and my
friends.
   I would study to show myself approved unto Thee. . . .
                                        A Spiritual Check-Up

Some years ago, in the midst of much toilsome work and not a few perplexities, I received a letter from a stranger. It was a lovely letter. It seemed to see right into my situation and, with almost uncanny discernment, to sense my need. . . . I looked at the postmark, half expecting to discover that it had been franked in heaven. . . . Though the letter required no answer . . . (my correspondent explained that he did not wish to add to my work) I sent a word of the warmest gratitude, and some months later we met.

Let me tell you a little of this obscure disciple and something of his secret service for our Lord. He is a shy man. It would be wrong to say that he has no gift in public speech, but he has a greater gift in writing. Years ago he went to God for guidance, asking how best he could serve the coming of the Kingdom, and it was revealed to him that a ministry awaited him in correspondence. . . . He accepted the commission. For years he has been fulfilling it. He does it with prayer and (as he believes) under guidance. The number of people he has encouraged must, by now, be immense. He writes to all kinds of folk—to friends, to acquaintances, to entire strangers; to the authors of books which have helped him; to people in public life who are carrying great responsibilities; to high and humble, known and unknown, rich and poor.

He writes to sick people and speaks of his admiration in their courage. He lets the lonely know that he remembers them. He backs up those who are battling for social righteousness, especially when they are maligned. A letter of comfort from him has soothed a hundred broken hearts. . . . He is a quietly happy man; happy with the happiness of those who have found their work . . . and do it.

(*continued* p 47)

. . . He offers no advice in his letters and makes it plain that he expects no reply. He specializes in appreciation. There are enough critics, he believes, eager to tell a man where he is wrong. . . . So often has he been assured of the *timeliness* of his letters' arrival that he cannot possibly doubt that he is working with Another.

Hugh Price Hughes is judged by some denominational historians to have been the most influential Methodist preacher after John Wesley himself. Do you know that he once resigned from the ministry? It was in the heat of an unpleasant controversy. . . . He took it back because of a letter he received; a warm, loving, constraining letter from Dr Ebenezer Jenkins who, in the controversy, was actually on the other side! But the letter melted the heart of Hugh Price Hughes. It was found in his desk when he died.

Sir Herbert Barker was on the lip once of abandoning his great work in manipulative surgery. He was sick and tired of being called a charlatan. It was a private letter from C. P. Scott, owner and editor of the *Manchester Guardian*, which made him change his resolution.

One of the most treasured letters I know is also the shortest. It was written by a little maiden of five years old in Westminster Hospital. In her own simple way she understood that she owed her life to the surgical skill of a doctor there, and when she was well enough she sat up in bed and called for pen and paper and just wrote: '*Dear You*'.

That was all! He described it as 'the shortest, the most charming, the most polished of letters'.

One of the most influential of the lesser-known letter-writers of our day was Dr Barkley. . . . Barkley's slogan was: '*Say it where it will count.*'

Methodist Magazine, 1947, pp 160–2

We see, moreover, how rich a service the sufferers render to our poor tormented race. Sympathy is a shallow stream in the souls of those who have not suffered. There is something unheeding and harsh in a man who has known nothing of pain. And sympathy is far too precious in this needy world to begrudge the price at which it must be purchased. When Richard Baxter lost his wife, he declared, in his . . . grief 'I will not be judged by any that never felt the like'. It was only another way of saying that he could not be comforted except by those who had. Suffering, in a disciple, can often be wrested to service. It is Christlike work to soothe and sympathize, and only those who have drunk the cup of sorrow are fully equipped to do it.

Furthermore, as we come to understand the family life in which God has placed us on this planet, and glimpse the purpose which His loving heart is working out, we come to understand also why we are exposed to grief and pain. Some of it is begotten by ignorance, and some by folly. Omnipotence could have avoided it all, but only at the price of invading our personality and making us marionettes. Can anyone, not utterly engulfed in sorrow, regret that God did not take that path: that His love would not compromise with sin: that He insisted that we bear the penalties of family life as we had enjoyed its privileges: that nothing would thwart Him in His purpose of keeping us in those conditions by which we might attain to the stature of men? Fellowship with God is the fine fruit of this discipline.

> *Nearness, likeness to our Lord*
> *Our exceeding great reward.*

Is it worth it? Aye! Though seven deaths lay between.

He is Able, pp 18–19

48

The immensity of the gift of the Holy Spirit at Pentecost may be measured in part by the change in the Apostles. They had a new sense of guidance. Peter knew when it happened that this was the day which Joel had foretold. Almost a third of the précis of his sermon preserved to us is given to proving that this was the day the prophet had foreseen. Between the Ascension and the gift of the Spirit they were still men groping in the twilight. They were convinced of the resurrection but they had no experience of clear guidance in their lives. . . . To fill the vacant place in the Apostolic band they cast lots! After Pentecost there was no more talk of lots. The greatest and most far-reaching decisions were now made at a higher level. 'It seemed good to the Holy Spirit and to us. . .' Not only had they a wonderful sense of guidance; their whole *strategy* changed. The period of secluded prayer in which they were instructed to await the gift of the Spirit was now past. They swept out into the stream of national life as a flood which none could ignore. . . . It is clear that to many of their contemporaries they hardly seemed the same men. From fearful, hunted, hiding men, they became fearless, hunting, noted men. Rabbits became ferrets on the Day of Pentecost.

The Pure in Heart, pp 28–9

This work is no monopoly of the ordained ministry . . . The laity . . . have a task not one whit less responsible than that of those of us who are separated to the work. When one thinks of the zeal of a convinced Communist or the hot enthusiasm of certain social philosophers running round with their latest nostrum to cure the world's ills, how strange it is that we can be so tepid in our vital task. . . . There are two reasons to explain our lack of zeal. (1) Many of us are unsure of the Gospel ourselves. Our religion is second-hand. We know God by hearsay only. . . . Consequently, not having any deep experience . . . we have nothing to give away. We are uncomfortable when we are confronted with our duty as evangelists because it reveals the poverty of our own spiritual life . . . the most that many of us can say is this 'I know a man who knows God and *he* might help you'. The second-hand character of testimony robs it of all power to persuade . . .

(2) The second reason . . . is the still, persistent thought that evangelism does not touch, in any large way, the world's need. Great events all seem to take place far above the heads of ordinary men and women. They want peace . . . they want to understand other nations . . . they think it terrible that millions are underfed, but it isn't clear to the ordinary man what he can do about it. . . . Two things should rebuke this hopelessness: (a) the recollection that the religion of Jesus Christ does not end (though it begins) in personal piety, and (b) that the power of even one man or woman with God is immensely potent.

Let me Commend, pp 22–3

Listen to the Parable of the Prodigal Son as Jesus *didn't* tell it:

And he arose and set out for his home, and when at last he arrived at the door, he banged and there was no response. He stood there in his piteous rags and hunger for a while, and then he knocked again and a third time; and finally a window opened and his father looked out and said: 'Oh, it's you! You're spent up, I suppose. You look a nice beauty. What have you come home for? You've had your share of everything. You know where to come when you're hungry . . .'

And he said 'Father, I have sinned against Heaven and in thy sight . . .' but his father banged the window and left him for a while on the doorstep. Presently his father opened the door and said 'You're an utter disgrace to me and to all your relatives. I'm ashamed of you; utterly ashamed. But I'm your parent, and I've thought it out, and I am prepared to put you on probation for three months, and if, at the end of three months I can find no fault in you, well, perhaps I'll have it in my heart to give you another start . . .'

That is the Parable of the Prodigal Son as Jesus *didn't* tell it. As you hear me say it, your heart cries out against its falsity. 'Lies!' you say. 'Lies!' And you are right; they *are* lies. 'And while he was yet a long way off his father saw him and had compassion and ran and fell on his neck and kissed him' (No probationary period, you notice. No talk of three months. No, it was instant. It was now! Now!) 'The ring, the ring, the robe, the robe'.

'Now is the acceptable time. *Today* if you will hear my voice.'

Westminster Sermons (vol. ii), pp 24–5

This is the supreme book. Begotten of God, it is daily employed by God. Prayer knits into it in a way altogether special. Of other books we say 'That man's thoughts are very helpful'. But with the illumination of the Holy Spirit on the Bible we say 'This is the Word of God'. As we appropriate the truths of the Bible we begin to base our thinking on its standards, to breathe its air. We begin to live in it.

The Bible is unique. It is the only full unfolding of the plan of God for earth. It is the only record of God's dealing with the most spiritually sensitive people of the ancient world. It is the only record of the life on God on earth. It is the only record of the beginning of the Christian Church.

The Bible is effective. It gives meaning to life. It is one of the chief ways by which God speaks to us still. It has fed the souls of millions for many hundreds of years. It has fully sustained people in the fiercest trials known to our race—sorrow, shame, pain, prison, despair, death.

The Bible is timeless. In its central meaning it is never 'dated'. It speaks eternal truth to every generation as it comes. The fiercest criticism leaves its spiritual truth undimmed. We can foresee no time when it will be surpassed.

Yet the Bible isn't all easy to understand. Picking bits at random can be dangerous. Only serious, reverent and prayerful study secures its treasures. This takes time—and we have crowded our lives with other things. So let us resolve to know this book better, to learn to live in it, to give time to it daily, to wait on the Holy Spirit before we turn a page, to let God apply it to our soul.

The Pattern of Prayer, pp 58–9

Of nothing do the witnesses of this experience speak more
than of the love of God which expanded their hearts, seeped
through their whole beings, and overflowed in love to all. That
it was supernatural love may be proven by the simple test . . . it
is not confined to the channels of natural affinity. Like their
Lord, the recipients of His love love where they do not like. It is
impossible to think that Christ *liked* rotting lepers, bloated
publicans, loose women or wild demoniacs; yet it is undeniable
that He *loved* them.

Those to whom, in response to faith, He gives this supernatural love, love in that way. It is not more of the love they
had before: it is love with a new quality. Like Saul Kane in
Masefield's *The Everlasting Mercy*, they feel 'that Christ has
given them birth, to brother all the souls on earth'. . . . Com-
mander Brengle's witness will serve as an example. He begins
his little book . . . with the startling sentence 'On January 9th,
1885, at about nine o'clock in the morning, God sanctified my
soul', and then goes on

'It was a Heaven of love that came into my heart. I walked out
over Boston Common before breakfast, weeping for joy and praising
God. Oh, how I loved! In that hour I knew Jesus, and I loved Him
till it seemed my heart would break in love. I loved the sparrows, I
loved the dogs, I loved the horses, I loved the little urchins on the
streets . . . . I loved the whole world.'*

The heart of the experience is love—and love is a gift. When
the moralist, in keen defence of ethical principle, asserts that
holiness *cannot* be given, this is the reply. The heart of holiness
so conceived is supernatural love—and love is a gift.

Love is the key to holiness.

The Path to Perfection, pp 157–8

---

* Brengle, *Helps to Holiness*, iiif.

He was born 6 B.C., of a young woman not married, in an out-of-the-way place called Bethlehem. He grew up in an insanitary village named Nazareth. With no known distinction of birth, belonging to a despised people, denied the best education of His day and race, He was trained as a carpenter. At about thirty years of age, He laid aside the tools of His trade and began to teach and preach and heal. Although the common people heard him gladly, He never touched world affairs in any obvious way. His whole life was lived in one obscure province of the Roman Empire, and His travels were limited to an area half the size of Wales. After three years of ministry, He was arrested on suspicion of leading a popular revolt, and was executed by crucifixion. The life which began in shadowed obscurity ended in public shame. But not *very* public. The whole matter seemed beneath the interest of 'people of quality', and His name was so unimportant that it wasn't even mentioned in any official document which has ever come to light.

Two thousand years have passed by. Nearly a third of the world worships Him. It is a safe guess to say that another third holds Him (as Mr Gandhi did) in enormous respect. He has inspired the mightiest music and the greatest art the world has known. People have died for Him in every generation since He Himself suffered. Multitudes would die for Him today. Indeed, some who deny belief in all religion consider that His rule of love would save the world.

Who was this strange peerless Person? The Christian Church is built on the conviction that He was God Himself.

Give God a Chance, p 40

... The real you is the self which Christ could make you. You were not made to grovel. You were not built to abide in sin. God made you for Himself, and deep-set in your heart there are longings after holiness, and every now and then the Spirit inflames them and you long for the great spaces in which the saint moves.

I was in the Zoo some time ago and lingered by the cages of the eagles. Somehow or other the sight of them hurt me. I looked at the great wing-spread of the King of Birds, and I felt sick at heart that they were caged. . . . Made for the skies . . . and crammed in a cage!

So many of us are like that; made for the skies and imprisoned in sin. When Jesus looks at us, He sees us as we are, but, with His double vision, He sees us also as we might be.

He looked on Simon and saw Peter. He looked on Saul and saw Paul. He looked on Augustine the rouè, and saw Augustine the saint. . . . If only we could see ourselves as Christ sees us! If we could stand at His elbow and get that double vision; the men and women we are; the men and women we *might* be! . . . See yourself then 'the man God meant'. Hold the picture in the eye of reverent imagination whenever you pray. Dwell (on your knees) on the thought that God could make you like *that* . . . and, as you dwell on it daily and in prayer, God will use your sanctified imagination to pull you up. The actual will turn into the ideal. The difference may be so marked that you will need a new name. To you, as to one long ago, He may say 'Thou art Simon . . . Thou shalt be called "Rock".'

Westminster Sermons (vol. i), pp 17–18

Does the story of Judas Iscariot speak . . . to our own condition? We learn from it . . . that it is possible to live near to
Christ and then to fall away . . . to be in His company, and be
regarded as one of His intimates, and then to be guilty of the
foulest betrayal. If any man . . . asserts in self-confidence that
'nothing could happen to me here' that man has added, by his
over-confidence, to the danger we mortals are always in.

I never go to Aber Falls, in North Wales, without feeling the
pathos of something that occurred there years ago. A brilliant
young barrister was climbing the mountain near the Falls with
a friend. His friend noticed the green slime on the rocks . . . and
called out 'Do be careful', to which young Payne replied: 'Oh,
it's as safe as anything. I *couldn't* fall here.' They were the last
words he uttered.

In second place, it is possible to be in the Church of God and
yet not be a disciple in heart. Was Judas ever a disciple in heart?
. . . No one can answer that question, but it is not to be doubted
that people can be in the Church today without any serious
commitment to Christ. . . . Indeed, their lack of loyalty can be
concealed almost from themselves. Until some severe test
comes, they are like everybody else. But a trial comes and they
are revealed. . . . Every Christian should periodically question
his own soul: 'Am I really in this because of devotion to my
Lord? Would I stand if a crucial test really came?'

There is a third thing. . . . With some natures there is nothing
so holy that money cannot besmirch it. Watch money. It is
enormously useful and so terribly dangerous.

They Met at Calvary, pp 38–9

A few years ago* *The Times* reported a strange case of crime
in a certain German town. A lady in that town found a basket
on her doorstep, and the basket contained a pigeon. There was
a note also inside, an urgent, imperative, threatening note
which said that if the lady did not fasten a certain sum of
money to the clip on the pigeon's leg and release the bird immediately, her house would be burnt down that night. The lady
immediately informed the police and the police acted with
amazing rapidity. . . . They chartered two aeroplanes and
having tied a streaming ribbon to the bird's neck they released
the bird and instructed the pilots to pursue it. The pigeon rose
in the air and wheeled round several times before it finally
took its course. The inhabitants of the town . . . stood in amaze-
ment at the strange gyrations of the two aeroplanes and feared
for their church steeple; but as soon as the pigeon flew on a
direct course the aeroplanes were in hot pursuit, while the
police followed, as best they could, in a high-powered car
below. Presently the pigeon flew down to a loft and one of the
aeroplanes took a photograph of the spot while the other
dropped a note to the police. The police dashed to the house
and discovered two brothers untying the tell-tale ribbon in
feverish haste from the bird's neck and they were placed under
immediate arrest. The men protested, however, that the bird
was not theirs. 'It just flew into our loft', they said; 'it is not our
bird.' 'Very well', said the officer; 'we will test that', and he
ordered the pigeon to be taken away and released from a
distant spot . . . and it came home. A second time it was taken
away and a second time it came home. A third time—and a
third time it came home. And every time . . . it deepened the
certitude of their guilt. Finally, they broke down and confessed.
. . . Sin is like that. It comes home.

Why Jesus Never Wrote a Book, pp 28–9

* 1932.

The essential element about a true and vital prayer meeting is that it should spring spontaneously out of an urgent situation. It should minister to keenly felt needs. The moment it becomes formal, either drop it or revitalize it; otherwise it will rapidly go sour. Do not let it linger on, or it will do more harm than good.

May I tell you about a real prayer meeting which I knew as a young man. I did not go to it; I belonged to it. It was part of my life. I and the other dozen lads were bound together by invisible but mighty ties. Our leader was an old engineman who worked in the shipyard. He was great in nothing except in soul. ... Every Friday night we met in a basement. Each week our leader asked one of us to conduct, another to give a short ten-minute talk. We began in fear and stuttering, but his wonderful smile carried us through. Yet all this (and it made preachers of some of us) was merely preliminary to the main business of prayer. We longed for the moment when we knelt on the floor, our elbows on our chairs, and one after another poured out our hearts to God. Sometimes between bursts of prayer someone would softly begin some old chorus which caught the mood of our supplication, and at times our hearts would melt and our tears flow as the warmth of the love of God flowed into us. Sometimes, if a lad was in deep trouble—and we were no strangers to sorrow and want in those days—or if we were constrained to lay before God some special concern, then prayer would pour out like a torrent until the very room echoed and shook with the power of pleading.

The Pattern of Prayer, pp 28–9

Some people have never been lonely. Born into a large family,
rich in relatives and friends, coping all the time with a glut of
social engagements, they simply do not understand what real
loneliness is. Loneliness is awful—especially to some temperaments. . . . Hospitality in Christian homes is the answer to
loneliness. . . .

People with no public gifts can do this. Let them open their
homes to the lonely. Let them say to the nurse off duty, or to the
lad in lodgings, or to the strangers in the neighbourhood:
'Come in.' Some people hesitate . . . because they suppose that
hospitality necessarily involves a lavish meal. But the lonely
are not looking for a banquet. Friendship and fellowship are
what they want. It is a thrill to them to be included in the
family life. A seat by the fire and a share in the talk are all they
ask.

Some people are hospitable but not in the way especially
commended in the New Testament. Those whom they invite
are always their already established friends . . . Jesus . . . meant
our hospitality to reach out beyond our own circle. Let it
reach out!

. . . So begin. Don't be vague with the invitation. Never say:
'You must come *sometime* . . .' A shy lad will never respond to
that. Nail him down. Make it Sunday at 4 or Thursday at 7.
Be precise. When he is established in your friendship he will
believe you when you say 'Come—*whenever you like*'.

Twelve Ways of Service, p 6

. . . For the modern pilgrim of perfection, the word 'sin' takes on a wider connotation. It is seen in social guises too; the selfishness which clings to dubious theories of economics, and which refuses to examine criticism directed against them, because these theories serve as a protective cushion to the conscience; the jealousy which guards existing privileges and will not meet a challenge concerning their legitimacy: the wilful ignorance of the circumstances of other people's lives though it is acknowledged that they share an equal place in God's regard.

Moreover, these aspiring souls find their consciences assailed by shafts which had not troubled them before: the absence of a really fair chance of rich Christian life for those of their fellows who are haunted by continual unemployment: the impossibility of finding a sense of divine vocation in work which is plainly inimical to the best interest of the race, or in tasks utterly mechanical and the tedium of which no effort is made to reduce: the subordination of industry to finance which has created centres of economic power exercising something analogous to tyranny over multitudes of men: the vast inequalities of opportunity which still exist in regard to health, education and leisure.

Those who would be perfect can no longer find their definition of sin exhausted by lewd thoughts, drunkenness and the use of a cinema on a Sunday. They see sin also in an evil social system, some of the buttresses of which may be set in their own class and in their own soul. And when they confess sin, they have need now to ask forgiveness, not only for the sins which they have long recognized as such, but also for their failure to follow their Master in the redemption of social life.

The Path to Perfection, p 183

Will you notice, in the first place, that they were *toil-worn* hands. The soldier noticed it; the soldier who nailed Him to the wood. As he stretched His arm along the cross-beam, and pointed his nail and the palm, it struck him—this was not the hand of some sedentary worker; this was not the hand of some *habitué* of the Court. This was the toil-worn hand of a working man.

Notice that. Jesus was a working-man. Oh! you don't realize the wonder of that until you think yourself back into the Greek and Roman world and consider their attitude to manual work. They *despised* it. It was the occupation of slaves. Plato and Aristotle were both great and clever men, but to both of them manual work was a thing of near-contempt. It was not an occupation for free men; it was a task only for the slave.

And this was God's answer to that; His reply to the ancient world's contempt for manual work. Peep into the carpenter's shop at Nazareth and see the incarnate Son of God bending His back at a bench; see Him ankle-deep in the shavings and perspiring as He toils. This is the answer of Almighty God to those who despise manual work.

Westminster Sermons (vol. i), p 90

Charles Wesley sang:

> In Jesus I believe, and shall
> *Believe* myself to Him.

Here speaks faith for holiness: faith fighting: faith booted: spurred and mounted: faith on the stretch: faith laughing again at impossibilities and crying 'It shall be done'.

The absence of that militant faith hinders the work of the Holy Spirit. The belief that the battle between the two natures must ever keep at the 'ding-dong' stage, keeps it there. We have to *reckon* ourselves dead to sin, and not in some anaemic way, and in the upper layers of the mind only, but with all the courage and persistence of faith. We shall *believe* for it. In intensity of concentration we shall direct our thoughts to God and His will to rid us of sin, trusting Him to mould our passivity into 'the mind that was in Christ'. No evil can have place in the mind that was in Christ.

We shall not forget the antinomy or turn a difference of emphasis into an 'either—or'. But we shall barely stop short of it. The work is the work of the Holy Spirit, but faith is the way He comes. The bias of our unredeemed nature in the presence of perfection is to put the emphasis upon 'I can't'. The energies of the Holy Spirit put the emphasis upon 'I can'. It is a moment-by-moment-life. Those who believe that the faith of a moment can receive holiness for ever have not proved their case. Life in God is like breathing: drawing in the life-giving Breath of the Spirit and exhaling the breath devitalized by use. . . . 'Moment by moment I'm kept in His love . . .'

The Pure in Heart, pp 40–1

. . . a great deal!—if he is utterly given to his task. Who among his neighbours at Down—in rural Kent, and only sixteen miles from London Bridge—knew that Charles Darwin would shake the world? Even to his own gardener he seemed half-mad at times, watching worms for forty years and ready, it was said, to give credence to any foolish idea that was put to him. . . . So unworldly! So foolish! And yet his work was so world-transforming too!

Who of those who saw the bearded figure of Karl Marx day after day in the library of the British Museum could have guessed that he would stamp his thought upon an age; that tens of thousands, still unborn, would make a holy bible of his writings and barely stop this side of idolatry in their awesome reverence of their 'master'?

. . . It is true that these illustrations are taken from outside the sphere of evangelism and the spread of the Christian Faith. But they militate against the current lie that individuals do not matter.

One person utterly given to his task can do much. If he cannot affect the thought of the world, he might greatly affect the thought of his village, city or state.

If, moreover, the task to which he gives himself is the proclamation of the Gospel of God, and the honour of God Himself be involved in its triumph, anything could happen.

Anything!

Let Me Commend, pp 27–8

God says 'Now' for the gift of the Holy Spirit—for cleansing and for power. One of the favourite words with John Wesley and Charles Wesley and all the leaders of the Evangelical Revival, was the word 'Now'.

It always *is* with true evangelical preaching: 'Now.'

When Wesley spoke about a birth in holiness happening in a moment, he shocked many of the religious people of the eighteenth century, and they said 'But it is absurd. You cannot be holy in a moment. It is a slow growth. This is dangerous blasphemy, in such a connection, to talk of "now".'

But they went on saying it. Charles Wesley sang:

> *Saviour, to Thee my soul looks up,*
> *My present Saviour Thou!*
> *In all the confidence of hope,*
> *I claim the blessing now.*

People said 'All growth is gradual, not sudden. It cannot be sudden'. And John Wesley said 'How is it with birth? There is a growth in the womb before birth and there is a long growth after birth, but birth itself is sudden. When that strange, mysterious downward thrust forces the child into life . . . it is sudden. You can mark it on the calendar and time it on the clock.' Said Wesley: 'It is like that in the things of the Spirit. There is a maturing before the moment, and there can be long development after the moment, but the moment itself is a moment—and that moment can be now.' Even now, at your earnest desiring, the Holy Spirit could enter your heart to cleanse it from evil, to break the power of cancelled sin, to give you freedom where before you were in bondage, and victory where before you were in defeat.

Westminster Sermons (vol. ii), pp 25–6

What devotion Wesley had to the holy book! How he loved to proclaim himself (despite his wide reading) as 'a man of one book'! How positive he was that this was, in the most special sense, God's own word. Yet the developing character of the Biblical revelation of God was axiomatic with John Wesley. He said flatly that the imprecatory Psalms were not fit to be read in public worship.

. . . The Bible, as the supreme book of religion, is there for us to read upon in entire confidence. . . . I want to come to the Bible in the spirit . . . of Dr Orchard's grandfather: 'This blessed Book!' Let me give my whole mind to it. Let me mine here for the richest ore in literature. Let me stay my soul on its dependable promises.

When the coffin is standing by the bed of my dearest, I can't afford to fall to wondering if Christ did (or did not) say 'In my Father's house are many mansions'. I know it's a translation of a translation. But is that the accurate sense of what He said? When the doctor gives me up, I can't fall to wondering if Christ is a dependable guide through life. I've proved Him so, and confirmed the Biblical promises through many years. I rest on them now. Come at it rightly and the Bible will never fail.

But someone may say 'How do you come at it rightly?' and I would say 'You must come to the word with the special help of the Holy Spirit'. The Bible was given by the inspiration of the Holy Spirit. It can only be properly read by the same divine help. He who gave it illuminates it. He who spoke through prophet and apostle knows best how to use what He has given.

The Pattern of Prayer, pp 57–8

Many people believe that, whatever value prayer may have to lift a man's feelings, it cannot possibly affect physical events, because the universe runs by unalterable law. . . . If fire burned today but didn't burn tomorrow, if water boiled at one temperature today and froze at the same temperature tomorrow, neither man nor beast could survive. Life is possible only because of these unchanging laws, and we should be grateful for their unchanging character, even if they seem to cancel out some of our prayers.

But—before we conclude that they do that—let us remember . . . laws interact with other laws. Iron will neither float nor hang in the air, but . . . planes don't break the law of gravity, for there are laws of aerodynamics as well. There are spiritual laws, too, which are not as firmly separated from physical laws as we thought at one time. It is likely . . . that some of Christ's miracles were performed by His use of higher laws. Scientists are themselves abandoning the old idea of 'cause and effect', if by those words are meant some completely rigid sequences which nothing can alter. One of them has said that . . . they can no longer talk of mechanical explanations, if only because they do not know what they mean by 'mechanics'. Perhaps we are helped a little here by what is called 'psycho-matic' sickness. People are sometimes made ill, not by a germ, but by a thought, a fear—and a thought or fear far deeper than the conscious mind. The effect is physical—sometimes awful and ugly—but the cause is mental and spiritual. People are sometimes cured that way too. There are many senses in which prayer changes things.

Give God a Chance, p 66

A certain church choir was giving a special week-night per-
formance in a Town Hall in aid of a civic fund. It was discovered, at the last moment, that the platform at the Town Hall
wasn't high enough, and another low platform had hastily to
be placed upon the first. It was not as large as the platform
proper, and left the choir on two levels. Some of the singers,
therefore, were obliged all the evening to stand lower than the
others, and one lady took umbrage at this. She hasn't been to
the choir since, and it occurred six months ago!

I think now that she feels the foolishness of it herself, but
pride complicates the matter and she cannot swallow it enough
to go back.

So she is out of the Royal Service, and miserable in her own
heart, and small in the judgement of others, all over the level of
a platform!

Don't feel too superior as I tell the story. Don't say 'I would
never do that!' (Maybe you couldn't get into a choir anyway!)
Search your own heart. It may be that upon *your* service there
has fallen at times a shadow no less disfiguring, and you have
been guilty also of an iniquity upon the holy thing.

Westminster Sermons (vol. i), pp 25–6

Some people think that all Church work takes place on Church premises. That is nonsense . . . like a soldier thinking he is a soldier only in barracks. Some of the most important Church work is done in the world. . . . Christian men with the necessary gifts should go into Parliament for Christ. They should go on the town or rural council. They should enter public life deliberately to secure the triumph of God's will in organized society.

They need, however, to measure themselves against the special perils of this form of service . . . there is an awful risk that the link with the Church will get severed, a risk that compromise, which is unavoidable in government, will attack moral principles. . . .

But social service is not linked to its public forms. Most large cities today have a Social Service Council which welcomes voluntary workers and undertakes many forms of service to needy people—hot meals for shut-ins, advice to families in difficulty . . . mobile libraries . . . Nor does service in citizenship end at this point. The modern Welfare State is ready to help people in a hundred ways not widely understood. That is why there are such places as Citizens' Advice Bureaux. Yet many of the most needy never go there. It is grand to have in any Church or neighbourhood someone expert in all these things and ready to put his knowledge at the service of others— a man who knows what form to get and how to fill it up; how to solve this pension problem and how to do that bit of legal business. . . . Thousands of simple folk are quite inexpert even in writing a clear letter. Is there a form of service here for you?

Twelve Ways of Service, p 7

. . . We may learn . . . how wrong it is ever to limit our Lord's forgiveness. After the betrayal, Judas took his own life. He forgot his betrayed Master's message of forgiveness. Perhaps he was not listening when Jesus said that the love of God was so mighty that it would always meet penitence with pardon. Perhaps he was wondering whether there was enough in the bag to take a little more!

But knowing what *you* know of the forgiveness of God, do you think that if Judas Iscariot had gone, not to hang himself, but to the Cross, and had flung himself before our dying Lord and said 'Lord Jesus, forgive me'—if he had done that, do you think that He who prayed for his murderers as they nailed Him to the wood, and who said to the dying thief, 'Today thou shalt be with me in paradise', that that same Saviour would have refused forgiveness to the man who had kissed Him into their arms?

I cannot believe it. It was the crowning error of Judas's miserable life. Do not add that sin to any others you have committed. Do not be like the man with whom I wrestled the other night to a late hour, who, having reviewed the enormities of his past, denied that God would forgive him, and went out, as Judas went out into the night, with the mark of Cain on him and without faith that God would ever wipe it away.

Put no limit to the grace of God!

They Met at Calvary, pp 39–40

Do I mark only my gloomy *hours?*
                              . . . unlike the sundial!

God have mercy on us; we are ungrateful creatures! . . . It is
the height of ingratitude to dwell on the shadows and half
forget the shine. When I lived in the beautiful old town of
Conway in North Wales, a friend came to see me from London.
He made the journey on a beautiful summer's day and he only
noticed that there was some grime at Stafford. Can you imagine the journey? The train threads its way slowly out of Euston
gathers speed as it passes Watford and soon it is hurrying
through the pleasant fields of Herts and Buckingham, North-
ampton and Warwick. What scenes of pastoral beauty stretch
away on either side. How the sun plays in splendour on tree
and hill, river and valley! Soon it reaches Rugby and from
Rugby to Tamworth and Lichfield; then it hurries through the
outskirts of the gloomy Potteries and pulls up pantingly at
Crewe. And from Crewe the train races across the Cheshire
plain with more beauty and sunshine, and then, through
Chester, with its walls and great cathedral, is soon roaring
down the North Wales coast. The sands of Dee stretch away to
the right and across the estuary, the sun plays on Hoylake and
West Kirby. The Welsh hills begin to rise on the left: there is a
glimpse of the Marble Church at Bodelwyddan: Rhyl: Aber-
gele: the beautiful sweep of Colwyn Bay: a peep of the little
Orme: Conway. The gate of glorious Snowdonia stands ajar.
And then my friend jumped out of the train and said, 'I'm glad
that's over: it was so grimy in the Potteries'. How long was he
in the Potteries? Two hundred miles of sunshine and beauty
and twenty-five of comparative gloom; and he noticed only the
gloom. And some of us are like that. We travel a road that is,
for the most part, a road of sunshine, and we dwell only upon
the shade.

Why Jesus Never Wrote a Book, pp 36–7

. . . Having accepted the forgiveness of God, *don't brood over the past*. There are many people in the family of God who do not doubt God's forgiveness, but they never seem able to forgive themselves. The memory of their sin lacerates them. It is hardly ever out of their minds. So far from being able, as some are, to forgive themselves lightly, they seem unable to forgive themselves at all. Just like some unhealed wound in the body, this unhealed wound in the spirit drains their strength, hinders their progress, pours pus into the blood-stream, and keeps them in a state of spiritual invalidism.

God has forgiven you; *forgive yourself*. Who are you to have superior moral values to the Almighty God? Here are two things which will help you to forgive yourself.

(i) Can't you see that your unwillingness to forgive yourself is a form of spiritual pride? What you are really saying, at the deep level of your mental and emotional life, is this: 'How could *I* ever have done that?' (Note the stress on the 'I'.) 'Me! A spiritual giant like me!' . . . Now, look! That self-hate is doing you no good. . . . It is like poison injected into your veins. Accept the forgiveness. You cannot undo the past. God has forgiven it, and, if God has forgiven you, who can justly accuse you? That is the first thing: *forgive yourself*.

(ii) Here is the second. In some mysterious way—beyond our human fathoming—*God can use sin* . . . the God who is mighty in creation is also mighty in transformation.

Westminster Sermons (vol. i), pp 149–50

Ten thousand thousand precious gifts
My daily thanks employ;
Nor is the least a thankful heart
That takes those gifts with joy.

Have you heard of the . . . minister who went to preach in a strange church and was told in the vestry that the front pews were always occupied by the inmates of a Home for the Blind? He was touched by the news. Turning to one of the church officials, he said, 'I wonder if they would like to choose a hymn: some comforting and familiar verses that would cheer their over-burdened hearts; something they know?' And while the church official went to inquire he pondered on their possible choice. Would it be—

>Lead, kindly light, amid the encircling gloom,
>Lead Thou me on;

or

>Come unto Me, ye weary,
>And I will give you rest!

or perhaps

>God moves in a mysterious way
>His wonders to perform;

or maybe

>When the weary, seeking rest
>To Thy goodness flee.

And then the official returned. 'They would like ninety-two,' he said. Ninety-two? The minister knew ninety-two. Ninety-two!

>When all Thy mercies, O my God,
>My rising soul surveys,
>Transported with the view, I'm lost
>In wonder, love and praise.

They were blind, and they wanted to sing—

>Through all eternity, to Thee
>A grateful song I'll raise;
>But O eternity's too short
>To utter all Thy praise!

And you can see! Open your eyes widely to the mercies of your God and 'be ye thankful'.

Why Jesus Never Wrote a Book, pp 38–9

. . . Sometimes the answer to prayer has been so singular in its attention to detail that one could barely refrain from laughing, as Sarah laughed, and St Teresa . . . I remember the old saint who had been a nurse in an aristocratic family but found her pension insufficient after the war. One week she had to meet a bill of £3 and had not so much as a shilling towards it. The thought of debt was dreadful to her and she begged God to undertake the burden and give her a settled mind. And as she read the scriptures, a great peace fell upon her heart with the words 'Thou shalt have plenty of silver'. Somehow she felt they were meant for her. She even declined a £1 note on the day before the bill was due because she could not feel that it was God's way of help. Then, in the hour of her need, when to some of her friends she seemed certain of disillusionment and not a little obstinate, her faith was triumphantly vindicated by the part repayment of a loan she had made to a neighbour years before and the very memory of which had almost slipped from her mind. Twenty-four half-crowns were put into her hand by an apologetic woman who begged to be excused for the delay and explained that only the most rigorous economy in her household had made possible the saving of an occasional coin. 'Thou shalt have plenty of silver.'

The old nurse laughed to save herself from crying, but the smiles and tears were all of joy.

He is Able, pp 24–5

There is that in the soul of man which *must* respond to the highest in virtue. It may not respond at once. Human nature can easily be over-faced by examples too remote and austere. Moreover, human nature can easily deny God because the whole race has long been in rebellion against Him. Yet there is that in human nature which calls out to the supreme examples of virtue: owns, as it were, the intention of God who made it, and feels the unmistakable homesickness of the soul.

And it is part of the service of the saints to awaken that homesickness of the soul in men and women. It does not exhaust their service to our poor race. Taken in its wholeness, their service is many-faceted. They often bring a revival of religion. It was of revival that Lacordaire was thinking when he said 'O God, give us some saints'. All France went to Ars in the second quarter of the nineteenth century to see the most lowly-born and ill-instructed priest in the country because he was a saint. The Church is revived by the power of the Holy Spirit through the saints.

The saints are the most convincing answer to atheism and agnosticism. . . . In some mystic way they make it impossible for others to live near them and disbelieve. In the mixed character of Voltaire—nobility and cynicism strangely blended —there was much mockery of religion. But a contented atheist he could not be. Asked by a sceptical friend one day if he had ever met anyone like Jesus Christ, he lapsed into silence and then answered with awe-ful seriousness: 'I once met Fletcher of Madeley.'

The Pure in Heart, p 60

There are more old people than there were. Medical skill has lengthened the span of life and people live longer than they did. Not only are there more old people. Their need *obtrudes* more. . . . There are lonely and half-unwanted old people all over our land. Some of these old people have been gathered into eventide homes . . . but only a handful of lonely old people are in communal homes. Many of the poorer ones are in drab back rooms, and not a few are finding life hard. Some feel that they are the survivors of their generation; some are literally the last members of their family; all of them feel the hurt of waning powers. . . .

Some of these old people have, in their day, been fine servants of God and the community. All their leisure may have been given in unpaid service to others, but a generation has arisen which knows not Joseph—and still less his quiet old widow. . . .

People who organize a Darby and Joan Club help them, or a Veterans' Society . . . but they need help and visitation in their own homes. Some grow sour as they grow old and are hard to help, but others are sweeter with passing time and live with one foot in heaven. Yet, sour or sweet, help them. A visit and a talk, a few flowers and little birthday remembrance, the latest news —by simple ministries like these they know they matter and they know that someone cares.

Twelve Ways of Service, pp 10–11

And . . . you say to me 'How is this delight obtained? What is the secret? If a man freely admits that he hasn't got it, what is the way to make it his own?' . . . Come with me in imagination to a home where a devoted daughter is tenderly caring for her aged mother, anticipating her wants and making life sweetly bearable, despite the prostration of old age. Let us ask this toiling daughter why she does all this? 'Is it merely because you were brought up that way and have just gone on? Are you afraid of what your relatives or neighbours would say if you neglected her? Are you just impelled with . . . a sense of "ought"?' She brushes all our feeble explanations aside: she says 'I delight to do it; it's all an outcome of my love'—and there I have the clue I want. Delight in service is explained by personal love.

And that is the secret of those who delight to do the will of God. They have seen God in Jesus and behind the dictate of conscience stands a loved and loving Person. Sin is not merely a broken rule; it is a wound in His heart. Goodness is not merely duty well done—it is a direct and deliberate serving of the Beloved and hence a dear delight. . . . I go to a lover of this Jesus and I say, 'Don't you get bored with church?' and he says 'No'. And I say, 'But frankly, don't you find the endless round of meetings rather irksome?' and he says 'No'. And I say, 'Honestly now, aren't there times when you want to have your fling?' and he says 'No, I *delight* to do His will, the will of my God.' . . . If you want to be strong in goodness, learn to love Jesus, because then it ceases to be a burden and becomes a delight.

Why Jesus Never Wrote a Book, pp 91–2

Henry Martyn . . . has been called 'the most heroic figure in the English Church since the time of Queen Elizabeth I' and, if that judgement savours of extravagance, no one familiar with the facts would think it wildly wrong. He was, indeed, a 'Confessor of the Faith'. After a brilliant career at Cambridge (Senior Wrangler before he was twenty: Smith's Prizeman: Fellow of St John's) he heard the call to the Mission Field and tossed aside half a dozen possible careers to carry the gospel abroad. He said, 'Here I am, Lord: send me to the ends of the earth; send me to the rough, the savage pagans of the wilderness; send me from all that is called comfort in earth; send me even to death itself if it be but in Thy service and in Thy Kingdom'.

That was how he gave himself, and, in that spirit, he prepared himself for India. Then something happened. He fell deeply in love with a girl named Lydia. He told her of his love and that he was under orders from heaven for India. Would she go with him? Together, they could do great things for God. All his heart pleaded with her to go. She would not go. If he stayed in England, she would marry him. If he went to India, he must go alone. So the question hammered in his brain: 'India or Lydia? Lydia or India? . . .'

He chose aright. He went to India and he went alone. He never knew that kind of affection again. He cried out in his pain 'My dear Lydia and my duty called me different ways. Yet God hath not forsaken me . . . I am born for God only. Christ is nearer to me than father, or mother, or sister' and (he might have added) than Lydia either.

That awful choice does not come to many Christians, but when it comes to the saint he knows how to answer it.

The Pure in Heart, pp 103–4

A change in oneself can mean a change in the whole scene
. . . I was asked once, when I was a minister in the North, if I
would find time to cheer up a young man who had been sent
into our neighbourhood to recuperate after a nervous breakdown. I promised to do my best. I sought the young man out,
and I began, but, O, it was hard work. 'This is a grey world',
he said. 'I see no purpose in it. It is dull, meaningless and evil.
Its pleasures soon pass. Its pains endure. I seriously ask myself
the question "Is life worth having?" '—and much more—*very*
much more—in the same strain.

I saw him once or twice a week for nearly two months, and
every conversation was the same—and then something happened to that young man! He fell in love. None of this nervous,
hesitant venturing into the waters. He took a header! And on
the day his engagement was announced . . . he came and saw
me, and began the conversation with words something like
this: 'This is a lovely world. Come out into the garden and
listen to that little bird singing fit to burst its heart. Isn't it a
glorious morning? How good it is to be alive.'

I listened to his raptures in reverent silence, and all my smiles
were up my sleeve. It was just the same old world he had been
castigating for months. Just the same; no better and no worse.
The change was all in him. I rounded off the little episode by
marrying them, and I pass the parable on to you. There are
people here who find life horribly dull, commonplace and
matter of fact, but if they fell in love with Jesus Christ, what a
difference it would make.

Westminster Sermons (vol. ii), p 33

'When in Rome do as Rome does!' Ah! you have heard that before. It is a common piece of worldly-wise advice. . . . I was a mere lad, with school barely behind me and my business career just about to begin. And some of my relatives had noticed in me what they regarded as puritanical leanings and they were fearful lest these eccentricities should hinder my prospects. 'Don't be a frost in society', they said. 'Don't be a gawk: accommodate yourself to people just as you find them and remember . . . when in Rome do as Rome does!' Ah! I see. If I find myself a member of a circle that drinks, I am to forget my abstinence vows and drink with them. If I find myself a member of a group that gambles, I am to cast my convictions to the winds and join in 'the little flutter' too. . . . You see? I am in Rome, I must do as Rome does. That is the voice of expediency and that is the voice that I beg you not to heed.

. . . from any angle you like it is bad advice. I cannot discover in it any redeeming aspect at all. If a man is to become, on grounds of policy, part and parcel of his environment whatever that . . . may be, any change of circumstances may send him straight to the devil. We cannot always control our circumstances. A young man gets a new post and finds himself among men in an office or workshop whose tastes are not his tastes and whose habits fill him with disgust. If he is to be loyal to his highest manhood . . . he must, at all costs, keep himself uncontaminated and live, in that alien environment, a precisely opposite life. If that is Rome, the sound advice to that young man is this—'Don't do as Rome does'.

Why Jesus Never Wrote a Book, pp 42–3

Not only is the saint free of worry and of condemnation. He is free of the fear that God's cause will not prevail.

An awful feeling of the senselessness of life oppresses many men. They have no answer to the hardest questions which have teased and tortured the mind of man since man began to think. 'Who am I?' (When the park-keeper, mistaking Schopen-hauer for a tramp, asked him in the Tiergarten at Frankfurt, 'Who are you?', Schopenhauer replied bitterly 'I wish to God I knew'.) 'Why am I here? Is there a meaning in life? Is there a God and is He kind? What comes after this?' A few who, at one time, persuaded themselves that something in humanity was worth salvaging, have more recently come to the conclusion that 'ours is a lost cause on this planet'. With nothing to look forward to, and no meaning in the medley, we must build our house 'on the rock of unyielding despair'.

A house built on the rock of unyielding despair cannot be an abode of joy. The saint builds his house on the Rock of Ages. He knows the answer to every question listed above. He did not come to those answers chiefly by ratiocination but by meditation. With a piercing perception in the spiritual world, not unlike the insight of the master musician or supreme painter in the world of art, he sees reality. . . . The saint is certain that God's purposes will prevail. The ultimate victory is sure. His Lord has overcome the world. When all things terrestrial look dark and forbidding, he cannot doubt. 'Be of good cheer', says Paul, on a sinking ship, 'for I believe God'. The saint is of good cheer for the same reason. He believes God.

The Pure in Heart, pp 113–14

If God is not there; if, being there, He is not love; if His best name is not Father . . . then the law of the jungle will prevail. The race is to the swift, and the prize is to the strong. The emancipated Hindu turned atheist is right. Repudiating the ancient gods of his people, he said: 'The real gods worshipped in the West are chemistry, electricity, nuclear fission. Let us fall down and worship them . . .' The swift and terrible destruction of all our civilization is at the end of that road.

But if a man receive the new life of the living God into his heart and bow before the Supreme Father in true devotion, his piety can never remain narrowly personal, but will overflow to the other members of the family as well.

Indeed, it will work out in all kinds of ways. It will encompass great principles and run down to details, too. Concievably, the devout Englishman at prayer might catch this counsel from his Father-God: 'You must pay more and not less for your sugar, if your black brother who cuts the cane in Jamaica is to have a living wage. You must pay more and not less for your tea, if your brown brother who picks the leaves in Ceylon is to have a living wage. . . .'

God—and economics! Is He interested, then, in a cup of tea? Is this what it means when piety is not narrowly personal and begins to encompass all life?

Let me Commend, pp 119–20

No one who believes in a God of love presumes to explain why some people go through life sick, maimed, blind, deaf or mad. . . . The faith and trust of some afflicted people is amazing; but whether they trust or doubt, their condition demands help. . . . Has anybody dear to you been seriously afflicted? If you cannot help them now, could you help someone like them? . . . Some sick people seem more neglected than others—particularly the old and chronic sick who fill those hospitals which used to be called 'infirmaries' and seem only waiting to die. Let me tell you how a friend of mine helped them.

He retired from business earlier than most men and went to live in a pleasant suburb of a large city. He soon discovered the cheerless state of the infirmaries. . . . He made friends with the authorities. . . . Having grace, he had charm and was hard to resist. Doors opened to him. Four or five afternoons a week he spent in the work. He used to put a good portable gramophone in the back of his car, and into the wards he would go. His arrangements were always elastic. If anyone was dying in a ward, or if, on a particular day, it was inconvenient to the sister-in-charge, he would smilingly make his way elsewhere. He ran competitions. 'Guess the name of this piece of music . . .' A pipeful of tobacco rewarded the old gentleman who won. When he was in the ward of old ladies he offered a few sweets as the prize. . . . Nor was this all. . . . He discovered and noted the inmates who never received visitors. He sent all the lonely souls a card on their birthday and took them a tiny gift as well. So the work grew under his hand. . . .

Twelve Ways of Service, pp 11–12

The peace of the saint, like the joy of the saint, is independent of happenings. The life he is learning to live is symbolized in his Lord asleep amid the storm on the lake—undisturbed calm in a raging world. The ugly arms of the Cross were stretching out to take the Master when He said 'Peace I leave with you; my peace I give unto you'. The peace of God does not require a mould of easy circumstance. Galilee in storm and Calvary in darkness both set it off.

The life of St Paul was a life of toil and suffering; sometimes of disappointment and apparent failure, or arduous travel, persistent persecution, and 'the care of all the churches'. Yet no one spoke more often, and with more conviction of 'the peace which passeth all understanding'.

People who suppose that the right mould of circumstance can produce this deep peace have been disappointed a thousand thousand times. Edward FitzGerald, the translator of the *Rubaiyat* of Omar Khayyàm, thought he knew the recipe. He lef the wife he was not happy with: took a place in the country, made a pattern of his days just calculated to foster congenial work, and kept *doves* (the birds of peace!) as a hobby—but he missed peace! It is the illusion of hard-worked townsmen that peace lives in the country: fret and rush and sin invade rural as well as urban hearts. It does not matter whether you live in a town or in a hamlet. It matters only whether or not you live in God.

The Pure in Heart, p 119

He has but one small weakness;
He cannot *make* a saint.
The Psychologist (G. A. Studdert-Kennedy)

The specialist may welcome you to his consulting room and examine the stuff of your dreams, or invite your ready answer to his series of harmless questions, and talk to you of trite irrelevancies. But finally, if he is a master of his science, he will drag out from your forgotten past the source of all your trouble . . . some unrealized want, it may be, some old sin, perhaps. Yes! He can do that and his results cannot easily be set aside. There is one thing, however, that alone he cannot do—he cannot deal with the sense of guilt. He may expose an old wound—but he cannot heal it. He may show you that your trouble is an ancient sin—but he cannot *forgive*. And that is what the sick soul needs most—forgiveness. . . . I can imagine his patience admitting the truth of his diagnosis. . . . 'But, sir, what is the cure? I want to be clean. . . . Can you take away the sense of guilt?' And the skilful psychoanalyst cannot do it. . . . A certain . . . nerve specialist . . . has said to certain of his patients, 'Go and hear Mr So-and-So preach. . . . He preaches the forgiveness of sins'. Ah! wise physician. True doctor of the sin-sick soul. There is discernment. He suspected the trouble—but he could not cure it. He saw the plague—but of himself he had no antidote. He sent them to the minister of Christ. To whom else could they go? You do not help me by stirring my sins unless you have news of a Saviour. There is only pain in parading the evil past unless you can provide a pardon. And that is why I say that there is no substitute for Christ with the sin-sick soul. He *only* can forgive.

Why Jesus Never Wrote a Book, pp 110–11

There is nothing dignified about a donkey. You can look at him from any angle you like and you will fail to find what men call 'presence'. He hasn't got it. He is an awkward, obstinate, and, some have thought, stupid beast. It is the presence of the donkey which makes Christ's triumphal march the most peculiar thing of its kind in history. Whoever heard of a conqueror riding in triumph on an ass? If any Gentiles had been present when the procession passed by, they must have been quietly amused. To give a common donkey a prominent position was enough to take the dignity out of any demonstration. . . . Not that it appeared in that light to the Jews! . . . The Jews' ideal man was a man of peace, and when the Messiah came he would come in the accoutrements of peace; not on a prancing steed and with the blare of trumpets, but meekly, riding upon an ass.

And, as I have been looking again into that curious processional scene, I feel somehow that the donkey didn't let it down at all. So far from dragging the lowly pomp down to *his* level, he seems rather to have been drawn up to *its*. He has caught a strange dignity and quiet consciousness of privilege. The scene is not ludicrous but royal. The awkward, obstinate and despised beast, has been chosen by the Son of God, and he seems aware of his elevation. . . . And I see a parable in that. Whatever Christ touched He dignified, and no matter how despised a person or creature may be, Christ has a use for him. Let me say that again. No matter how ordinary, ill-educated, disfigured, ill-born, one-talented or obscure a man or woman may be, Christ has a use for them, and He gives them dignity by that use.

Westminster Sermons (vol. ii), pp 57–9

History has a way of proving the relevance of many things which the wise of this world had wiped away contemptuously . . . when I came to Athens! Ah! 'nor tongue nor pen can show'. I sat most of a day and gazed at the Parthenon and, as the sun sank, its horizontal rays played on the iron in the Pentelic marble and turned the gleaming whiteness into a glorious rose-red. 'If it could move one to tears in ruin', I asked myself, 'what must it have been like when it was whole?' And then I remembered the day when a man came to the Areopagus (which is really a rocky spur of the Acropolis) and preached Christ. What a foolish babbler Paul must have appeared then! How utterly irrelevant he would seem to be, telling his improbable tale in the shadow of the Parthenon, and to men who read Plato and Aristotle, too. Nor could he stop short of his whole piece. On he went—to the Resurrection itself and to their open mockery. Fancy trying to put that over on Athenians! Really! It was too funny . . .

Let history judge! The message of that poor babbler smashed the ancient Paganism, despite its philosophy, and its ritual, and its lovely temples; took, indeed, in the passing of four centuries, the glorious Parthenon itself, and turned it into a Christian church for a thousand years.

Irrelevant? It cannot be denied that the message seemed such. But nothing uttered in the ancient world was more relevant than Christ. . . . If the leaders of advanced thought in that period had been told that the cure for the malady [of their day] was in the life and words of a Jewish carpenter, whom some fanatics believed had risen from the dead, they would barely have paused to sneer. The very suggestion would have dipped beneath contempt.

Let me Commend, pp 14, 15

There can be little doubt that many people hesitate to take the initial step of faith in religion because of the tragedies of life: floods, famines, earthquakes, cancers and a host of other things put the possibility for them of a Loving God beyond the reach of rational thought. Some of them wish they *could* believe but wishing doesn't make it so. They have said in their heart: 'There is no God.'

Tolstoy in his *Confessions* has a four-fold classification of how people stand up to tragedy. Some are just scared and mentally fly from it. They may soak in drink . . . to forget. Some despair and commit suicide (or want to). Some are grimly stoical: their heads are 'bloody but unbowed'. Finally, there are those who meet it bravely; not with full understanding but with courage; not claiming to *know* but refusing to strangle the deep conviction of their soul that there is sense in it somewhere. . . .

I wonder! Isn't there a further category or, at least, an enlargement of the fourth? Christianity teaches that suffering can be *used*; that even while a full understanding of origins and purposes eludes our mind, the brave and the bold (by the help of God) can turn the disaster into triumph and force the loss to yield a gain. . . . Tragedy is often fruitful of good. Lighthouses are built by drowned sailors. Roads are widened by mangled corpses. Frustration and testing have had a major part in the higher triumphs of our race.

And if anybody enquires how Christians came to believe that tragedy can be *used*, the short answer is that they learned it at Calvary. In Christ upon the Cross they see God meeting sin with love; wresting earth's worst to heaven's best.

The Little Book of Sermons, pp 32–3

Because Christ founded it. Deliberately so. He said 'On this rock will I build my Church'. The Church was not the idea or invention of the disciples—as though they said after Christ's death 'Let's have a get-together'! It was founded of set purpose by Christ Himself and is, therefore (so Christians believe), a divine institution.

Without claiming to understand all that Christ had in mind when founding the Church, we can, at least, see some things. Life is not *purely* private and individual. Life *is* personal, but that involves relationships and social life also. How much of a man's life is left, if you take out what he is as son, brother, husband, father, friend, workman, citizen . . .? We are social beings. . . . The fulness of the Christian life cannot be known except in fellowship—fellowship with God and fellowship with one another. Moreover, the purposes of God in this world require a social organism by which to express themselves. Far as the Church has fallen below the intention of her divine Founder she is still His best instrument in this world for doing His will. No one knows better than the leaders and members of the Church how unworthy their witness is, but they know, even in this failure, that it is part of their task to offer the world a picture of what the world might be if it sincerely tried to do the will of God. The Church deplores her divisions, but her different branches are less in rivalry with each other, and love and understanding leap over the barriers which still remain. . . . If the nations were as near and as sincerely respectful to one another, as the branches of the Church now are, it would be a different world.

Give God a Chance, p 84

In the last twenty-five years the world has grown suddenly small. By wireless, nation speaks to nation, and the plane has made the wide globe a neighbourhood. The cinema has penetrated the jungle and hungry multitudes have seen the opulent life which Hollywood portrays. The nineteen richest countries in the world have sixteen per cent of the world's people and two-thirds of the world's income. The fifteen poorest countries have over half the world's people and nine per cent of the world's income. . . . This awful inequality lies behind most of the world's unrest.

Christian missions are only a pin's head in this enormous territory of need, but they are an important pin's head. . . . To go as a Missionary doctor, teacher, nurse, or evangelist is noble service.

. . . But work for the wider world is increasingly done at home. People from abroad are flooding into Britain to be trained . . . and to take their share in unskilled labour also. . . . They are a field for service. The scant courtesy with which some of our fellow-countrymen treat them will have awful consequences unless it is offset by the greater courtesy and kindness of others. To send back the future leaders of young nations to their own lands with bitterness in their souls is to rend the Commonwealth and make world peace harder to achieve.

Service for the wider world is at everyone's doorstep today. Befriend the stranger in our midst. Open the home and the hostel and the Church to them.

Open your heart as well.

Twelve Ways of Service, pp 13–14

There is something in man which earth can never satisfy. It is common for people to say and to believe that if they only had this or that coveted thing they would always be happy, and some of them die believing it. But the evidence of those who obtain the 'treasure' does not bear them out. It satisfied for a little while . . . and then there was the old, persistent hunger again, clamorous as ever.

No one will deny that to lack enough money to meet the simple needs of life is to miss happiness, but it is a widespread error to suppose that a lot of money means a lot of joy. Jay Gould, the famous American millionaire, who died possessing fifty million dollars, summed up his life in these words: 'I suppose I am the most miserable devil on earth'.

Some people set their mind on a coveted position and believe that complete satisfaction for them would come by its achievement; they work and scheme and plan to obtain that high post, but the satisfaction of arriving soon fades. When Benjamin Disraeli, twice Prime Minister of England, reviewed his life, he said 'Youth is a mistake; manhood a struggle; old age a regret'. . . . Fame is the will-o'-the-wisp which beckons others on. . . . Sir Walter Scott achieved it—great, and worthy, and deserved fame—but there was that in him which not all the praise of men could satisfy. When he was dying, he said, 'Bring me the book'. 'The book?' they said. 'What book?' 'There is only *one* book', he answered, a little wearily. 'Bring me the Bible.'

Westminster Sermons (vol. i), pp 30–1

During the war* a certain famous battalion was ministered to by a very popular padre. Almost everybody liked him. He was such an understanding fellow. If anyone was expressing himself in lurid language the Chaplain had a wonderful gift of being deaf. . . . Nobody was ever rebuked by a word or look from him. . . . One day he was moved . . . and when the new Chaplain arrived the battalion laughed for a week. Everybody was nudging everybody else and saying 'Have you seen the new padre?' and then there was a shout of laughter. . . . He was straight from College, a pink and white curate . . . and he walked about in a tunic that seemed to fit him where it touched. . . . And that wasn't all. Whenever he was excited he stammered. He provoked more fun in a week than the Concert Party could produce in a month. None the less, there was a hero in that little man's soul, and it peeped out on the first important dinner he attended in the Officers' Mess. The Colonel presided as usual, and as usual expressed his annoyance on some minor matter with the most colourful and obscene language that the little curate had ever heard. Nobody took any notice. They knew the Colonel. But suddenly . . . they became aware that the new padre was on his feet stammering violently and turning alternately red and white. . . . He said, 'Pardon me . . . s-s-sir, b-but you are a s-soldier and you w-w-would expect a m-man to do his duty and it's my d-duty to tell you that your language is an offence to God and to man'. There was an awful silence. Then the Colonel spoke. With a final oath, he said, 'The man's right! . . . Bring me a red-cross box at once'. . . . Henceforth, in that Mess, a man was fined a shilling a swear. Hats off to the little padre! He was a hero. They don't give those heroes the V.C., but their names are written in the Lamb's Book of Life.

Why Jesus Never Wrote a Book, pp 45–6

* World War I.

Christians are completely convinced that He did. If it is said that nobody else ever did, it can be said also that nobody else has influenced the world as He has done. If He was unique in life, is it a thing incredible that He should be unique in His way of leaving it? Something astonishing happened to found the Christian Church. To suppose that a bunch of Galilean fishermen did it without some amazing event is harder to believe than the miracle itself. Nor was it a tale which slowly grew with the years. It was being told three days after His death, and publicly and effectively preached within eight weeks.

No rival theory has withstood careful examination. It has been said . . . that His friends stole the body away. But can you really believe that? If you do, you will also have to believe that His disciples spent the rest of their lives preaching a lie they had invented themselves, and that finally they were prepared to be executed for it. Some have said that it was all hallucination. But hallucination normally turns on expectation—and they were *not* expecting it. . . . Hallucination can account for some queer things, but not this. So *many* saw Him—on one occasion, five hundred at once.

This thing happened. . . . Think of the quality of His life; think of His impact on all subsequent history; think what He does still with men and women. . . . Part of His mission on earth was to show men and women that death is not a blind alley but a highway to life.

He came back from the dead to prove it.

Give God a Chance, p 47

[Pilate] did endeavour feebly to administer justice. When they first brought their unresisting captive to him, he refused to hear them except on a stated political charge. When he had examined the prisoner, and assured himself of His innocence, he stated that fact definitely before them all. . . . He seized on their own custom and offered Jesus as the prisoner who should be released at the feast. But to this the Jews replied with their last and strongest argument: 'If thou let this man go thou art not Caesar's friend. . . .' Their case was won then. The fierce struggle in the mind of Pilate was over. Superstitious fear, the good in him, and his sense of justice on the one side, stood opposed to private ambition and his sense of security on the other; and the selfish element won. He could not risk further complications at Rome. Deliberately, he condemned an innocent man to death . . . he preferred his social standing to any spiritual stability. He would not be a just man, if to be a just man, he must be a poor man. Moral values clashed with earthly values—and he chose the earthly.

. . . We must all face this issue sooner or later. To every man and woman the inevitable choice comes . . . 'Which is first in my life—the spiritual or the material?' . . . There are the higher aspirations of our soul, and the lower, coarser tendencies of our nature. We are constantly legislating between the two. Our best self points out the hard and costly way; our lower self derides it and urges us to 'play for safety'. Our best self challenges us to be the highest we have power to be; our lower self tells us that we must always take care of 'number one'.

They Met at Calvary, pp 54–5

Scientists are agreed that pearls are the product of pain. Sometimes the pain is caused by a microscopic worm and sometimes by a boring parasite. In this latter case, the shell of the oyster or mussel gets pierced, chipped or perforated and some alien substance (a speck of sand, it may be) gets inside. Immediately, all the resources of the tiny organism rush to the spot where the breach has been made. On the entry of that foreign irritant the unsuspected healing powers of the little creature are marshalled at the point of peril . . . powers that otherwise would have remained for ever dormant are called out by this new emergency: the foreign irritant is covered and the wound is healed—by a pearl. No other gem has so fascinating a history. . . . It is a symbol of stress; it is a healed wound; it is the enduring token of a tiny creature's struggle to preserve its life. We do not normally associate pearls with pain. Pearls are for the ball-room; pearls are for the hours of entertainment and of relaxation; pearls will share in the sparkle and gaiety of those who agree to forget for a while that life has its sombre and saddening sides. But pearls are not so made! Their history contrasts strangely with their use. They are the product not of pleasure, but of pain. They are healed wounds. If there had been no wound there could have been no pearl. Some oysters are never wounded and the men that seek for gems throw them aside.

Why Jesus Never Wrote a Book, pp 47–8

There is a terrible courage in the saints . . . almost the first thing a trained hagiographer would say of the saints is that they are brave. Many of them were not brave by nature. Henry Martyn was timid and nervous. St Francis de Sales was afraid of the dark and of evil spirits. Miriam Booth was not physically courageous. Yet these, and the vast holy company to which they belonged, did things incredibly brave and make it seem the more miraculous because of the sensitive imagination that must have vividly foreseen the probable consequence of their deeds.

Henry Martyn, seeking to present a Persian New Testament at the court of the Shah of Persia, went *alone* into that centre of fanatical Moslems to offer the Book. Attending the Vizier's levee, he found himself surrounded by an angry group who demanded that he recite the Moslem Creed. 'Say it', they said. 'Say "God is God and Mohammed is the prophet of God".' The whole court awaited that lonely man's reply. His voice rang out 'God is God and Jesus is the Son of God.' It would have been heroic in a grenadier but from this one-time timid, nervous, imaginative man? . . . Yet these splendid moments are not the best illustration of the courage of the saints. . . . It is the harder kind of courage with which the record of their days abounds: cold courage displayed over long years: costly loyalty in the face of loneliness and persecution: unflinching faith in prison and in scorn. . . . The biographer of John Howe truly says: 'The brief horrors of the stake—the momentary pang which at once dismissed the weary spirit to its everlasting rest, would often have been gladly preferred to that slow, protracted torture, which was inflicted on many of the sufferers for religion during the seventeenth century.'*

The Pure in Heart, pp 128–9

---

* Rogers, *Life of Howe*, p 123.

It was just getting the 'me' into the Cross which made all the difference to the greatest figures of evangelical religion. It was that realization that made them the men they were. It was true of Paul . . . it was true of Luther. In his early years he was a rigid Roman monk, laboriously working his passage to heaven by midnight vigils, and flagellations, and fastings, and still never feeling that his sins were forgiven, until that ever-memorable day when the pronouns came alive to him, and he cried: 'The Son of God, who loved *me*, and gave Himself up for *me*.' Writing his commentary on Galatians years afterwards he said: 'Read therefore with great vehemency these words "*me* and for *me*", and so inwardly practise with thyself, that thou, with a sure faith, mayst conceive and print this "me" in thy heart, and apply it to thyself, not doubting but thou art of the number of those to whom this "me" belongeth.'

It was so with John Wesley too. Whatever it was that happened in Aldersgate Street on 24th May 1738, there is no question that the pronouns came alive. He says himself '. . . an assurance was given me that He had taken away *my* sins, even *mine*, and saved *me* from the law of sin and death'. Nor was it different with Charles, his brother, who came into the experience a day or two before John. The 'me' came into it suddenly for him. He cried:

> I felt the Lord's atoning blood
> Close to my soul applied;
> *Me*, *me* He loved—the Son of God,
> For *me*, for *me* He died.

They Met at Calvary, p 78

It is dubious whether anyone today . . . can imagine the horror which struck the world when Alaric sacked Rome in the year A.D. 410. It did, indeed, seem like the end of all things. To Jerome, in his cell at Bethlehem, it appeared to be the 'day of wrath' and 'day of mourning. . . .' . . . When one thinks of the extent and strength and durability of the Roman empire, it must have seemed to multitudes that the very pillars of the Universe had snapped before their eyes. . . . Thousands of simple people who, for all the faults of the Imperial City, had enjoyed 'the peace of Rome', must have waited in fearful expectation of what the coming months and years would bring.

If one had told them in the year A.D. 413 that a bishop in Africa was writing a book, *The City of God*, would it have seemed relevant to them? Would anything said or written by an ecclesiastic who never went beyond the confines of Africa and Numidia during his episcopate . . . seem fully matched to the world's awful need . . .? No!

. . . To us it seems the most relevant thing of all. . . . Augustine soars above his fellows as one of the greatest figures in the Evangelistic Succession, and, however blind his contemporaries were to his greatness, we now know (and the thinking world has long known) that *his* was the word matched to the world's need, and his relevance centres in this: that, with all his haste in writing, and all his necessary modifications, his word was vital because his word was Christ.

Let me Commend, pp 15–17

. . . We notice the ennobling power of suffering in the lives of the people who suffer. The Gentiles were evangelized by an Apostle with a stake in his flesh, and you cannot separate his sufferings from his successes. It was the blinded Milton who sang so divinely in *Paradise Lost*. It was the prisoned Bunyan who wrote the world's greatest allegory. It was the deafened Beethoven who composed the immortal Ninth Symphony. Who will say that their distresses had nothing to do with their triumphs? I am myself acquainted with a lady in London who will illustrate my meaning. In the short space of a few months she lost by death the three people for whom she lived. Her mother—by shock in an air-raid; her little sister—by meningitis; her fiancé—killed at the front. It wasn't a wound; it was a rent. We didn't see her for a week when the last blow fell, but when she came among us again we saw that a strange spiritual alchemy had begun. She seemed possessed by an unearthly peace. Christ in her was busy staunching the bleeding by tireless devotion to the needs of other people. A large part of an important Mission depends on her today; she wields an immense influence over scores of young people: the wound in her soul is healed by a Christ-made pearl and its lustre irradiates all whom she meets. Busy on the necessary business of this life, she nevertheless treads already, by anticipation, the golden streets of that celestial city.

Why Jesus Never Wrote a Book, pp 49–50

The very mould of your life, and of which you complain so bitterly, may be capable of transformation, if you are transformed yourself. There are awful frustrations in life, and sometimes we can only endure them. But the greatest frustration is the sin inside us and when that is dealt with, it sometimes happens that the external frustrations frustrate us no more.

You have not forgotten, I suppose, the workman who was chaffed by his workmates because he lived a life of strict sobriety, never gambled, and always spoke of the Bible with reverence.

'If you believe in the Bible', they said 'you must believe that water was turned into wine.' 'I believe more than that', he said. His mind went back to his evil early days and his pre-conversion years.

'I have seen', he said, 'beer turned into furniture. Betting-slips turned into food. I have seen a woman, miserable because she was married to a gambling addict, made radiantly and permanently happy because her man was changed before her eyes. Of course I believe in miracles.'

A changed man changes his environment.

Westminster Sermons (vol. ii), pp 35–6

Salvation is by a Saviour, not by a system. The Saviour's plan will only be worked effectively by those who have His Spirit and who have known His personal salvation within themselves. . . .

There is no system devisable by man which will work with automatism to perfection, and which an evil will cannot subvert. The deepest personal religion is called for from all who would fulfil the enlarging opportunities of God's new order on earth, and the demand is made to Christians in every stratum of our present social life. From some it will require the surrender of exclusive privilege and extreme wealth: from others it will call for victory over sloth and self-indulgence: from all it demands honest labour of brain and hand. . . . There will be much for the pilgrims of perfection to learn: patience with the slow development of those who have been unprivileged in time past and may be loath to learn: patience with those in whom it seems hard to create any desire for nobler things: courage to face the subtle evasions of sin in their own souls and to overcome the temptation to return to the narrow concept of holiness because it was less costly and more comfortable. . . . To shape this God-inspired order, and effectively to work it, will demand more than the average in moral achievement. But those in whom God's perfecting process is at work will not be unequal to it. Self and society are not at war in them. Because supernatural love fills their consecrated hearts, and directs their keen minds, they are the true pioneers of the new order, and they march in the van of the victorious host of God. Nor have they parted with the text they loved so dearly in their most individualistic days—but they see more in it: 'For God so loved the *world*, that He gave His only begotten Son'.

The Path to Perfection, pp 183–4

No. Not deeply. God did not make us to be happy at any price, and good if we could manage it. He made us to be good —and deeply happy as a consequence. Don't confuse this with priggishness. I am not describing people who feel morally superior to others and are proud because of it. That is probably the most detestable of sins and led Christ to say some of the severest things which ever fell from His lips.

The full answer to the question . . . runs right down to those deeper layers of our nature. . . . We always knew that it was right to do right, that kindness was better than cruelty and the truth than a lie. If these things are basic to our human nature —however much they may be overlaid by our habit of lying to ourselves when we want something which our conscience disapproves—how can we hope to be happy if we are deliberately running against them?

We can be happy *for a time*. We can ignore the disapproval inside us. We can do the very things our moral sense warns us against (in order to silence it if we can) but we can't be deeply and constantly happy. When we are alone, the inner voice awakes again in disapproval, and although it weakens with years of neglect, it is doubtful if it is ever completely silenced. Always it speaks at any rate of the decencies, and there is the power of authority in what it says.

Give God a Chance, p 90

Nor is the urgency of the task [of evangelism] to be found only in the world's condition. It is to be found in our human awareness of the passage of time . . . it isn't hard to point to changes in ourselves. The comb passes through the hair more swiftly. Something of resilience has gone . . . a great many opportunities have passed for ever. We dare not fritter any more away. The night cometh when no man can work. A double urgency therefore hangs over the enterprise. The world's condition cries aloud for the eternal Gospel, and the galloping years carry away our chances of serving it. Nor does the wisest among us know what opportunities are left nor how soon upon our day of life the night will fall.

A friend of mine told me once that he had reduced a normal life to the length of one day in order to test how far he was forward on the pilgrimage of life. He assumed that life was seventy years and that a normal day runs from seven o'clock in the morning till eleven o'clock at night. That being so, he worked it out *roughly* like this: At 20 years of age it is half-past eleven; at 30 it is two o'clock; at 40 it is four o'clock; at 50, half-past six; at 60, a quarter to nine.

What time is it with you?

Whatever the time o'day, let us do all we can . . . let us go on with a fine scorn of earthly fame and fortune, and let it be our high resolve never to be traitorous in heart.

. . . And if, at the end of the day, a little time is allowed to sit over the fire and think, though we know ourselves to be unprofitable servants and base no hopes of the future on our own endeavours, it will not be without comfort to remember that we laboured while it was day.

Methodism: Her Unfinished Task, pp 121–2

I well remember a member of my congregation coming to my door one day in deep distress. Her daughter had recently been admitted as a patient to the eye hospital, and had gone in with every hope of recovery. But the disease proved more deadly than anyone guessed, and, on the day when my visitor stumbled over my step, the blow had fallen. The doctors foresaw that she would be blind in three weeks or a month, and suggested that it would be best if the mother broke the news to her girl. She, poor soul, had come to pass the terrible task on to me. I went with lagging footsteps to the hospital, and I can see the little private ward now as I saw it then. The single bed, the locker, the polished floor, the drawn blind, and the patient turning her fast dimming eyes towards me. I talked of trivialities for some minutes, scheming for an opening, and half afraid that she would hear my thumping heart. Then she guessed! Perhaps I paused too long, or she divined it by some vibrant note in my voice, for suddenly she burst out with a half-suppressed sob, 'Oh! I believe that God is going to take my sight away'.

It was a hideous moment, and an ugly phrase. My divided heart in that minute was half in prayer to God, and half in talk with her. I remembered a story I had heard of a missionary in India, and what he had said when he lost his little girl, and I said 'Jessie, I wouldn't let Him', and when she begged me to explain, I falteringly asked if she thought (not at once, but in three weeks or a month!) she could pray a prayer like this: 'Father, if for any reason known to Thee, I must lose my sight, I will not let it be taken from me. I will give it to Thee.'

And in three weeks or a month, she prayed that prayer. It was not easy. Does anyone think it was? One day she clutched at my hand and declared that she simply could not live in this world without a bit of light, but she offered the prayer before the last glimpse of day vanished for ever. Peace came with the prayer. She carries the cross willingly, not grudgingly, or of necessity, but with a cheerful courage. She is sweet to live with, and God uses her for the comfort and help of others.

He is Able, pp 20–1

There is something in man which earth cannot satisfy; not even the best things of earth. The testimony of those who have achieved coveted things is emphatic and uniform; there still remains a longing, and a hunger, and a heart-ache which nothing material or terrestrial seems able to meet. We live on earth and yet, somehow, we do not *belong* to it. In certain ways we have kinship with the beasts, but, so far as we can judge, earth satisfies them.

> *Irks care the crop-full bird?*
> *Frets doubt the maw-crammed beast?*

Earth does not satisfy us. I cannot help but feel that that is an impressive fact. I warn you against supposing that, if only you had more of this or more of that, you would be completely satisfied. It is an illusion. Earth *cannot* satisfy you. William Watson—in his poem *World-Strangeness*—asked

> *In this house with starry dome,*
> *Floored with gemlike plains and seas,*
> *Shall I never feel at home,*
> *Never wholly be at ease?*

Never!
You weren't meant to.

Westminster Sermons (vol. i), p 32

When M. Vianney arrived in Ars, the village had sunk very
low. Sunday was desecrated: the cabarets and dance-halls were
full: ignorance was widespread: foul language was too common
for comment: drunkenness, blasphemy, impurity and lying
were the features of that rural life. The Curé declared instant
war on all this wickedness, but the powers of darkness con-
tested the field for ten years with a venom and tenacity and
resource which made this obscure village the scene of a major
contest of hell and heaven. Almost the first thing to go in the
mud was the Curé's reputation. Slanderous stories were spread
that he attracted girls to his house for immoral purposes and
spent the nights in debauchery. His pale face and wasted frame
—the fruit of fastings and midnight prayers—were offered as
evidence of his evil living. He was the subject of obscene songs
and scurrilous anonymous letters. A woman of the streets
paraded under his window night after night, accusing him . . .
of being the father of her child. . . .

But he won! God used his unwavering faith, and the time
came when the cabarets and dance-halls folded up: when the
foul language was heard in Ars no more: when the church was
crowded with eager worshippers. . . . Congratulated by a visitor
from Paris on the purity of Ars, a resident said: 'We are no
better than other people but there are some things you cannot
do when there is a saint about.'

The Pure in Heart, pp 149–50

It moved in the heart of this felon [the penitent thief] as he hung on the cross that he had witnessed something not of this earth. He had seen them nail the Nazarene to the wood, watched the blood spurt, forethought his own immediate agony in the writhing body of Jesus, and heard through the hammer-strokes—not the torrent of curses that was customary —but a prayer that shivered to the sky and struck into the soul of that convicted thief as nothing else had done in years: 'Father . . . forgive them . . . they know not what they do.'

He believed it then—all he had heard of Jesus. He had done nothing amiss. However fairly he himself was condemned, it was a filthy parody of injustice to nail this unearthly prisoner to the cross. As the shadows gathered about him, and he heard the blasphemous railings of his companion in crime, he rebuked him. Evil man though he was, he feared God. No man is wholly evil in whose soul lingers some fear of God. And as he spoke, faith rose in his soul . . . and rushed in appeal from his parched lips. 'Jesus,' he cried '. . . remember me when thou comest in Thy Kingdom'. . . . Oh! the joy—and the pain—for Jesus. He had said 'And I, if I be lifted up from the earth, will draw all men unto Me'. And He was lifted up—and they were coming. Already! The first of many millions.

> *The dying thief rejoiced to see*
> *That fountain in his day;*
> *And there may I . . .*

And there may you!

You. Repentance—by a cross!

They Met at Calvary, pp 61–2

New Zealand is a fascinating country to those who are interested in geography and travel. Do you know that there are no dangerous wild animals and no dangerous reptiles native to New Zealand at all? Not one! Apart from its human occupants a child could have wandered through its primeval forests unharmed. Do you know also that New Zealand is the home of more flightless birds than any other country?—the Kiwi, the Kakapo, the Penguin and the Weka Rail. These birds had wings but lost them by neglecting their use. Scholars say they neglected them because food was always abundant and there was no danger near—no fearsome beast or reptile. And the cost of their immunity was the power of their wings. They had no necessity to fly; now they have no ability to fly.

My friends, it would have been the same with us. The dangers that we dread compel us to expand the wings of the spirit. It is our need that drives us to the bosom of our God. I put it to you that you pray most when you feel you need most. When sickness, worry, depression, loss and the dark mysteriousness of life has you in its grip; then it is you pray most. If earth offered all we asked, we should have been superior beasts without a thought above the clouds.

Why Jesus Never Wrote a Book, pp 50–1

We need revival. Prayer is the way. . . . The 1859 revival had no outstanding leaders at all! But—like all the others—it had the great prelude of prayer. We need assurance. Many—even in the Churches—are groping. . . . How can we be sure of our faith? Prayer is the way. We need warmer relationships between the denominations. Holding conversations and fashioning a formula has its part to play no doubt, but the love which makes us cling to one another is born in corporate prayer. We need to integrate our Methodism. Church amalgamations are resisted in many areas still for lack of love. . . . Hearts are fused in the fellowship of prayer.

. . . We need to recover again the power of corporate prayer. Something is added to prayer offered in fellowship which is not given in the same degree to the same prayers offered by the same people in separateness. . . . Through 200 years of Methodism, men powerful in winning souls have ascribed their success to the fact that the prayer meeting was the central meeting of the week—honoured by all; undertaken with business thoroughness; consisting of no haphazard railing to heaven, but preceded by thought and conversation concerning the right 'objectives' of the praying. . . . This is our great need —the recovery of range and depth and listening and love in prayer. Oratory, organization, mass meetings are not basic. We want a prayer-cell in every home, and we want our Churches to be a cluster of them. . . . Nothing we do is more important than this. The people who brush prayer aside . . . forget that many of the things we would do would be different if we prayed first for God's plan, rather than asked for His blessing on ours.

The Pattern of Prayer, pp 14–15

I heard recently of a young man who had been in great trouble. His wife had gone blind. While her sun was still climbing the sky it was blotted from the heavens and midnight descended before it was noon. Her chief delight in life had been their lovely garden; all her leisure was given to the cultivation of flowers and no small part of her bitterness arose from the thought that the garden had gone from her for ever.

But her devoted husband has tried to give her the garden again and in a novel way. He has taken up all the plants that were there merely for their looks, and he has replaced them by plants whose chief merit is their smell. Out with the asters and in with the thyme. Out with the peonies and in with lavender. Out with the marguerites and in with stocks, pinks and carnations. Out with the rhododendrons and in with more roses. And my last news of that heroic couple is that the wife has her garden again and her husband has the joy of giving it to her. By another sense she retains her own. Books are closed, and life in the house grows irksome, but spring in the garden is still precious, though the joy of it comes another way. That seems to me to be a parable of the way God deals with His aged saints when their powers begin to decay. He finds a secret stair to their soul. He is constant when their joys have fled and He tells them things He does not tell us. I am not disposed to dread old age when the saints open to me the treasury of their God-given wisdom.

He is Able, pp 27–8

It may be doubted whether—even in the Church today—
there are many whom St Paul would recognize as saints. He saw
a colourless group of worshipping people one day at Ephesus
but he knew that they were not the real thing. They had not
received the Holy Spirit and Christ was not being formed
afresh in them. He would be similarly disappointed in many of
our Churches today.

When the Holy Spirit fills a human heart and Christ is being
formed within, it is impossible to conceal it. Supernatural love
streams from it. Joy bubbles out of it. Peace and serenity shine
in it. Saintliness is the most winning and attractive thing in the
world. It cares. It is so unselfcentred, so sincere, so guileless, so
radiantly good. . . . Most of us have known someone with this
quality of life, and their memory stays with us through all the
years.

But how few they are! Even Church-people are often unloving, fault-finding, selfish, and querulous. They worry—showing
that they do not trust. They can be filled with fear, jealousy, be
greedy for praise, and insistent on their own way. People who
never go to church watch them and wonder what difference
Christianity is supposed to make. 'I can live as good as that,'
they think, 'and I don't need to go to church to do it.' Some
people who keep the churches open, keep other people away. If
Christianity can do no more for people than this, it's a fraud.

But it can! The saints prove it. In them the appeal of Christ is
well-nigh irresistible. If there were more saints, the Church
would challenge the world.

You Can be a Saint, pp 6–7

People often talk about 'the secret of the saints' but . . . it must be an open secret. . . . The saints attend to God. How mild the word seems for the absorbing, adoring, passionate gaze they fix on Him, but that is the essence of it. . . . They attend to God. They attend to God, of course, in prayer. There is no instance of one great in sanctity who was not great in prayer.

The 'secret' of St John Bosco turns out to be the secret of prayer. In nineteen hours a day he never lost conscious communion with God. St Aloysius Gonzaga could not tear himself away from prayer. To the fixed prayer-pattern of his days, Fletcher of Madeley spent two whole nights a week in prayer. With St Francis of Assisi, all life was prayer. Alexander Grant called prayer his 'Fourth Dimension'. Thomas Collins was wrapt in God for hours on end, and would wander in the country for a day of prayer. They said of St Gerard Majella that 'for him, everything was prayer'. Everything was prayer, also, for the Sadhu Sundar Singh, though within two or three years of his conversion, he had ceased to pray for things and prayed only for God. St Thérèse of Lisieux found a similar development in her absorbing prayer. She said 'I am no longer able to ask eagerly for anything save the perfect accompaniment of God's designs on my soul'. All progress with Catherine Booth was progress in prayer. 'Oh to live in the spirit of prayer!' she cries. 'I feel it is the real secret of religion.' Lost in prayer at times, Henry Martyn 'knew not how to leave off'. David Hill spent whole nights on his knees. . . . It was in prayer that John Woolman found renewal from all the toils and trials of the day. . . .

The Pure in Heart, pp 197–8

There was once a man who was courteous and considerate in all the business relationships of life and had a reputation also for being a very fine man in the church. Yet he stored up his ill-humour for the home, and he was a cross-grained and irritable creature in the house. The members of his family heard other folk praising him but they were loyal to their relationship and never gave him away. None the less, they couldn't help wishing sometimes that he would be as nice in the home as he was in the world.

Art thou that man?

There was once a young woman who had grown up in the Sunday school. She liked her teachers and they liked her and they thought 'Some day she will be a teacher too'. But somehow or other she passed through the school and never really consecrated her life to Christ. Finally she drifted away from the church and gave little, or no, thought to the deeper things. Dress and boys—both natural things—occupied most of her thought. And yet sometimes she was seized by a strange dissatisfaction. She felt that life had not given her the greatest thing of all; now and then she met people who were alight with God and who seemed to know Christ and be certain of Him. And she wished with all her heart that she might know Him too.

Art thou that woman?

There was once a young man who had been cradled in a Christian home. . . . He thought himself a man of the world and to all appearances the church had failed with him. None the less, there were times when he wished with all his heart that he was clean. . . .

Art thou that man?

Why Jesus Never Wrote a Book, pp 58–9

Two major revolutions . . . stirred Europe in the eighteenth century: the French Revolution . . . and the Industrial Revolution in England. In their different ways they have had a large share in shaping the modern world . . . the two Revolutions worked themselves up and out, and fear stalked Europe for years. If people dreaded the bloody horrors of France more than they feared industrialization, nobody denied that they were days of crisis, and many Christians lived in imminent expectation of the end of the world.

But at the same time (one feels half apologetic for mentioning such a 'trifle' on the background of those grim world events) another movement was active, too. . . . Bands of preachers were going all over England and Wales, and penetrating Ireland, Scotland and America, too. They owed their origin, under God, to an Oxford don who had passed through a remarkable religious experience in 1738. . . . Their message was Christ. They penetrated into nearly every part of the British Isles . . . in America, the greatest of them* was said to have marked out the United States with the hoof-marks of his beasts, and Calvin Coolidge said of him, 'He is entitled to rank as one of the builders of our nation'.

To the worldly-wise, it was all supremely unimportant. The only notice the 'intelligentsia' have ever taken of 'hot-gospellers' has been one of amused contempt, and in this century it was no exception. But the work went on. . . . History has passed its own verdict on the relevance of all this. . . . G. M. Trevelyan comments on the 'profound effects upon England for generations' of the coincidence in time of Wesley and the Industrial Revolution. . . . Of one thing only were [those Methodist preachers] sure. They must preach Christ.

Let me Commend, pp 18–20

* Francis Asbury.

April 23   *The Jews have no dealings with the Samaritans—*
but He changed all that

Most people who study the Scriptures know that there was enmity between the Jews and the Samaritans. It had . . . its roots in history. It went back to the year 722 B.C. when Sargon, the king of Assyria, sacked Samaria and carried away the Ten Tribes into captivity . . . and when he sowed that devastated area with his Assyrian settlers, they found a remnant of the Israelites still in occupation of the land. In course of time, the Israelites and the Assyrians inter-married, and made one people, who were called 'Samaritans'. . . . The Jews said: 'They are not of the pure stock of Israel.' Nor did the Samaritans improve their position in the eyes of the Jews when they . . . took the Pentateuch and said 'This is our Holy Book as well'; and said 'We will have a holy mount of our own', and they fixed it at Mount Gerizim in Samaria. . . . Among the Jews, the word 'Samaritan' was about the nastiest term you could use. It meant 'dog'. It meant 'devil'. It meant 'illegitimate'. Among the Samaritans the term 'Jew' meant 'snob', 'stiff-necked', 'haughty'.

If you had called a Jew, in the time of Jesus, a 'Samaritan' it would have been the dirtiest insult you could have thought of. But if you were to call *me* a 'Samaritan' today, it would be one of the highest compliments you would pay me! I should be flattered. You would mean that I was full of the milk of human kindness and bursting with practical zeal. What has happened to the word? It has been completely changed.

Jesus changed it. He told a story . . . a simple story about a robber-infested road, a bleeding victim, a callous priest and Levite, a despised Samaritan, a wondering inn-keeper, a re-ceipted bill. Jesus . . . picked that word out of the gutter . . . and made it adjectival of the saints.

Westminster Sermons (vol. ii), pp 39–40

Faith in the New Testament is variously described, and each description adds something to its rich reality. In the Gospels it is commonly associated with Our Lord's healing miracles. His healing touch rests on the subject of His cure. He seeks to create faith when it is not present, and He is temporarily defeated—as at Nazareth—when unbelief is entrenched and immovable. . . . Faith provides a point of entry. Where people believe, the power gets through. Where people believe utterly, it comes through as a flood.

In the letters of St Paul, faith is conceived as personal trust. In the abandonment of oneself to Christ, deliverance is found from moral defeat and from straining self-effort, and the life of God flows so omnipotently into the soul of the consenting disciple that it is no longer himself who is living in the body but Christ living in Him. In the letter to the Hebrews—and this is the clue we are seeking—faith is a form of insight: it is the power to see Reality behind Appearance: it is the vision, in this world of time and sense, of the world which is unseen and eternal. . . .

Faith affirms that behind this world there is another—a world more real than the world of experience, the pulsating power of which (pouring through believing men and women) can transform the world which we see. Because it goes *beyond* reason, it cannot be proved *by* reason, but it is not necessarily contradictory *of* reason. It ventures out beyond what reason has proved and it calls reason to lumber forward and sustain faith. But, at the last, it lives not by logic but by conviction.

The Pure in Heart, pp 214–15

Many Christians live on a sub-Christian level. That is not a judgement made in spiritual pride, nor yet a judgement which necessarily omits the critic himself. Its truth is keenly felt by sensitive souls in the Church, even more, perhaps, than by those outside. The Church is living far below the New Testament offer and promise. There is not enough difference between the people inside the Church and those outside to be impressive. Men cheerfully ignore the Christian faith, repudiate public worship, private prayer, and all the means of grace, and live, so they believe, as good a life as their church-attending neighbours. And in thousands and thousands of instances the professing Christian lacks that quality of life which would inevitably, though unconsciously, rebuke such inverted Pharasaism, and make it self-conscious and ashamed.

Not even her most earnest devotees would claim that the Church is a mighty and effective instrument for God in this world. Without belittling her thousand secret philanthropies or abating one jot of the claim that, with all her faults, she is the nearest expression of God's will in this world, it remains true that, in the western world, she is disunited, enfeebled, and in retreat. The gates of hell prevail against her.

In her multitude of needs, what need, if any, out-tops all the rest? The need for holiness. Like the word of God it 'is living, and active, and sharper than any two-edged sword, and piercing even to the dividing of soul and spirit'.

The Path to Perfection, pp 192–3

Slowly, the awareness of what had happened grew upon [the disciples] in the days succeeding Pentecost. The Saviour had fulfilled His word. The Holy Spirit was within them—to make them holy too; to impart His own fruit (love, joy, peace, patience, kindness, goodness, faithfulness, humility and self-control); to convict the world of sin through them and make them mighty in evangelism.

So—to evangelism they went. No dependable record survives of their travels. Did Thomas get to India, as some believe? Did all the Apostles but John die for the faith? We do not know. But wherever they went, the Holy Spirit went *in* them, breaking the sin in their nature, moulding them to holiness, pleading in prayer, exalting the Saviour, convicting the world of sin.

From the earliest years of the Church the threefold blessing was in use. The grace of the Lord Jesus Christ, the love of God, the fellowship of the Holy Spirit. . . . I say again: these men were devout Jews and never departed from the central conviction of Judaism. God is One. But One in Three, and Three in One. Creator; Redeemer; Sanctifier. The Father in majesty; the Son in suffering; the Spirit in striving. And it was from the Church's experience that this doctrine arose. It wasn't fashioned (as some seem to suppose) to make a simple thing difficult for ordinary people. 'This is how we met God', said the Apostles in effect, and the Church sought, as she formulated her doctrine, to put into ordered thought an experience implicit in all parts of the New Testament.

Westminster Sermons (vol. ii), pp 117–18

Conscience has sometimes been called the 'Voice of God' and, while the definition is by no means silly, it is capable of misunderstanding. I once overheard two young mothers talking on the same day about the vaccination of their respective babies. One said 'I *must* get it done. It is on my conscience'. The other said 'I am not having it done. It is against my conscience'. They were really using the word . . . to mean 'judgement'. All men and women have a moral sense. They know what the word 'ought' means. 'Ought' is quite different from 'I want', or 'it suits my game', or 'it is the custom', or 'it would be wise'. I can be opposed to all these things and still be *commanding*. '*I ought*' is different and universal. People who deny the existence of God have it . . . [they] trace this moral sense to what society has found convenient, and it is made imperative (they think) because 'our group' is behind it, and it was built into us in childhood.

But this is not deep enough. The sense of shame and pollution we feel when we run contrary to a sensitive conscience requires more explanation than a social convenience. . . . Nor is it true to say that all morals vary according to the tribe or race. *Some* things vary; but the agreements on the major matters are widespread and striking. . . . Those who believe in God find the origin of the moral order in the divine mind. None the less, we must remember that the moral sense requires education, and Christians believe that the best way to educate it is to think much on the God revealed by Jesus Christ, to talk and listen to Him, to worship, and to read with understanding the book in which His unfolding purpose has been made plain.

Give God a Chance, p 91

[Faith] cannot be confined to the intellect. It is a movement of the whole personality. Emotion and will are involved. The vision calls to venture. What nearly all men see as an occasional glimpse the saint sees (except when some dark-night settles on his soul) with steadiness. What most men ignore, the saint embraces. He sees it so clearly that, unless he acted in harmony with what he sees, he would go mad. To men who do not see what he sees, his conduct seems at times bizarre and quixotic, but it is utterly rational in the light of the spiritual world on which his steady gaze is fixed.

One day in Dothan, according to the old story, the king of Syria flung a wide circle of horses, chariots and armed men around the city of Elisha the prophet, and, when the prophet's servant woke next morning and saw the city besieged, he was undone. But Elisha himself was quite unperturbed. It was a nice morning, no doubt, and with God on the throne of the universe, there was no cause for alarm. But to quieten the fears of his servant, Elisha asked a boon of God: 'Lord, I pray Thee, open his eyes that he may see!' And the Lord opened the eyes of the young man; and he saw; and behold, the mountain was full of horses and chariots of fire about Elisha.

Here is a parable for us. The saint sees the spiritual forces of the invisible world. He lives in their light.

> *Lo! to faith's enlightened sight,*
> *All the mountain flames with light. . . .*

The Pure in Heart, p 215

. . . Often in the language of Scripture. God selects a text or passage we have known for years and makes it radiate with a new light. It is as though He says: 'This is the relevant word for you now!' Sometimes it is a couplet from the hymn book, or a chapter in a modern book of devotion, or a phrase from a praying friend. But we know it by the different, shining, commanding quality. It is as though He says: 'This is it.'

Sometimes God borrows our own tongue and talks to us. How wonderful these secret conversations of the soul can be! I wish lack of space and some proper reticence did not prevent me writing of some of my own experiences here. The greatest spiritual hours of my life have been in these conversations. You raise a question with God and go on talking of your perplexity, and He seems to take over, asking you questions and elucidating answers which were sometimes inside you already and sometimes come direct from Him. You get to the point where you hardly know who is asking and who is answering: but it doesn't matter. The blessed session ends leaving you lost in wonder, love and praise. You can go a long time on the memory of one such exalted hour. Should the time come in which He seems for a while not to answer, you can say in complete trust 'I have heard God speak. I can bear His silence. He will speak again when He is ready.'

The Pattern of Prayer, pp 22–3

The time to disbelieve in a general providence watching over this universe will come when seed-time and harvest fail; when the sun is blotted out from the sky; when children are begotten and bring no protective love in the hearts of their mothers; when rain no longer falls to irrigate the parched earth; when disease is the rule and not the exception; when men lose the power of sleep, that blessed providence of nature in which we get both our courage and our strength.

When these fail, these firm and general blessings, these pillars of our universe, this framework of our days—then disbelieve in a general providence and cry it from the housetops that God has forgotten to be gracious. But while the sun is there, and the gentle rain, the fecund earth, and all the melting loveliness of hill and vale and tree and flower; while mother love is discoverable at every level of our social life, and all the *constant* forces of the world are on our side, then let us believe in the general providence of God and say, with Isaac Watts,

> *Thy providence is kind and large,*
> *Both man and beast Thy bounty share.*

The earthquake, famine and flood, are not the rule of this universe; they are the exception. God is working with us to a better understanding of them. Volcanoes will lose much of their terror when men are careful not to build their dwellings on the lip of these vent-holes of nature. . . . And all who toil in the service of mankind against these dark evils may know that they have a senior Colleague in God. . . .

Providence, pp 9–10

Some time ago a poor drunkard came into this church and committed his life to Christ. Twenty years before he had been a church official in the Midlands, but he came to London, took to drink, and drifted to the gutter. When he capitulated to Christ he had a pathetic hope that his thirst might be quenched by some stroke of omnipotence.

It wasn't.

There began on that day when he surrendered to our Lord a long guerrilla warfare in his soul between the deadly craving and the keeping power of Christ.

As his new friend, I suggested that, on any day in which he found the fight especially hard, he might drop in and we could have a prayer together. He dropped in quite often. His drawn face told his own story. We would go into the little chapel at once and pray.

One day, as I was praying with him, he broke down completely. The contrast between his earlier life of holy service, and the revolting bestiality to which drunkenness had brought him, was too much. He sobbed like a child and said:

'I know I'm in the gutter. I *know* it. But oh! . . . I don't belong there, do I? Tell me, I don't belong there . . .'

I put my arm around him. I felt a great elation even in the embarrassment of his tears. He had lost his way . . . but not his address. 'No,' I said quite positively, 'you don't belong there. . . . You belong to God. At the last, *heaven is your home.*'

Westminster Sermons (vol. i), pp 36–7

I was in Wookey the other day, Wookey in Somerset . . . I thought on its famous son. Born in the home of the curate and baptized 'Cyril Arthur' by his father, he came, after schooling, to London, and was soon a power in Fleet Street. He had a flair for journalism. Education for all had produced millions of shallow readers. What could they read? He gave them—naming it after himself—*Pearson's Weekly*, *Home Notes*, *Pearson's Magazine*, the *Daily Express*. The little lad from Wookey had arrived.

And then (it was 1913) in the midst of an amazing career, he went blind. . . . Would you call that a cross? To live for books —and go blind? What did he do? He had his doubly dark hours, I have no doubt, but he did not rebel, or curse God, or turn sour. Did he remember the training of his early years? his boyhood prayers? his father's training? I do not know. I know this. He offered to God his weakness and disability, and asked the Almighty if He had use for a blind man. And God whispered in his ear.

He obeyed! Henceforth . . . he dedicated all that remained of life to those who walked in darkness. . . . He became—noble contradiction of the New Testament word—the Blind Leader of the Blind. Soon he founded St Dunstan's; welcomed home despairing boys as they streamed back blinded from the First World War; taught them to hope again, to laugh, to work, to be wanted; taught them because he knew it all himself; gave them the tonic of a purpose of life. Well—what do you say? Did God make redemptive use of Cyril Pearson's cross? . . . He could do the same with your trouble.

They Met at Calvary, pp 63–4

They say that Christ does not so much save us *from* sinning as *in* sinning; that there is something to be forgiven in the best deed of the best man on the best day of his life; that we are sinners dyed in the wool, and not even grace can make us other than we are.

They believe that even to aspire to this quality of life is vanity and illusion, and that God can do nothing with sin but forgive it.

It is best to avoid the word 'perfect'. Though the term is biblical, it has been fruitful of such wide misunderstanding, and it so often misdirects the interest of people from sanctity that it is best to keep the biblical use of the word 'saint'.

To the objections of those who say that we cannot have this high quality of life we assert that the Bible commands it, promises it, illustrates it, and that there have been saints through all the centuries since the Holy Spirit was given.

We hold also that God can do more with sin than cancel it.

> 'He breaks the *power* of cancelled sin
> And sets the prisoner free . . .'

We contend that the New Testament is not so much concerned with how God can *call* sinners holy, but how He can *make* them such.

We believe that to put anything beyond the power of grace borders on the blasphemous.

The people who say that you can't have this quality of life are mistaken.

You Can Be a Saint, pp 10–11

Is it surprising, do you think, that the disciples should fail to recognize their God? I do not think so—if we remember that men are always more attracted by the spectacular than the truly great. If God had come to earth in a chariot of fire multitudes would have knelt before him. But He was born as we are born and His coming was marked only by a few. If He had moved among men in dazzling apparel, with a glance of flame and a voice of thunder, He would have subdued kingdoms, but He came in the dress of a common workman, spoke with a Galilean accent, and so blended the sublime with the normal that only the few saw that the sublime was there. . . . The unusual and the ostentatious are always more attractive than that which is truly grand. A normal healthy baby is a more glorious sight than a poor malformed infant, but the gaping multitude ignores the normal child and crowds the showman's booth to see some sad monstrosity. . . .

I once stood at sunset with a group of friends waiting for a firework display. It was to begin at dark. While we waited I looked behind me and saw the sun sinking in a sea of glory, and I said to them 'Look at the sunset!' Nobody looked. They were waiting for a common squib.

. . . Many people are making this same mistake today. They are seeking at a distance the God Who stands at the door of their heart. . . . I believe that some of you have only to quiet the deafening noises of the world and you will hear Him say 'Have I been so long time with you and yet hast thou not known Me?'

Why Jesus Never Wrote a Book, pp 67–8

The breath-taking claim of the New Testament in regard to holiness is that while man is helpless and hopeless alone, by the power of the indwelling Spirit he can do more than keep the ancient code: he can reach up to the dizzy heights of holiness revealed by Jesus and scale the serene summit itself. To a man who, in his own strength, had failed to keep the Ten Commandments, the new view of righteousness would be hard to the point of absurdity. It is as though, having failed to climb the Rigi, at less than 6,000 feet, he was taken to the Jüngfrau and told that *this* was the height he must scale. And, while he stares in dumb incredulity at the impossible, it is whispered to him that, if he will trust himself to the power generated in the works near Lauterbrünnen, he can rise mysteriously 11,000 feet to the Jüngfraujoch and a dependable guide will conduct him thence to the summit. 'There is a way for man to rise . . .'

A Holy Spirit's energies! That is the teaching of the New Testament. Being holy by the indwelling of the Holy Spirit, men are being made righteous, even in the enlarged sense of righteousness which Jesus taught. Even the *order* is important. It is a religious rather than an ethical order. The New Testament does not call men 'holy' because they are righteous but because they are becoming righteous by the indwelling of the Holy Spirit. The Holy Spirit indwells them, *in order to* make them holy. And that is the way of it. A Holy Spirit's energies. The utterly impossible in righteousness is made gloriously possible by the life of God in the soul of man.

The Pure in Heart, pp 32–3

Prayer, in its essence, is fellowship with God; it is talking, and listening to, and loving the Supreme Being who made and maintains this universe. That such fellowship is possible is so amazing a fact that it ought not to surprise us that some people find it incredible. . . . Prayer, at its best, opens earth to Heaven. . . . If this earth was widely open to Heaven by prayer, and we were obedient to the guidance which came, earth would be transformed. War would go; race and class hatred; hunger, disease. . . .

Some people doubt this. 'If prayer is so mighty', they say, 'why hasn't it been the means of more change than has appeared until now?' . . . The answer to this is threefold: (i) There hasn't been enough prayer (ii) The prayer has often been of poor quality (iii) We have not been obedient to God's guidance when it came.

. . . So much of our prayer is selfish. It is 'Gimme . . . Gimme . . . Gimme'. We are not much better than the little boy who told the vicar that he didn't pray every night, because there were some nights when he didn't want anything. So much of our prayer is coldly dutiful. It is better than no prayer at all, of course. But prayer without love has no suction. It doesn't draw the blessing down. The sick are not healed—or sustained in their serenity. God is not truly adored. Our neighbours are not blessed. We can't say prayer has failed if it has only been of that quality. Such prayer isn't the real thing. Some of us have to learn something we have mistakenly supposed that we have understood all our lives.

The Pattern of Prayer, pp 78–9

Heine, the exiled German poet, loved all things beautiful but he discovered the limit of beauty's power to heal. He knelt in tears before the Venus de Milo, holding out vain hands to that serene torso, and cried 'It is beautiful but it has no arms'. Art has no arms to lift one up in life's bitterest hour. The most exquisite painting is a sublime irrelevance. The most finished statuary is chill. Art alone cannot succour and if great art cannot do it, poor art cannot help. The man who modestly explains that, being no connoisseur in art he would turn for comfort to the cinema in any hour of sorrow, fosters a vain hope. If great art fails, poor art will not succeed. . . . If Venus de Milo falls short, no painted film star can save. If Handel misses the mark, jazz is hopeless. . . . Where is comfort? What sure word can be relied on when all the world has gone suddenly grey? Who is able? Who can heal?

Christ is able! Christ is willing. Let the broken-hearted make their way to Jesus. He and He alone has a word adequate to their need. No sorrow is outside the compass of His help. How tender He is towards those who suffer shame begotten by another's sin. . . . So close He comes to tormented hearts in an hour like that and keeps them poised in a tempest of gossip. None knows more of the burdens of sin than He, nor how heavily the weight falls on those who were innocent of the great transgression. For this cause He endured the Cross, despising the shame, and as the comfort of His understanding sympathy seeps into the soul, a new courage comes to face the world and to walk about among our fellows with quiet dignity.

He is Able, pp 33–4

We assert that all men can be saved and, theoretically no doubt, we mean it. In Christ, we have been taught that there cannot be Greek and Jew, circumcision and uncircumcision, barbarian, Scythian, bondman, freeman, but Christ is all, and in all. And now take a glance at the modern world we are considering, and at the activities of those who fight our faith. On 12th August [1951] in East Berlin, the Communists had a youth rally. . . . A million and a half youth were there. They were from almost every country of the globe. They marched. They marched for eight hours. 'It was like a rally of the Hitler Youth', you say. Yes! But with this difference. It was an *international* rally. In Lenin, they say, there cannot be Greek and Jew. . . . Scythian, bondman, freeman, but Lenin is all, and in all. And, look, they were there from South Africa, too—the most racially divided land in the world: a land where a Christian Church (on Calvinist and Old Testament principles) can disenfranchise the people to whom the land originally belonged and work for eternal separateness.

But there was no *apartheid* in the Communist delegation from South Africa to Berlin. White and black, they marched together. 'We really *are* one in Lenin', they say. 'The Christians say it also, but it is all humbug . . . they can't even worship in the same church.' People wonder sometimes how the Communists get such a grip on youth. One of the reasons may be here. Have we failed with the application of our own principles? When we said '*All* men may be saved' did we mean it—and mean it fully—mean to work it out?

Proceedings of the Eighth Ecumenical Methodist Conference,
1951, pp 74–5

Nothing but an increase of saints will make the church powerful in the world. The Holy Spirit is the Lord and Giver of Life. As He comes to sanctify, so He comes in power. The world could not long ignore a holy church. The church is not despised because it is holy: it is despised because it is not holy enough. There is not enough difference between the people inside the church and those outside to be impressive. A church in which saints were as common as now they are rare would convict the world, if only by contrast. Sanctity cannot be ignored. Even a little bit is potent. So far from the gates of hell prevailing against it, it hammers on their triple steel.

The saints are the chief hope of re-union. They link loving hands while mere ecclesiastics eye each other with suspicion and moil for a formula. Deep calleth unto deep. All the saints belong to one communion. That truth is obscured now by church divisions but only in the Church Militant. When the saints meet at the throne in the Church Triumphant they meet with the ardour of love.

Holding up the saints before the people helps them in a dozen different ways. They see the Lord reflected in His servants. They see what God can do with human nature. 'This you can be!' Unaware of themselves, that is what the saints are saying all the time.

It would never occur to them to say it aloud. It is doubtful if they ever think it. . . . If they could be persuaded to admit their progress and talk of it at all, the language of their heart would be this: 'If God could do this in *me*, He could do it in anyone.'

The Pure in Heart, pp 60–1

Sanctity is a gift of God: it is not a human achievement. You cannot *make* the peace of God . . . you can only *let* it—let it enter your heart and let it *rule*.

. . . It comes of the goodness of God in response to faith. Our salvation came that way; our sanctification comes that way also. The first thing to settle with oneself and an open Bible is whether God intends this thing. . . . Being sure of that, have *faith* for it. Dare to believe that God is able and God is willing. Stand on His promise and believe that His grace is greater than your inbred sin. See yourself as He would make you. . . . Say to yourself (as you forget yourself in the service of others) 'He intends this. It is His Will. Nothing can ultimately defeat the purpose of God. He will make me holy.'

. . . At the beginning of each new day . . . *see* yourself in Him. It is still you . . . but oh! how different: Christ formed afresh in you. Positively (in imagination) see it done. Hold it clear in your mind and warm in your heart, and say to yourself

> The most impossible of all
>   Is that I e'er from sin should cease.
> Yet shall it be, *I know it shall*,
>   Jesus, look to Thy faithfulness . . .

And He will look to it! . . . It is the deep unbelief in God's power to change us which keeps us unchanged—negative, inferior, jealous, ill-tempered, sour and mean. Faith for the opposite would open our hearts to all the resources of heaven and we should witness the miracle of a personality truly changed.

He is able. He is willing. Doubt no more.

You Can Be a Saint, pp 16–17

Most of us can have a greater mastery over wandering thoughts than we enjoy at present. Concentration and consecration are nearer together than we know.

One of the chief perils of this breathless age is that we shall come to our prayers breathless also. Gabbling one's prayer is a poor occupation at any time—even if the gabbling isn't vocalized and we just rush through them in our mind. Let us learn to be quiet within; to come to God, however brief our time of prayer, unhurried; to be *still* before him, recognizing that the day has nothing more important than this intercourse with heaven.

It may help someone if I confess that my own battle with wandering thoughts turns chiefly on the many engagements which each day brings. The quiet of prayer is invaded by the thought of a mass of correspondence to be handled; a cluttered desk awaiting my attention; *this* duty, *that* duty . . . and these distractions seem to stand in serried ranks, bidding me leave the quiet and get on with my work (always with the subtle insinuation that the work is more important than the prayer!).

I have learned through the years how to outwit that kind of distraction. Instead of fighting those thoughts away, I lift them right into my prayers. I go through the whole day slowly with God, meeting my duties in prayer before I meet them in fact, and I have two immense gains from that discipline. When I have looked them in the face in that way, they lie down and don't interrupt the rest of my prayers. And when I come to deal with the duties that I have already met in reverent imagination, I seem more the master of them and better able to make those duties a maximum for God.

Teach us to Pray, pp 18–19

The life of God does not depend on circumstances. When it first spread through the world, the Romans were masters, and . . . they persecuted the people who possessed it, and cast them to the lions. But those victims were the happy ones. The harder, more terrible sentence passed on Christians in those days was *damnatus ad metalla*—condemned to the mines. Their sufferings there beggar description. Under the scourge they rowed their own galleys to North Africa, and then trekked through the scorching mountains to the Numidian mines. Arrived at the mines, their chains were shortened so that never again could they stand upright. They were branded on the forehead . . . as like as not, one eye would be gouged out, and with a lamp and a mallet thrust into their hands they were whipped underground never to return. . . . They worked under gaolers who killed for amusement. If the poor prisoners were fortunate they caught the prevalent fever and died. Yet many lived on. . . . Many, it seems, wrote messages with charcoal on the smooth rock; prayers some of them, and the dear names of remembered friends. But one word appears again and again and again . . . *Vita, Vita, Vita*. Life! They had it! There! When circumstances were so hard that they could barely have been harder in Belsen. Life! Life that was 'life indeed'.

This is the spiritual life the evangelist comes to offer, and even though many who claim it live with half their treasure unappropriated, the offer is there, and whosoever will, may come.

Let me Commend, pp 30–1

The saint never gives up. He goes on serving, loving, helping. . . . He aches for souls. Neither indifference, nor slander, nor injury, can stop him. He does not make a motive of gratitude. His great motive is his utter love of God.

God gave this mighty love to Catherine Booth. Even as a girl, she said that she was willing to die for her father's salvation . . . she said that the all-absorbing question of her husband's life (and it was no less true of herself) was how best to reach and save the masses. Many a time she cried 'O! the value of souls! They are worth all the trouble and sacrifice involved —yea, a thousand times over'. . . . Or consider the life of John Woolman, the Quaker saint. His biographer says: 'The keynote of his message was always and ever love. Love to God and love to man. This single note runs through his life and writings like a silver thread'. It was still true of him when he came to die. On his deathbed he had no pre-occupation about heaven: no mention of crowns, harps, raptures 'but the same tender and touching concern for suffering humanity, relieved only by the thought of the paternity of God, and His love and omnipotence'.

From his loving service of men, the saint never retires. Men have wondered what kept John Wesley in the saddle for fifty-three years 'contesting the three kingdoms for Christ'. . . . They have wondered what kept David Livingstone in the jungle of Africa for thirty-three years, and Peter Claver tending the poor slaves at Cartagena for thirty-eight. None of these men retired. Death alone ended their labours. . . . It is not in normal nature to love like that; it is a *given* love. They had sought it and received it from God and they were consumed by its scorching flame.

The Pure in Heart, pp 104–5

This offer of new life in Christ is sometimes expressed in five 'universals'; certainly the chief leaders of the great eighteenth century Revival saw it that way, and held that the New Testament sustained their beliefs.

1. All men need this life.
2. All men may have this life.
3. All men who have this life, know that they have it.
4. All men must witness to its possession.
5. All men must press on to perfection.

An outline of the evangelist's task lies in these five 'universals'.

1. He must convince heedless men, living (some of them) an animal life, drugging their conscience and believing a lie, that for all their talk of life they've never had it.

2. When desire awakens in them and their conscience condemns, the evangelist must convince them that the offer is for *them*.

3. To have this quality of life, and not to know it, is impossible. Yet the evangelist must teach his convert not to live on fluctuating feeling, but to know his possession of this new life by the inward witness and moral power of God.

4. Nor can he allow a convert . . . to carry this treasure about as though it were a guilty secret. . . . The plain duty and high privilege of witnessing, he must impress on every one.

5. Finally, he must make clear to those new-born in the life of God, that this life, like all life, involves growth; that no limit need be put to its development; that whatever decay mars the life of men, no decay mars the life of God. And *this* is the life of God! Therefore it is 'nor wanting, nor wasting'.

Let me Commend, pp 31–2

Nothing is real but love
(*Laplace's* final *judgement*)

. . . the centrality and might of love. . . the dying words of Laplace 'Science is mere trifling. Nothing is real but love' . . . science itself is 'discovering' love, and an international congress on mental health declared that the taproot of mental ills is lack of it. Child psychologists have said that the question whether children should be smacked or not is unimportant so long as the child is loved. Sociologists trace delinquency to a lack of love, and some criminologists see, in its absence, the early cause of crime.

. . . They see this God-like love as the matrix of mature personality, as though this human nature had been divinely made to come to health and wholeness in that very environment. . . . Love is the soil in which our nature grows. Properly understood, it lives by giving, not by taking. It has amazing therapeutic value. The love that cures delinquency is not a sentimental feeling—now hot, now cold—but a love which holds the wayward to the highest and can never be sinned away. Only the crassly ignorant would confuse this quality of love with ephemeral feeling and foolish indulgence. It is strong, wise, uncompromising with evil, and always working to the best. It never 'appeases'.

Nonetheless, it is love, the very sun and breath of vital life. . . . If those people are emotionally ill who hate others, that man is also emotionally ill who hates himself. He lacks that quiet dignity which belongs to a child of God, a sense of belonging, of being precious in heaven and not wholly inadequate on earth. . . . The Bible student may be forgiven, as he watches the work of scientists in pursuit of the secrets of mental health, for concluding that they are heading again towards the deep and timeless truths of the scriptures.

The Pure in Heart, pp 248–9

He comes to a man who is living for money—and how many there are! You can live for money without having much of it. You live for it when you think it is the only thing worth living for. He comes to a man living for money, and He says: 'May I come in?' And the man says: 'Welcome, Lord—if you are content with things at my level.' And then the luminous eyes of Jesus search his soul, and he sees at a glance what Jesus will do with him and his money. He will give him a sense of steward- ship. He will teach him dispersal, tithing, large generosity. The man fears—and shuts the door in His face. He will not receive Him, because 'His face is as though He would go to Jerusalem'.

Some years ago I went to Pompeii and saw that city so strangely hidden in the dust and ashes of the centuries. I went to the very edge of the new excavations and watched the tragedy as though it had happened only the year before. I saw at Pompeii, not far from one of the gateways, the skeleton of a man who, to all appearances, had not fled when the volcano gave its first warnings but had run back for his trinkets. And there is his skeleton now—and the trinkets! They are gold, but they looked strangely green and mouldy lying at his side. He ran back for the bangles and he lost his life. O! the folly of it; that people should put such surpassing value on the treasures of this earth and not see . . . the treasures laid up in heaven; the things which time cannot tarnish; which will shine in time and in eternity, too.

Westminster Sermons (vol. ii), p 43

1. What do you think is the best definition of prayer?
2. How do you distinguish affirmative prayer from petition?
3. Why is it very important to think before you pray?
4. Is there such a thing as 'unanswered' prayer?
5. To what thoughts does your mind normally turn when you are not thinking of anything in particular?
6. 'No holiness without prayer; no revival without prayer; no mastery of life without prayer'. Do you agree? Are you sure?
7. A man said 'I pray, but I always have to push myself to it. How can I love prayer?' What advice would you give him?
8. A housewife enquires: 'Is washing-up a good time for extra moments of prayer?' Answer her.
9. A child asks 'Is it right to pray about exams?' Give a careful reply.
10. Is there a risk in prayer?
11. Are you prepared to see yourself in Christ?
12. Are you ready to be made honest 'in the inward parts'?
13. Can you say (and mean) 'Create in me a clean heart, O God'?
14. Do you want purity of heart before everything?
15. Are you trying to use prayer just to get things?
16. When we listen, God speaks. Are you ready to obey?

The Pattern of Prayer, p 35

[*The book contains no answers to what Dr Sangster himself might have called 'these piercing questions': but very evidently they are questions to which we must find an answer.*—Ed.]

138

It has struck many discerning observers of the modern Church that very many of her members lack any sense of goal. Even to the thoughtful, membership of the body of Christ is just . . . membership. Their eyes are not held by a vision of glory and they are not dumb before the wonder of God's uttermost purpose in their lives. There is little about them to suggest resolute pilgrims knowing their goal and holding on their course with unswerving zeal, displaying that 'toil unsevered from tranquillity' but yearly maturing and refining for heaven in everyone's gaze but their own. They do not seem that kind of pilgrim. Indeed, the general scene is so frosty, and the gait so waddling, and the journey so undirected that, as has been remarked, they seem more like penguins than pilgrims.

A clear conviction received into the mind that God is able, and willing, and eager, to deal drastically with sin in us, the sins of the mind as well as the sins of the flesh, the jealousies, pettinesses, irritabilities, resentments, egotisms: the earnest attending to God that one may receive this *present* salvation, and know in experience the deep difference between a straining effort to do the thing oneself, and the bewilderingly wonderful awareness that God has done something Himself; such a conviction and such an experience beckon the pilgrim on and make it obvious to all that he is a man on a journey with a pre-view of his goal. Indeed, he sings as he travels: the note is set to aspiration rather than complete and present achievement, but he puts no limits to the power of his God.

> *O that I now, from sin released,*
>   *Thy word may to the utmost prove,*
> *Enter into the promised rest,*
>   *The Canaan of Thy perfect love!*

The Path to Perfection, pp 193–4

The shortest way to be sure about anything is to accept it on high authority, and—if we deal specifically with the Christian Religion—the highest authority is the Bible and the Church. Many people have come to satisfying conviction by the simple acceptance of the teaching of the Bible clearly interpreted in the living Church.

But the difficulty about this for other people is that, before you can have conviction this way, you must first accept the authority of the authority. How do they know that the Bible is dependable and the Church is its true interpreter?

It is not irrational to take things on high authority. If a surgeon says he must cut our body open and take something out, we let him. ·. . . If a ship is in a violent storm at sea, no sane person suggests that the thousand passengers meet in the saloon and decide by majority vote how the ship should be handled; they trust the expert knowledge of the handful of officers and, in particular, of the captain himself. It isn't irrational to take things on authority; it is our daily habit. *We are careful in our selection of the authority* . . . but we rely on authority. 'But isn't the Church itself divided', people say, 'and don't scholars differ on Bible interpretation?' The Church is divided on some things, but increasing love is drawing the varied parts of it together . . . there is only one *major* matter of conduct on which the Church is divided—whether or not Christians should go to war. On nearly every really important moral question the Church speaks with one voice. There is authority here—high authority. . . . The Way of Authority is still a way worthy of respect.

Give God a Chance, p 21

Phocas was living in the first years of the fourth century in a cottage outside the city gate. . . . Phocas was a Christian. He made no secret of it. Hundreds must have tasted the simple hospitality of his cottage home. And then the Diocletian persecution broke out. . . . In some secret assembly Phocas was named as a Christian. . . . The lictors were despatched in haste to Sinope to identify and execute the criminal on the spot. So it happened that, tired with their journey, the executioners were nearing the gate of Sinope one hot afternoon when they were hailed from a cottage garden by an old man who begged them to pause awhile and refresh themselves. . . . 'What is your business?' said their host. They told him. . . . They were seeking a certain Phocas. Did their host know him! The man was a dangerous Christian and had to be executed immediately. 'I know him well', said Phocas. 'He is quite near. . . . Let us attend to it in the morning.' When his guests retired, Phocas sat thinking. Escape was easy. He had only to go. . . . Fellow Christians would hide him. When the persecution was over, he could emerge again. Nobody will ever know what arguments weighed most with Phocas. . . . If he ran, would it be cowardly? . . . And what of the executioners?—decent fellows as they seemed; just doing their duty? . . . Their own lives might be forfeit for his. . . .

Next morning he told them. 'I am he', he said. Bishop Asterius, who tells the story, said that they stood 'motionless' in astonishment . . . shrinking from a deed so foul upon a man so kind. He overcame their reluctance. Death, he told them, had no terrors for him. They had their duty to do, and he had nothing but love in his heart for them. A sword swept, and all that was mortal of Phocas mingled with the garden he had loved so well.

The Pure in Heart, pp 107–8

Paul said [Epaphras] 'laboured greatly in prayer'. . . . He was
a good colleague and a faithful minister *because* his character
was founded in prayer. Paul tells us that his prayer was largely
intercessory. . . . He was praying for them. What an insight
Paul must have had into the character of Epaphras when they
prayed together at Rome! Epaphras shared Paul's imprison-
ment while he stayed with him and when he prayed for the
church at Colossae Paul saw him in a new light. Like some
modern minister praying with his church roll open before him,
praying for his people one by one, I imagine that Epaphras in
memory went through his distant flock member by member.
This was when he remembered their limitations and difficulties:
he prayed for them with insight and fervency and Paul's heart
glowed.

Men and women . . . if your heart has said in response to this
story, 'I should like to be like that', be sure of this—the secret
of this man's spiritual success was his prayer-life. He was great
in soul because he prayed much and because he prayed with the
unselfishness that marked all he did. Copy him in this and you
will be easy to work with and careless about credit: you will
learn his secret of co-operative service. Follow him here and
and your judgements of others will be sweetened and you will be
known for your charity of thought. Earnest and persistent prayer
was the secret of his sanctity. That secret is available to us all.
My biography or your biography may be written in few words
or many (perhaps not written at all), but I will not grieve and I
think you will not grieve if at our passing it can truthfully be
said of us, 'He was a good colleague, was swift to see and ready
to speak of the good in others and reinforced all his service with
persistent prayer'.

Why Jesus Never Wrote a Book, pp 118–19

It is freely allowed that no man is a hero to his valet. The world may speak of him in superlative terms, but the servant who sees him at all odd hours—at night when he is overtired; in the morning before he is properly awake; when business over-presses; when disappointment comes; when he is off-guard and under no temptation to pose—this man does not normally think of his master as a hero. He knows the other side.

It is easily possible to know too much about some people. I remember from my college days that the head gardener never came to the college chapel when a student was planned to preach. He said, half in jest and half in earnest 'I know 'em. I'm like the man who works at a jam factory; he has no taste for jam.'

Who was it first claimed that Jesus was sinless and used of him the awesome name of God? The disciples! The men who had shared every kind of experience with Him that mortals could share; who had seen Him at all hours of day and night; who had seen Him tired, hungry, disappointed; scorned, abused, and hunted to death; who had ridden with Him on a wave of popularity and hidden with Him from inquisitive miracle-mongers; who had met Him when He came down from a sleepless night of prayer on the hillside, and known Him physically overworked and emotionally over-wrought . . . these were the men—eleven of them, who, with amazing unanimity, declared Him, at the last, to be the sinless One. . . . No thinking man can doubt the quality of Christ's character . . . if he give attentive heed to the unanimous testimony of the men who knew Him best.

Westminster Sermons (vol. i), pp 40–1

Among the many misunderstandings which have affected the common mind of man concerning the religion of Jesus Christ, none is more perplexing or more false than the widespread idea that to receive it is to be made miserable. . . . The fact that there is a cross at the heart of the Christian faith, and that following Christ involves some rigorous self-denials, does not alter—and cannot alter—this central truth: the fruit of the Spirit is joy.

Nor is the word translated 'joy' a weak word. It is not resignation wearing a wan smile. It is exuberant, and on occasion, boisterous. People too much imprisoned in the proprieties, and stiff with 'good manners' have even thought . . . that there was a touch of the vulgar in Christian joy. It cannot be denied. Tertullian said 'The Christian saint is hilarious'.

. . . The summons to rejoice is sounded no less than seventy times in the New Testament. . . . Honest men at Pentecost thought that the apostles were drunk, and, whenever the living water has burst fresh from the rock again, the same exuberant gladness has been manifested. The early Franciscans had it; the early Methodists; the early Salvationists. . . . When Dr Farmer, organist at Harrow, pleaded with the Salvationist drummer not to hit the drum so hard, the beaming bandsman replied: 'Lor' bless you, sir, since I've been converted, I'm so happy, I could burst the blooming drum.'

We know the people who disapprove this kind of thing with a slight pursing of the lips. . . . Neither the early Franciscans, Methodists nor Salvationists need mind the implied disapproval. With the experience of Pentecost in mind, the apostles would have understood.

The Pure in Heart, pp 109–10

Nothing . . . can really rob this day of its immense significance in the life of John Wesley. It is the manner of men new-
born in God (or, if the phrasing is preferred, of men, who,
being already in God, are lifted to some new level of life in
Him) to speak of their experience in ways which seem to others
extravagant—and even sometimes to themselves in the cooler
atmosphere of later years. But let us submit the question to a
plain pragmatic test. This will be far more fruitful than arguments as old and sterile as the vain discussion of whether the
spark or the barrel of gunpowder had more to do with the
explosion. A plain, pragmatic test is not inappropriate to one
who applied the same test so often himself, and who has been
recognized as, in some senses, the forerunner of Schleiermacher
in theology and William James in philosophy. Is it in serious
dispute that before this day John Wesley was a man marvellously equipped but pitifully ineffective, and that after this day
he was an apostle?* Let his *feelings* be left aside for the moment,
for he put only the slightest stress upon them himself: neither
the warmed heart of May 24th, 1738, nor the doubts of June
27th, 1766, need confuse the question. *What of the work?* What
of the influence, religious and humanitarian, of the formerly
frustrated man before whom the mountains now became as a
plain? On those who depreciate the importance of Wesley's visit
to Aldersgate Street must rest the onus of explaining what, on
their thesis, is surely inexplicable. To say that the man had been
found of God would seem to them to beg the question, but not
even they will deny that he had found himself. The Revival had
begun.

The Path to Perfection, pp 97–8

---

* Piette, *The Rediscovery of John Wesley in the Evolution of Protestan-
tism*, 478 f., cf. Cell, 49f.

There was the man who carried the Cross for Him: Simon of Cyrene. I know he was *compelled* to do it. A prisoner was supposed to carry his own cross to the place of execution, but our blessed Lord could not do it. Weakened by the bloody sweat, and the lashings of the pillar, and all the burden of the world's pain thrust through the channels of His mighty heart, He fell beneath the load.

The soldiers caught hold of a man in the crowd, and made him carry the Cross. I don't suppose he wanted to. I imagine he felt as you would feel, if you were looking on at some trouble in the streets and were suddenly pounced upon to take part in it. Your first thought would be 'I want to keep out of this'. But when he was dragged forward and saw that piteous, blood-stained figure, and the unearthly look of the Son of God, don't you think some pity stirred in his heart? Don't you think he said within himself 'Well, I am not going to be crucified, but I can at least carry the Cross for him'?

Anyhow, he did. He carried the Cross for Jesus. I am grateful to Simon of Cyrene for that.

They Met at Calvary, pp 67–8

Christ promised His companionship to His followers when He had gone from their sight. He said in effect, 'I shall still be with you: indeed, in some senses, you will be better off'. That was His plain promise to the disciples and through them to us. Moreover, the disciples realized that His presence was with them. . . . there is not one word of complaint in the New Testament that Jesus Christ was no longer with His infant Church. Would it not have been natural if, at each crisis in its perilous beginnings, they had uttered some vain wish for His counsel and help?

Jesus would have been only forty-nine when Paul left Antioch for his first missionary journey, and Aristotle says that a man is at his best at forty-nine. He would have been only fifty-five at the heated Conference in Jerusalem and only fifty-seven when Paul first preached His name in Corinth. Would it not have been natural if they had cried now and then, 'If only the Lord was with us now?' And yet they never did; not once! And why? Because He *was* with them: they knew they had Him: they had not to moan over an absent Leader: they had rather to rejoice in One Who was ever gloriously near.

When one reads the history of the Bonapartist party in France after the exile of Napoleon, . . . their constant moan is 'If only the Emperor were with us now!' When one reads the history of the Liberal Party after the death of Gladstone, the one recurring thought is this, 'If only Gladstone were with us now!' . . . you never hear the Apostles say that. Nay, rather, they say, 'We have Him!' 'Lo! He is with us always even unto the end of the world.'

Why Jesus Never Wrote a Book, p 69

Pleasure and happiness are sometimes mistaken for Christian joy. A worldling has his pleasures. Indeed, he often counts himself an expert in pleasure. Are there not many wholesome pleasures in life—sweet, God-given, and lovely things which the Father meant us to enjoy? . . . Yet pleasure and Christian joy cannot be identified. (i) Pleasure depends on circumstances. It requires a measure of health. It demands that the conditions of life be kindly. . . . It can be filched from us . . . by irritating trifles like tooth-ache or sea-sickness. Christian joy is completely independent of health or circumstances. It appears in the saints when 'strength and health and friends' are gone. . . . (ii) Moreover, pleasures come and go. What pleases the youth does not please the man. . . . Confectionery, a bicycle, games, the theatre, an arm-chair . . . the things that give us pleasure change with changing years. The joy of God is constant. Children may know it. It can be the strong stay of youth: the means by which the middle-aged may bear the heat and burden of the day: the secret exultation of those who grow old. (iii) Again, pleasure satiates . . . When the point of satiety is passed revulsion sets in. . . . Joy never satiates. . . . Joy rises to rise again. . . . (iv) Moreover, pleasure always remains superficial. It exists only by ignoring the hard unanswered questions of life. It is like the gaiety of Christmas in a home in which religion means nothing: a party but a party without purpose: fun and frolic but an empty aching heart beneath: a coronation and no monarch.

Joy is deep. It bubbles from utter contentment. The smile is not only on the lips but in the eyes and in the heart. It may flame into rapture or sink into peace, but it possesses the whole personality. It is true bliss.

The Pure in Heart, pp 110–11

The power clearly comes from God, and He is more eager to give it than we are to receive. It does not depend upon remote committees. . . . It can't be 'administered' into us; it comes in through adoration. . . . Our administrators are doing all they can do. The inspiration—for lack of which we are in danger of dying—comes this other way. In such contacts as I had with Dr Scott Lidgett I seldom found him peeved, though I recall one occasion. . . . He commented tartly to me on the current criticism of the leaders of the Church. . . . The people whose Church 'work' it appeared to be to comment adversely on the men whom they had themselves shared in choosing were saying at the time . . . 'Why don't you give us a lead?' 'What do they mean?' the old veteran asked me. 'Sometimes they complain at the lead we give them. Now they complain because we don't give them enough. Don't they know what the Church is for and where we are seeking to go?' . . . I felt some sympathy with the old man. It may have been an excess of assurance on my part, but even as a probationer I knew what the Church was for and where we were seeking to go. The Church (I would have told anyone who asked me) was—1. for the worship of God, 2. for making good men and women, 3. for Christianizing the social order. I didn't wait for a Presidential pronouncement to learn that.

. . . What do these people mean who ask for a lead? Do they want another 'call' from the Conference?* I think we've had too many 'calls'. These 'calls' are seldom followed up. . . . It is for us to do what needs to be done in sufficient numbers and with sufficient seriousness and the miracle will happen. The Church will throb and thrill with new life.

The Pattern of Prayer, pp 80–1

---

* *The annual Methodist Conference – the 'parliament' of Methodism.*

. . . Emerson said it over seventy years ago. . . . Discerning men had known it long before Emerson. It comes dangerously near to self-condemnation to say that one is friendless. It begs the rejoinder: 'Have you been a friend?' Christ enlarges our capacity for friendship. He increases our love, turns our generous thought out upon others, makes us unconsciously more attractive, and adds a charm that does not belong to nature alone. The Greek word *charis* which is translated in the New Testament as 'grace' also meant 'charm'. The grace of the Lord Jesus Christ adds charm to unlovely sinners. It lights them up from inside. Everyone has noticed how radiant two people become who fall in love and find their love reciprocated. The love of Christ irradiates this poor human nature more permanently than that, and heightens human attractiveness in many ways. His presence in the heart removes the barriers to fellowship. Pride prevented us enjoying the company of those we thought our social inferiors, but pride is banished now. Jealousy hindered intimate friendship with our colleagues, and those who surpassed us in similar tasks, but jealousy has perished in the fire of His love. Our bias to believe the worst of people has been turned into a bias to believe the best, and fellowship flourishes in the atmosphere of expectant faith. So the circle of our friendship widens. Love begets love. In this world's goods we may be poor, but we are rich towards heaven and affluent in friends.

He is Able, p 41–2

Who got more from the natural world than St Francis of Assisi, to whom the birds and the beasts became as his kinsmen?—and the sun and the wind, morning and evening, flower water and burning fire, all spoke of the love of God. Go through his hymn, 'All creatures of our God and King', and sense a quality of natural bliss unspiritual people never know.

... I stood outside a church one Sunday evening and watched the worshippers disperse. God had come very near to His people that evening. The aweful hush of His presence was on them as they turned to walk quietly home. A crowded motor-coach, returning with revellers from the seaside, was checked by the traffic for a minute. The occupants were flushed with too much drink: they were wearing paper caps and false noses and singing scraps of comic songs. For some reason, the dispersing worshippers appeared amusing to them. They flung streamers of coloured paper over the people leaving church, and one bibulous passenger called out 'Why don't you enjoy yourself?'

Two ways of life had met for an instant. The coach rolled on with that question hanging on the air: 'Why don't you enjoy yourself?' It is those who think they are artists in enjoying themselves who so signally fail; whose enjoyment leaves a 'hang-over'.

Bliss is the prerogative of the saint.

The Pure in Heart, pp 111–12

People who have put stress upon holiness have sometimes been suspected by their evangelical friends of being disloyal to the gospel—of having . . . reverted to 'salvation by works'.

It isn't true. Their salvation and sanctification are both by grace through faith. Their absorbing interest in good works is not in their *merit* but in their *witness*. The transformed life shows that grace has come. . . .

One keeps the fruit of the Spirit (shown plainest in this transformed life) as one keeps open to the Spirit's inflow. The discipline of the devotional life is not a fretting effort to be good in our own strength (which invariably leads to nerve-strain and breakdown), but in that ordered daily devotional life which holds us open all the while to the in-breathing of God. . . . The secret of the saints is in two words: they *attend* and *obey*.

. . . The life of the saint is really a moment-by-moment life. It isn't that he really 'keeps' anything—except that he keeps himself low at the feet of his Lord. Indeed, he comes at times to doubt if he even does that and whether, in his faithful waiting upon Jesus, there isn't more of the help of God than the constancy of his own will.

But certainly he judges every day ill-spent which does not include some time given to gazing steadily on his blessed Master and unmistakably (though to him unconsciously) he comes to mirror the Lord he loves and adores.

You Can be a Saint, pp 18–19

How does one put oneself in the way of receiving guidance
from God?

You are in the spirit of prayer, withdrawn from the world.
You are in the conscious presence of God. Self is no longer at
the centre. As things cross your mind, they have no immediate
self-reference, as alas! they do in normal life. (How will that
affect *me?* What do *I* get out of it!) You see things differently
because you see them in the light of God. Conscience is at its
tenderest. Spiritual perception is sharp and penetrating. It is
God and you.

Listen! Something comes—clearly, maybe, or not so clear. If
it is something to do, make a note of it and get it done as soon
as possible; a letter to write, a call to make, an apology possibly. With the majority of things that come there is no moral
uncertainty, and a critic might say 'I could have thought of
these things myself'. He could—but he didn't. When a thing is
plainly right it is, perhaps, an academic question whether I
thought of it myself or whether God told me. But one thing is
certain. I 'thought' of far, far fewer sweet things to do (and
hard things to do!) before I learned to listen to God than I do
now it is my daily practice. So perhaps it was God after all . . .
helping me to think!

If you feel uncertain whether what comes to you in the quietness is of God, test it by its harmony with all that you know of
Jesus, and discuss it in confidence with some wise and keen
Christian friend. . . . God's guidance *does* run counter at times
to our best judgement. Paul's fine judgement directed him once to
Bithynia, but the Spirit stayed him and God called him (against
his judgement!) to Macedonia, to Europe—and to us.

Teach us to Pray, pp 25–6

Three . . . affirmations, rooted in the New Testament, have been happily stressed . . . by evangelists in recent years.

1. Once for All.
2. All or Nothing.
3. Here and Now.

The first affirmation is of God; the second of man; and the third of God and man.

1. *Once for All.* However sure we may be that God has fresh light to break out of His Word, when The Word became flesh, God spoke for all time. All else is ancillary, comment, interpretation.

2. *All or Nothing.* The response of a mortal to his God must, in the end, be utter . . . a dedication deliberately defective is dishonouring to God and limits the Holy One of Israel.

3. *Here and Now.* There is nothing more glorious in the gospel offer than this. The evangelist can cry from the housetops that God will meet the sinner where he is. *Just* where he is! He can say 'Here'. And 'Now!' It is no accident that gospel songs in all generations have had the note of urgency and of immediate offer. 'Make no delay', 'Do not tarry.' 'Now, poor sinner.' 'Now to be Thine, yea, Thine alone.' Charles Wesley's adoring soul had grasped the precious truth of it when he cried:

> Father, *now* accept of mine,
> 　Which *now*, through Christ, I offer Thee;
> Tell me *now*, in love divine,
> 　That Thou hast pardoned me.

Let me Commend, pp 33–4

All down the ages godly men and women have possessed this experience: they have borne the burdens of life more easily: they have wept less bitterly in their sorrows and they have smiled in the face of death, because He was with them, ruling their heart, controlling their life and never deserting them. And such people are with us today. I do not doubt that there are people known to us all who can say with humble boldness. 'He dwells in me, and I know it.'

What are the marks of His nearness? How can we confidently assert His presence with us? One mark . . . is a keener appetite for spiritual things. You may feel it in the presence of a good man: in your heart the wish may form: 'I should like to be like him.' Or you may feel it in the hour of public worship—and unsatisfied longing after higher things. . . . The very craving after God is, in itself, a signal mark of His presence, for these desires are not generated in our hearts by ourselves. We are stirred to them by a movement of the Holy Spirit. God is already at hand.

. . . The line between seeking and finding is not always easy to draw. In one sense you have God, before you can seek Him. The man in whose heart God has no place at all feels no need of Him and wonders why other people should get hot about it. Really to want Him means that the journey is well begun.

Why Jesus Never Wrote a Book, pp 69–70

[The saint] cannot worry. For him, all the big questions are answered. Because he is sure of God, and sure of God's nature as Love, he cannot worry. The All-Great is the All-Loving, too. . . . He believes God. He rejoices in the Lord. Fear, anxiety, fretfulness, apprehension, have no place in the heart of one who is utterly sure that all things rest in those loving hands. . . . Not only is he free of worry, he is free of guilt. This must be said with care because there is a worry in which the saint has a keener sense of sin than the normal mortal. Having seen more of God's holiness, he has felt more of his own pollution. . . . He knows himself a sinner in a way that no . . . Pharisee knows himself a sinner. Having caught a gleam of the burning purity of God, he is scorched with horror at the sin of his own soul, and yet the horror heightens the joy. Guilty—but there is now no condemnation to them that are in Christ Jesus. Profane—but he is wrapped in the righteousness of his Lord. False and full of sin he is—yet he is to be made full of truth and grace. He which began a good work in him, will perfect it until the day of Jesus Christ.

Both—and both together! Yet the joy prevails. The saint accepts God's forgiveness. He does not demand the impossible —peace as the fruit of being clean in his own eyes. He surrenders the pride which tries to persuade him that forgiveness must be earned. If he finds it hard to forgive himself, he none the less accepts the free and full forgiveness of God and dwells, not on his own failures, but on his Lord's triumph. Wretchedness is not a direct fruit of the Spirit. It is the shadow cast on the life of the saint by his glimpse of God's awful purity. They love heaven more who have seen hell.

The Pure in Heart, pp 112–13

During the First World War our authorities were greatly troubled by the trench-fever that was so affecting the soldiers, and they could not discover how it was communicated. The opinion had been expressed that it was spread by lice, and they sent for a remarkable man, a Mr Bacot, who had made a particular study of lice. They told him their need, and Mr Bacot went to work. He took the lice, put them into small pill-boxes with an aperture on the underside, and strapped them on his wrist beneath his cuffs. He let the evil things live on him. He went about his work receiving hundreds of bites a day, and the people who knew what he was doing saw him sitting in the tube trains with these slight bulges beneath his sleeve.

He began to get results. To save our men in their need he went to France, to Egypt and to Poland too, exposing himself every day to hundreds of bites, and then testing out in his own body, when the infection was given, the power of a cure. Finally, he became completely infected with typhus, and died. His story is just another of the splendid martyrdoms to science that our records hold.

He who was clean became unclean that he might save others. Jesus . . . knew no sin, and yet He entered into the experience of sin—the awful sense of separation from His father. The cry of dereliction shows it. Whatever sin-bearing means, it means this; the consequences fell upon Him. 'Him who knew no sin, He made to be sin on our behalf.'

Westminster Sermons (vol. ii), pp 54–5

. . . There are not a few acute observers of modern Church life and thought who remark upon the wide neglect of the doctrine of the Holy Spirit and would explain the lack of spiritual power chiefly by this. That the doctrine is neglected few will deny. Some scholars reject the 'personality' of the Spirit and would prefer to be called 'binitarians' than 'trinitarians'. The mass of Church people receive the doctrines of the Spirit's 'personality' and His power 'as taught', but their powerless lives remind one of none so much as the men of Ephesus whom Paul challenged with the words 'Did ye receive the Holy Ghost when ye believed?'* . . . Wesley says that it is the Holy Spirit which is responsible for 'the conversion and entire sanctification of our hearts and lives. . . .' Wesley's precursors in this teaching are not less emphatic. . . . Scougal affirms it.† Marshall makes it clear‡. All claim that the New Testament is behind them. . . .

Is it only a coincidence that, in an age when the doctrine of the Holy Spirit is neglected, the Church is feeble and ineffective, and does not seem to be rich in lovely lives of compelling Christlikeness? Or have we a hint here that the wise will be swift to heed? Power was promised with the Holy Spirit and the first fruit of the Spirit is love. Christians today need power and perfect love. On the plain promise of Christ, God is pledged to give the Holy Spirit to them that ask Him. And then to 'let go and let God!' Just to *receive* the Holy Spirit! To believe and find it true! To practise the moment-by-moment life! Busy but not harassed! On the stretch for the Kingdom but not way-worn! Buying up the moments in this royal service but all quiet within!

The Path to Perfection, pp 194–6

---

* Acts 19[2]
† *The Life of God in the soul of man*, 9.
‡ *The Gospel Mystery of Sanctification*, 127.

In the terrible floods that swept up the Conemaugh Valley in 1889 and utterly devastated the city of Johnstown, a strange providence seemed to watch over a little community of nuns. The Mother Superior, chancing to look out of the window, saw the torrent sweeping down the doomed valley and immediately lifted her heart to God in passionate prayer for guidance. It came to her immediately that she was to take her little flock to the chapel and remain there in prayer.

When the flood had passed, the little chapel was the only building in the immediate neighbourhood which remained intact. We do not suggest that God stayed the flood at that point; we do suggest that He responded to a devout woman's plea for direction, and led her to the one place within reach where she, and those in her care, would be safe. . . . We are not prisoners of law, the laws are capable of adaptation. Nor is our prayer a vain pursuit; in addition to all its other gain it opens the human mind to providential guidance.

Jesus said 'I know my sheep'. The individual was not lost in the flock. He knows His sheep still. The special needs of all the separate ones are known to Him, and the Arab physician was right when he rose to the bewildered faith that 'the All Great (were) the All-Loving too'.

God cares. He not only cares—He can succour. When He denies, it is the denial of love. Even in the shadows we have a song that can cheer the heart:

> *I'd rather walk in the dark with God*
> *Than go alone in the light.*

Providence, pp 15–16

There are people who hesitate to embark on the adventure of faith because they think that all religion may be 'wishful thinking'. Men cannot face the idea of a godless meaningless universe (they suspect) and they invent, therefore, a supreme and kindly Being behind things. But He may be only the fruit of their fears and wishes, and have no basis in reality at all.

Let us look at that possibility. The world itself is not the fruit of wishful thinking. Geology has taught us nothing if it has not taught us that the world was here long before man came to 'think' it. . . . Nor is the moral sense in man. People who believe that all religious experience is a delusion sometimes say that folk who think that they listen to God speaking inside them always hear what they want to hear. It isn't true. The animal in man might think that he had a right to any woman he could persuade, but the God he meets within him withstands his wild appetites and requires that he be loyal to his mate. The coward and scheme in man often thinks that a lie is not only convenient but permissible, yet the God he meets inside him insists on the truth, whatever the personal cost.

Wishful thinking? No doubt there *is* such a thing, and we have all been guilty on occasion of half-believing something to be true because we *wanted* to believe it. But that cannot explain religion. The God who confronts us in our conscience with moral commandments which run directly opposite to our lusting desires isn't a figment of our wishful thinking. He is the great Other, whom someday we must all meet.

Give God a Chance, p 28

. . . Nor do the saints kill self-centredness by aiming directly at it. Too much conscious self-denial leaves a man self-absorbed and too much aware of what he has sacrificed. Try and read the mind of St Francis of Assisi in the moment before he kissed the leper. Imagine him saying to himself 'I am aiming at sanctity and I must kill the self. Here is a leper. I neither like the look nor the smell of him but, as I wish to be a saint, I must miss no opportunity of clouting my inclinations. Here goes. . . .' Not thus are saints made. Neither by seeking to obliterate the self, pursuing the fantasy of pure altruism, or consciously aiming at self-denial. They kill self-centredness by the same sovereign means they have used in all their scaling of the heights. They just gaze on God in adoration . . . they look at Him and He looks at them. Their adoring contemplation receives the life of God in the Person of the Holy Spirit into their own awe-struck souls, and the Holy Ghost beats down the sin in them and builds up the good. . .

Nor is it hard to understand what might be called the divine psychology of the operation. They *see* God in Christ. They see vividly. They see not only with the mind but with the heart. They are compounded of holy longing . . . they are fixed in this absorbed concentration, desiring only God.

Is it any wonder that they become like Him? If we thought only in terms of the mechanics of the mind, and allowed little for the power of the Holy Ghost, it would still be easy to understand. They hold the mirror of their lives steadily before their Lord and the very mirror is transformed. Grace, of course, enables them.

The Pure in Heart, p 231

Every man or woman who *really* meets Jesus feels the impress and challenge of His life. There is something utterly unique in meeting Him. Everybody here who has had the experience—and a multitude of you have—is behind me in this assertion. When Christ looks at you, you know that He sees you through and through; your secret hopes, your nameless fears, your gusty passions, your dirty, furtive sins. You cannot pose to Him.

Yet, when you see how truly He loves you though He knows the worst about you, and 'beckons you His road' . . . all that is decent in you leaps out in response. Your heart cries out for Him. You know it. You feel it. You would be lying if you denied that He pulled the heart out of you.

That's the proof you were seeking. He embodies all that you have 'willed or hoped or dreamed of good'. He does not need to display any other credentials. Your heart knows Him; cries out to Him; will not be satisfied without Him.

Oh! you *can* run away from Him like the Rich Young Ruler, but it is only your body that will run. Your heart will play you traitor. It knows its Lover and will abide with Him. Having truly seen Him once, it will hunger for Him for ever.

'None but Christ can *satisfy*.' Though you live a whole long life through in wilful rebellion, and will not have this Man to rule over you, nothing and no one else can give you peace.

Therefore, I say, if you would prove Him, meet Him. Open your heart to Him. Fashion your lips in prayer. And . . . listen . . . He will make your heart burn within you, and He will stir in you longings after the noblest life.

Westminster Sermons (vol. i), pp 45–6

Did you ever hear of Dr Brackett? Perhaps not. He ministered, as a medical practitioner, in a small town in the southern parts of the United States. But I think you ought to know about Dr Brackett.

He specialized in serving poor people who had no money. He would get up on the coldest night and go for miles to help some needy soul. Everybody knew his surgery. It was on the main street over a clothing store, and there was a plate at the doorway. He never married. He fell in love, but on the day of his wedding he was called out to the birth of a Mexican child, and his girl gave him up. She said that a man who would fail to appear at his wedding for the sake of a Mexican child would not be any good as her husband. A lot of people agreed with her, but not, I need not say, the parents of that little Mexican child.

He died not long since. He was over seventy. It was the biggest funeral they had ever had in that town or neighbourhood. And then they began to argue about a fitting memorial —what should be inscribed upon it, and how tall it should be. But, as often happens, it all ended in talk, and the only people who seemed really worried were the parents of the child he had delivered all those years before, on the day which should have been his wedding day. They settled the memorial in the end. It was the undertaker who discovered what they had done. Too poor themselves to put up a stone, they went at night and took from the door of his old office the brass plate that had been there so many years. Passing through the cemetery, the undertaker noticed it. Embedded in a mass of flowers, he read the old inscription:

Dr Brackett
Office Upstairs.

They Met at Calvary, pp 72–3

. . . I felt I had lost God. Spiritual things had become unreal to me. Doubts darkened my mind. I lost appetite for the holy vocation to which I believed God had called me. The conviction grew in my heart that the one thing an honourable man could do would be to give it up. And yet I wanted God. In those months of awful darkness, nothing was more sure to me than my hunger for Him. All the varied wants of my heart had become resolved into the one great cry of the questing soul, 'Oh, that I knew where I might find Him!' One night I had reached the breaking point. My mind was wearing with the effort of pondering these problems over and over again. My heart was sick with hope long deferred. I sat at midnight in the darkness of my study on the border of despair, when a friend came to me with words of unsurpassed comfort. He knew my need. He said, 'You are chasing your shadow: the hunger within you is a mark of His presence'. I know those words will not seem magical to you, but I have no language to describe the effect they had then upon me. To my poor soul they were the authentic words of the living God. I grasped the truth of what he said. This hunger!—the one consuming passion of my soul —a mark of His presence. The God I had sought far was here at home. He was *in* my heart: the hunger as well as the food. He seemed to say 'Have I been so long time with you and yet hast thou not known Me?' In that moment I knew the trembling joy of having God in my heart and *knowing* He was there. And that was the real beginning of an intimate experience of God in me. If you deeply want Him, in some measure you already have Him. Turn and recognize His presence. Turn and obey the command He lays upon you. The greatest thing in earth and heaven is within your grasp.

Why Jesus Never Wrote a Book, pp 70–1

The peace of the saint . . . is based on [his] utter faith in God. He believes! He does not *pretend* to believe. He does not *half*-believe. He does not believe today and doubt tomorrow. He *believes!*

He believes in God—the God that Jesus revealed. He believes that the hairs of our head are numbered and that not even a sparrow falls to the ground but the Father knows. He believes that the universe is in the keeping of Infinite Wisdom and Infinite Love. In ways he cannot fully understand, he believes that God directs the course of history, and cares, at the same time, for each individual soul. . . .

Nothing can happen in the universe (he holds) but by the permission of God. God would not permit anything to happen utterly infertile of good. If it were possible to conceive anything out of which infinite wisdom could not bring good, God would not allow it. In that deep sense, therefore, the saint says:

> *Whate'er events betide,*
> *Thy will they all perform.*

He does not sit impassive to events. His love of his fellows would not allow it. He does not withdraw from events by intellectual pride, or the wrong religious detachment. He is certain that God loves persons, but he remembers also that God so loved the *world.* . . . The peace of the saint is set deep in the rock of reality. It is based on his utter faith in God.

The Pure in Heart, pp 119–20

The real war . . . is the war of ideas. The honest Communist and the honest Capitalist have more in common than they know. . . . The *sincere* devotees of these opposing ways of life honestly want a fairer distribution of things, a chance for fuller life for all, a practical recognition of the brotherhood of man. . . . Both creeds have their martyrs. Men die only for what they passionately believe.

. . . What are the basic, and, it may be, the deadly differences? What is at war in the war of ideas?

Is God there or is He not? Is man His child with a life after death—or just what he eats? Is the last explanation of the universe spiritual or material?

Communism tries to satisfy man's craving for a spiritual purpose by persuading him that there is none—that only materialism is real. But some people who profess to believe in the spiritual prove by their deeds that they also are materialists at heart. They don't deeply believe in Christianity. They just want to 'use' it. 'If it will pay debts, check the cosh-boys, reduce the expense of prisons, let us have it. It will be good for "the masses".' This kind of religion will not dam the red tide. It doesn't deserve to. Only real religion will do that—personal and utter dedication, sacrifice till it hurts, the spirit of Christ in the day-to-day contacts of life. The finest schemes fail on the selfishness of man. Christianity teaches a secret neither communism nor capitalism knows: *how to die to self*. The possession and practice of that secret would make us invincible in the war of ideas.

Revival: The Need and the Way, pp 8–9

... Some would say 'a crowded Church' but every devout preacher knows that a crowd is not an achievement but only an opportunity. Some would say 'Any Church where the Sacrament of Holy Communion is regularly celebrated', but that rule ... would shut out all Quakers and Salvationists, and Jesus would never do that. Some would say 'Any Church which gives large sums to Overseas Missions' ... some, 'Any Church where worship is sincerely offered', but the worship of some people never expresses itself in any kind of service to others, and something must be deficient there. Some will suggest 'A Church rich in prayer meetings', but we all know that prayer meetings vary very widely. ... This question is harder than we thought.

... I think I would say 'Any Church filled with the love which is the life of God'. 'Filled. ...' A church is a public place. Anyone can come. A malicious gossip might regularly attend a church and pump the poison of scandal into the fellowship of God's people, and there would be no easy way to prevent it. But if the central fellowship was 'filled with the love which is the life of God' the poison would be sterilized. The 'anti-bodies' in love would master the evil in the gossip, and the health of the body would be maintained. So we will keep ... to that definition—

'A successful Church is any Church filled with that love which is the life of God.'

The Pattern of Prayer, p 82

Let us accept the principle of discipline in life. God has put us in a world where all kinds of distress can overtake us, where ignorance, folly or sin (our own or another's) may provoke calamity at any time. It does not contradict His love: it is a condition of our freedom, and a necessary element in our schooling. Let us accept it *willingly*. There is no situation out of which, granted our willingness, He cannot work good. Surely therefore, self-pity is a mean and mistaken state of mind, and this personal commiseration must be abandoned. The place of disciples is in the company of those strong souls who, in every age, have borne the buffetings of circumstance with fortitude and cheerfulness, and who say with Browning:—

> *I count life just a stuff*
> *To try the soul's strength on, educe the man.*

. . . An emotion, as the word implies, is a movement *outwards*. Pity, therefore, should go out to others. It is perverted when it is turned inward, and made into self-pity. We live in a love-hungry world, and a pity-provoking world: it is not seemly, or kind, or just, to expend our pity on ourselves. It should:

> *Raise the fallen, cheer the faint,*
> *Heal the sick, and lead the blind.*

It should foster all fruitful philanthropies and never turn back upon itself.

He is Able, pp 48–9

Three chief attitudes . . . may be distinguished among Christians. Some are *resigned* to it. An awful and inescapable trouble may invade their life and, for a while, they are rebellious; bitter; in arms against God. They cannot overcome a sense of resentment. Then, by grace, they resign themselves to the will of God.

Resignation is better than rebellion, yet resignation is not a full Christian grace. Beneath all resignation there is . . . rebellion. . . .Some are *conformed* to God's will. That was the stage which Paul was on at one part of his journey, and a stage which all the saints pass through. . . . Peter was conformed from a foul-mouthed blasphemous fisherman to the leader of all the apostles. Augustine was conformed from a loose, low, incontinent man, who had turned his fine intellect against the Faith, into its glorious defender. . . . But those who linger at the stage where their will is being conformed to the will of God lack spontaneity, mobility, or gaiety. . . . The saint is *abandoned* to God's will. St Francis de Sales sought to express this abandonment in a variety of ways. It is the mobility of the voyager who moves with the motion of the vessel in which he has embarked; a servant in attendance on his lord going only where his master goes: a child leaving to his mother the care of willing, choosing, acting for him, content to be in her safe and tender keeping. . . . It is the attitude of the Virgin Mary (as Father Caussade says) who meets the annunciation with the words: 'Behold the handmaiden of the Lord. Be it unto me according to Thy will.'

The Pure in Heart, pp 120–1

I am not in any doubt that people who are advanced in the school of prayer spend more time in intercession than in any other of the segments of prayer—and often more time in intercession than in all the others put together. The need is so wide. The effects can be so powerful. The sheer unselfishness of it is so compelling that it is no wonder that the weight of their intercourse with heaven falls here.

Is there anything that we can learn about intercession which will deepen our desire for it and increase our skill?

Most people need to be more *particular* and more *methodical*. By 'particular', in this connection, I mean that we ought to pray for persons more than for areas. I don't know how it is with others, but when, say overseas missions are in my mind, I can't pray with any sense of effectiveness for 'China' or 'India'. My thoughts splay out over those vast sub-continents and I have a jumble of images in my mind made up of coolies and temples and elephants and tea-pickers, and while I would not say that God can do nothing with my prayers, I know within myself that this is not praying at its best. But, if I fix my mind on a missionary I know in either of those countries; inform myself of his exact situation; enter (perhaps by personal correspondence, or through a magazine, or circular letter) into his very circumstances, I can lay hold on that man in his need, and on God in His power, and I can pray the blessing down.

Teach us to Pray, p 27

Not even when Rome fell was fear as widespread, or as well-founded, as today. Most of the scientists are scared men. Clearly, war does not end war. Science only gives more terrible weapons with which to wage it. . . . Proud of its achievements it may be, and jealous to be master in its own house, but the achievements threaten the very structure of civilization. . . . Is it possible for the evangelist to relate his message to this world-despair?

Nobody is honestly content with things as they are. If men are less willing than once they were to admit personal sin, they are even eager to admit frustration and 'world sin'. Millions starve . . . and need not. Blind racial hate and ideological antagonisms swell, and fester, and threaten, at any time, to burst. Men batten on black markets, and are the direct cause of the slow death of innocent children. . . . Is this the brave new world? Is this the best that men can do with all their wit? Is it not plain that what is needed is the wide recovery and respect for spiritual authority and the whole moral counsel of God?

So the herald of the Kingdom demands to be heard . . . 'Man is sick inside. The disease is in the will more than in the mind. . . . When man *sees* what is wrong, he can't mend it. It is new life we need: the life of God.'

'I offer it to you—in Christ', says the evangelist. 'Here and now! It is potent. It can only enter the world through persons, but, so entering, the world itself can be transformed by its power.'

Let me Commend, pp 38–9

Saints revenge themselves in a manner all their own. Their Master taught them the method. It is not a case of lighting a fire around the martyrs' feet, but of heaping coals of fire on their traducers' heads. . . . There is no revenge like the revenge of a saint.

My father watched the rise of the Salvation Army and observed at close quarters the scurrilous attacks upon the early Salvationists by the Skeleton Army. Composed for the most part of bibulous thugs, the Skeleton Army bore down on the Salvationists wherever they assembled, and pelted them with filth and stones, inflicting upon them, at times, the most serious harm. Outside the 'Eagle' Tavern in City Road, London, a Salvationist was offering Christ to the people one day when a half-drunk man came out of the public house and, with one savage blow, knocked the preacher from his box. As he fell, the soldier of Christ struck his head against the kerb with such force that everyone thought he was dead. Then he came round, staggered to his feet, and saw, through his swimming eyes, the brute who had done it—almost sobered now with fright. Raising his hand in love, he said: 'God bless you' as he resumed his address. My father witnessed the incident and knew in that moment that the Skeleton Army was defeated, and that these new soldiers of the Cross would march around the world.

The Pure in Heart, pp 127–8

The people are not happy and they see no prospect of peace. Look at the faces of people in the streets, in the buses, and on the trains. When their faces are in repose they do not look happy. The only hope of happiness which millions entertain is to win something big on the pools.

Real religion makes people happy, as happy as the day is long. They get up in the morning with brightness and go to work with zest. They have the answer to all the dark mysteries of life—suffering, bereavement, death. Nor is there any particular mystery about it. Anybody who was completely sure that the world is in the hands of a good God could be happy. Not even hydrogen bombs tossed about by half-mad men can damage the throne of God.

Real religion gives people peace. Nobody knows if there is going to be a Third World War; the Cabinet Ministers don't know, and Commissars don't know either. It *could* happen. The little carefree children may be growing up for that.

There is only one place where peace can be found today. Deep in the heart of those who have religion. It does not depend on circumstances; it depends on conviction and communion. Those who are waiting for peace until all men love one another will be disappointed. Peace is there to be taken and it can be taken now.

But it must be taken from God! Britain has many needs, but this is her greatest. *She needs a Revival of Religion.*

Revival: The Need and the Way, p 9

. . . I fancy you would tell [your would-be consoler] all your heart. 'Sir, I am bereaved. I have laid in the grave the body of a dear one but I cannot bury my love. I carry it about with me. It is a great joy and a great pain. My heart is weak perhaps but I crave for something more than the most that you have offered. I long for household voices gone, for vanished smiles I long. Sir, will I meet my dear one again?' And that philosopher shakes his head and smiles sadly. 'You nourish a baseless hope,' he says. 'Learn to be content with the seventy years that this life offers and school yourself to be satisfied with that.' And so you turn away from him with a great longing in your heart. A busy life has not left you time for philosophy and you cannot argue against the academic mind. None the less, you feel that he is wrong. Vague reasons take shape in your thought: the persistence of love: the soul's instinctive plea for fellowship beyond: the very justice of the universe seems at stake. . . . But is this all that one can rest in? Is there nothing more warm and more certain? Don't come to me for it. I cannot help you . . . unless . . . unless I open this book again and point you to the words of Him Who merits all your love. Listen! 'In My Father's house are many mansions . . . I go to prepare a place for you'. 'He that heareth My word and believeth on Him that sent Me, hath everlasting life.'

Precious promise. Unimpeachable assurance from the Best of whom we've ever heard. What consolation for a broken heart! . . . There is no substitute for Him. He has outlived all His rivals for 2000 years and He has outlived them all because they are not really rivals at all. To whom else *can* we go? He has the words of eternal life.

Why Jesus Never Wrote a Book, pp 112–13

Almost everything which gives preciousness and meaning to life.

Some people dispute that. 'Without religion', they say 'you still have life, love, flowers, music . . . and lots of other wonderful things. Enjoy them and be thankful.' Yes, but a doom hangs over them. Nothing, in this life, stays. Death parts the most loyal lovers, flowers fade, the music dies on the ear. Without religion there is no sense in things. Did you watch your own dear child die? Do you remember the look in her eyes? 'So what? Put the body in the earth. There's no sense in things.' No, but there's infinite sadness in them. Don't pretend that life on those terms *satisfies* you. An eminent unbeliever says that the most you can achieve on this road is 'unyielding despair'. Don't try to deceive yourself that you like it that way. It's religion or the dark.

Other things gnaw at you, too. What of the awful injustices of life—the blind, and lame, and maimed and mad? Are they just unlucky? It's foolish to say that all questions about 'the meaning of life' are 'meaningless'. People will go on seeking meaning. . . . Every uncomplicated man wants to make sense of things, and deep in his mind is the belief that there *is* sense in life somewhere. Religion is seeking the sense. It does not claim to clear up all mysteries, but it claims to have the clue to meaning. . . . Nothing else in life even offers the hope. If you are sincere in saying that you have had all of life you want, what a poor life you've had!

Give God a Chance, p 35

175

In classical Greek the word peace was mainly negative, implying freedom from war, but in New Testament usage the word gathers up the positive elements in the Hebrew term *shalom*, and cannot fully be understood apart from it. The central meaning is harmony within a total community. Elements which might otherwise be diverse and opposed are affectionately related as in a good family or a loyal nation. . . . So peace and righteousness are woven together by the spiritual leaders of Israel, and lasting peace becomes an element of the Messianic hope.

. . . This promise is fulfilled in Jesus. . . . In Him is peace. . . . In Jesus, all men may be at peace with God, and it is the central secret, therefore, of eternal life. In Jesus, all believers may be at peace with one another, and can even face without fear a militantly hostile world, because peace garrisons their heart. . . .

The saint has a serenity no worldling possesses. He did not make it—any more than he makes the other fruit of the Spirit. It is all a glorious consequence of God in the soul. It appears as an unearthly serenity. All that modern 'mind-healers' mean by poise and intregration, the saint has—and more; deeper, more securely based, and set in the rock of reality. His is peace 'in the inward parts': not faked: not kept in place by mental gymnastics, which are often so difficult as to be self-defeating. He is in the world but not of it. Worldly perplexities dash upon him but cannot pierce him. And the peace he receives, he radiates to all who are around.

The Pure in Heart, pp 116–17

There was the soldier who moistened his lips when He cried: 'I thirst.' Have you ever really thirsted? I wonder. The only time I ever thirsted was when I was travelling across the desert; the car broke down, and we were far from water of any kind. I would say quite positively that thirst is far more terrible than hunger.

Think of the day of the Crucifixion: the heat, and the noise, and the dust, and the pain—and the thirst. The only cry of physical torment wrung from the lips of our dying Lord was this: 'I thirst.'

Seven times He spoke—but only once of His own suffering: 'I thirst.' And then that rough soldier darted forward and moistened His lips . . . a spot of pity in the midst of hate. . . . There is often a kind heart beneath a rough exterior.

I soldiered once with a blaspheming Irishman who was my pet aversion, but one day, as we marched, we fell in with what today would be called a horde of 'displaced persons', and there was a little child among them utterly lost. And then that blaspheming Irishman tossed his rifle to a comrade, picked up the little girl, and carried her on his shoulder for miles and miles and miles. I always looked on him differently after that.

And there was a rough soldier who moistened my Saviour's lips.

They Met at Calvary, pp 68–9

. . . His words may still seem ordinary to you. The first thing God said to the little housemaid, whom Spurgeon was fond of quoting, was 'Sweep under the mats'. I talked once to a junior shop assistant who, before the sense of God's reality came to him, had been slack in his prescribed tasks. 'But', he said 'I always do the front down now with water and the hard broom'. Only last week I read of a hearty and humorous young saint whose first clearly recognized word from God was a condemnation of his flirtatious habits. Oh yes, it is ordinary—absurdly so! But then God is concerned with these ordinary things. Duties matter to Him. It is when we attend to these little things immediately at hand that He can lead us on to higher things. Trust His love. He will not greet you with a metaphysical abstraction. He will speak of something known to you already—some neglected task, some old sin, some nurtured grudge—but the growing awareness of God for you depends on your response to that word.

My friends, God is at hand. In the condemnation of conscience, in the keener appetite for spiritual things, in the common duties of every day, God is calling us. O don't search afar: don't wait for some blinding vision. He is near you: nearer to some of you than you know. You did not think that simple craving could possibly be He. Yet it is. He has found voice in the very citadel of your heart: the keep of the castle walls calls out for its rightful Lord. Be wise! Fling wide the gates and, welcomed and crowned, revered and exalted, the King of Glory shall come in.

Why Jesus Never Wrote a Book, pp 72–3

There is in the saint a glad out-running to the will of God: an eagerness for it. Speaking of Our Lord's delight in doing His Father's will, Robertson Nicoll says: 'He did not merely accept the will of God when it was brought to Him and laid upon Him. Rather, He went out to meet that loving will, and fell upon its neck and kissed it.' The saints emulate their Lord in that. They run out to meet that loving will. . . . Events, therefore, cannot destroy this central peace. The 'tragedy' which would steal peace from another man they embrace as a disguised blessing and are thrilled to be allowed in some mysterious way to 'make up' the sufferings of their Lord.

. . . The Sahdu [Sundar Singh] . . . was preaching the Gospel in a forbidden area. He 'could not from His praise forbear'. Arrested and convicted, he was condemned to be stripped . . . and exposed for a night and a day in the market place, his body being covered with leeches. When the authorities assembled the next morning, they expected to find him dead or crazed in agony. He was not dead. He was alive and so calm of countenance that they were awestruck and convinced of his possession by some supernatural power. They immediately ordered his release. Though he fell unconscious at the word of dismissal, his unruffled calm was still with him when he came round, and still with him as he slowly crawled away. Speaking of the experience afterwards, he said that 'all the while he enjoyed an experience of *intense* inward Peace'. In this impressive proof that the fruit of the Spirit is peace, we may find an anticipation also that the fruit of the Spirit is longsuffering.

The Pure in Heart, pp 121–2

What kind of pride could be the impediment to revival?

Pride in our *learning* perhaps? Academics have seemed more important to us than sanctity. We have moved away from the simplicity of the gospel. . . . John Wesley was a scholarly man, but he said: 'Religion is the most simple thing that can be conceived. It is only humble, gentle, patient love.'

Pride in our *organization* perhaps! Ecclesiastical machinery has become a fetish with some of us . . . we have come to think it mattered *in itself*. . . . Did we want to prove to business men that we are as 'efficient' as they are when it wasn't efficiency they chiefly asked from us?

Pride in our *past* perhaps! We have boasted—in all denominations—of our traditions. 'Ours is the only Church which *really* goes back to the Apostles'. 'Ours is the *established* Church!' 'Ours is the Church which revived religion in the 18th century.' 'Our Church is *truly* Bible-based'. . . . God help us! It is pride which has ensnared us again.

'If My people . . . shall humble themselves *and pray*. . . .'

'If My people . . . shall humble themselves and pray *and seek My face*. . . .' That kind of praying, the unhurried waiting before God which isn't just words and a breathless eagerness to 'get it finished' but a true seeking of His face, an encounter, a meeting with God. If (humbled before Him) we will pray like that—we are coming near to revival.

Revival: The Need and the Way, pp 13–14

If your Church is failing, put this question to yourself: What can I do about it? It would be wrong for me to guess what God will say to you, but I'm bound to admit that to me (and to most of my friends who have submitted to this test) He said at once: 'How much of this love have you got yourself?' Then He began a most unhurried and loving probe. 'Are you prone to criticism? to jealousy? to whining? Do most things which come up have an immediate self-reference to your mind? Do you bear resentment? . . . If it is My love you want flowing through you, you must learn that it is divinely possible to ache with love and pity over the most vicious and repulsive people—even while you hate their sin.'

This kind of scrutiny from Heaven, if a man will submit to it, can turn him inside out, and make him a different kind of Christian from what he had ever dreamed. It isn't done in one session. It may take many weeks . . . but the moment will come when you will face in stark helplessness another question: How can I get this love? You will know you haven't got it. You will know how much you want it, for yourself and for the Church. . .

It is a gift of God. You cannot get it by your own will. . . . No sinner can say with sense: 'Go to! I will have love.' You cannot get it by reason. John Wesley said: 'Reason cannot produce the love of God. . . . Love never flowed from any fountain but gratitude to our Creator.' If you want the way . . . put into one word, it is the word 'Attend'. Attend to God in prayer. See Him as revealed by Jesus. Look . . . look . . . look. Longing will awake in you, and longing and loving (in this context) are almost indistinguishable.

The Pattern of Prayer, pp 83–4

When Molly Ellis was kidnapped at Kohat in April, 1923, and snatched away by the same treacherous hands which had murdered her mother, all the world shuddered with horror, and a punitive campaign was discussed. But the soldiers never marched. The girl was rescued by an unarmed Englishwoman who pierced those iron hills and brought her back in safety again. How came this woman to have such power? In this way. She was a nurse, and married to a missionary doctor. One night, years before, her husband was stabbed to the heart in his own porch by one of the people he had served so well. So Mrs Starr was widowed within two years of her marriage, but the only revenge she took on the murderers of her husband was to go on nursing them still. That was all. She went on nursing them still. The Afridis live for vengeance, and maintain their blood-feuds for generations, but service so sublime as this clutched even at their hard hearts. Her power among them could not be denied. Sir John Maffey, the Chief Commissioner of the District, said that she made a mark upon them better than all the drums and tramplings of an army corps. It was the fine fruit of forgiveness. What if it does sometimes fail? A doctor does not cease to be a respected physician because his remedy does not always cure. Forgiveness is not to be waved aside as foolish if it fails to evoke response in *every* heart.

The Cross stands and holds wide appealing arms to all who thirst after revenge. It seems to say 'This is how Jesus dealt with hate'. He held it to Him, and quelled it in His Mighty heart of love. The boomerang lost its spring because the venom which flew out in His murder did not fly back again in revenge. So He appeals to us still and having caught the vision, we can do no other. We *must* forgive.

He is Able, p 57

[The saints'] joy, like a dazzling rainbow, must ever be seen against a dark sky. Richard Baxter in Kidderminster seldom knew an hour free from pain. Fletcher of Madeley said that 'some lessons we can never learn but under the Cross' and he wanted to be like his Lord 'despised and rejected of men'. He confessed himself '*well pleased* to suffer'. St Francis of Assisi came to believe that 'there was nothing for him but to suffer . . . and he resigned himself to God's will'. The sufferings of the early Quakers are dreadful to contemplate . . . Thérèse of Lisieux said: 'Suffering became my treasure. I found in it charms that held me spellbound.'

. . . What is not fully clear . . . is what part the suffering is playing in the shaping of the saints—why God stands a handsbreadth off at times, and seems indifferent to the prolongation of their woe. The saints themselves do not talk like this. Their utter trust in God's wisdom and love forbids such questionings. . . . If there is some alchemy of the spirit which really transforms [pain] it must be very deep. The nature of pain is not altered by a metaphor. If pain refines one soul, it embitters another. It cannot be suffering as suffering which works a blessed work in the soul of the saint. It must be suffering received in the meekness of the Holy Spirit: suffering willingly accepted in the belief that God can do something with it. At least a little of heaven must mingle with these stresses of earth. Only God Himself could beget such triumph in the soul of man.

The Pure in Heart, pp 123–4

The ordinary man, when he thinks at all, is half-paralysed at the thought that he does not matter. The world is run, he believes . . . by 'high-ups'. For all the lip-service paid to him by politicians, he feels that he is just 'one of the masses'. He suspects that he is planned-for, planned-on and planned-over, but not treated as a person. . . . He feels, at times, less than a pawn in a game played over his head by the people in authority, and he awaits the next crisis, or the next depression, or the next war, powerless himself to put it off.

. . . The evangelist treats him as a person; assures him . . . that he is dear to God—dear enough to shed the precious blood. . . . He is, so the preacher affirms, so intimately known to God that the hairs of his head are all numbered, and God has set such store on winning his love that He gives His own Son for the gift of a sinner's heart. If he will trust God for it, new life will flow into him—the life of God. It is wonderful for a 'mass-man' to become an individual; a *person*. . . . 'Meeting' with God does it. Cardinal Newman knew, in the hour of his conversion, 'two and two only absolutely and luminously self-evident beings, myself and my Creator'. Luther knew it. He said 'It is the personal pronouns that matter'. . . .

In an age of personal futility, the evangelist has a sovereign opportunity so to offer the life of God to people that futility will vanish in conscious effectiveness, and each new-born soul know himself a person in the sight of his Maker.

Let me Commend, pp 40–1

When Jacob lay down to sleep he had no expectation of meeting God. He had not been thinking much about God for some time. The stirrings of his conscience which he had tried to stifle had had the effect of pushing God out of his thought. And besides, who ever would expect to meet God in a desolate wilderness of that character, wild and unfrequented, unknown to worship and unhallowed by praise?

Yet it was just there that God held tryst with Jacob—just there where all the appurtenances of the holy place were wanting and where men would least expect to hear Him speak. I cannot imagine what Jacob would have chosen had he been privileged to choose the spot, but I do not think it would have been the bare and barren hillside where, as a fugitive from justice, he made the moss his couch and a pillow of stone. Yet God came to him there. . . . God is constantly seeking to meet us in the common and unexpected moments of life. He does not wait for what we are pleased to call the 'grand moments' but He will make the common place the grand. We walk about blind to the glory that is around us because we do not expect to find it there. We mortgage the joys of the present, the quiet homely joys of humdrum days, to our anticipations of some distant time of overwhelming happiness of a kind that never comes to most people. God has not concealed our happiness in some fabled El Dorado. It is all around us if we would only learn to see it in common things.

Why Jesus Never Wrote a Book, pp 74-5

Every week the minister must meet the broken-hearted. I say again: *you* may forget it; *we* can't.

If I had no crucified Saviour with whom to greet those who have been broken by the tragedies of life, I would not know what to say to them. How could I speak to that girl whose young husband was actually killed on their honeymoon? How could I speak to those parents whose longed-for child turned out to be a cretin? How could I speak to that poor polio victim twenty years in an iron lung? How could one speak to the multitude of sufferers in a world like this if one had no crucified Saviour to speak about?

To all those whose minds reel in sorrow; to all those who feel resentful because life has done to them its worst; to all those tempted to believe there is no God in Heaven or, at least, no God of love, He comes and He shows them His hands. More eloquently than any words those pierced hands say: 'I have suffered.'

There are tears in things . . . and there were tears on the face of Jesus Christ. Not for His own suffering, but for that of others, is it not recorded that Jesus wept? He weeps with the sufferers still; with you who are suffering, and whose hearts may be bitter or resentful, even while I speak to you. You can't steel yourself against this suffering life. You need the 'inside word' He brings. Can you resist the appeal of those eyes 'majestic after death'? He has suffered. He knows the answers. He could bring even you to utter peace.

Westminster Sermons (vol. ii), p 73

To the natural mind, the idea of anybody else living *in us* seems plain silly or a bit of religious mumbo-jumbo. 'How can anybody else live in me?' the man in the street asks. . . .

Perhaps the only way to convince him of the possibility is to display this quality of life yourself. The life of Christ is so potent, so radiant, so engaging that men can't resist it. When they really see the appearance of His life in us, it fascinates and holds them.

How, then, does it come? What must a man do who . . . wants that divine life in his own stunted soul?

He must believe in its *possibility*. The promise of Christ, the testimony of the Apostles, the experience of the church must wipe unbelief from the mind.

He must want it—*ardently*. God is drawn into our souls by 'the lure of strong desire'. Desire is inflamed by constant study of the life of Christ in the New Testament. Desire is inflamed, also, by the study of the saints. Desire is inflamed by prayer. . . .

He must open his *mind* to Christ's incoming and, because that is not so simple as it sounds, it is there that he needs especial help. . . . How can we give Him our mind?

Is it as hard as that? All our school-days our teachers urged us to 'give our minds' to things. There is nothing mysterious here. It is all summarized in the word 'attention'. We give our mind to Christ when we attend to Him; think of Him; talk to Him; work with Him; rest with Him; walk with Him . . . and the more we give Him our minds, the more He gives us His.

How to Live in Christ, pp 4–5

. . . We have our part to play—small, but not unimportant. Should a millionaire give a fortune to a pauper, the pauper must take it. If the King grants a pardon to a felon, the felon must accept it. When a mortal goes to God for forgiveness and the Holy Spirit, he must receive the gift and, if he is wise, receive it daily for each new day as it comes.

That is where discipline comes into the holy life: not the toilsome, straining, failing effort to be good; but the faithful attending on God to receive. . . . The fact of one high moment cannot secure holiness for ever; it is a life of intimate relationship (which issues in mystic indwelling) and faithfulness shows itself in our consistency in attending.

Wesley was a man of iron discipline from his youth up. During the years which he spent in what he afterwards came to regard as his 'legal night', he was unshaken in discipline, and when illumination came he carried the discipline over to be the servant of his enlightened mind. It stood him in good stead. Early and late and often in the day, he waited on God and his waiting had its rich reward.

Most Christians reverse Wesley's order. Enlightenment comes first and they need to forge the discipline afterwards. Some fail to do it, and the precious thing they found slips from them. They may even come to doubt if they discovered any secret at all, and in chill cynicism write it off as the ebullience of adolescence. They have ceased to wait upon God and this is the heavy price. There can be no continuance of the holy life in the soul of any man who does not continually wait on God. Only those who 'attend the whispers' of His grace can hear Him 'inly speak'.

The Path to Perfection, pp 197–8

It is easier in some ways to believe that Christ was an impostor or mad than to believe that He was just a good man.

He made such immense claims for Himself. He said: 'The Son of Man is Lord of the Sabbath' (Luke 6⁵), 'I am the way, the truth and the life' (John 14⁶). [*See also* John 14⁹, Mark 8³⁵.]

He forgave sins. He said 'Be of good cheer; thy sins are forgiven' (Matthew 9²), 'The Son of Man has power on earth to forgive sins' (Luke 5²⁴). [*See also* Luke 7⁴⁷, John 8¹¹.] The bystanders saw the point of all this and asked in bewilderment 'Who can forgive sins, but God alone?' (Luke 5²¹).

He had no sense of sin Himself. Every good man has a sense of sin. The better the man, the keener his sense of sin. . . . He said one day . . . 'Which of you convicteth me of sin?' (John 8⁴⁶).

He accepted worship. Worship belongs only to God, Any good man would be appalled at being worshipped. Christ accepted worship. [*See* Matthew 14³³, 28⁹, John 9³⁸.]

Add all this up. Christians have felt driven to choose between three possibilities: that He was an impostor, quite mad, or . . . God. For nearly two thousand years they have made answer 'Very God of Very God'.

Give God a Chance, p 43

Without suffering, the saint cannot be known. Many people with many of the marks of holiness fail to pass this test. Their character disintegrates under suffering. Loving, joyous, kind and good enough they have been, this test defeats them. God forbid that we, who have not reached their spiritual stature, nor been subjected to so stern a test, should feel any superiority over the defeated ones. But so it is!

Years ago, I had in my pastoral care a man with many of the marks of a saint. Indeed, in my heart, I put him in that category. He fell ill, gravely and painfully ill. 'What a privilege the nurses will find it', I thought to myself, 'even to minister to such a man.' They found it no privilege. To the distress of doctors and nurses, and to the utter confusion of his pastor, his character broke up under this discipline. He was querulous, self-pitying, constantly complaining; almost in arms against God. So splendid his past had been! So like a saint he seemed! But this fruit of the Spirit did not appear in him, and in its failure to appear, made one wonder whether his joy and peace were not so much celestial fruit as the bloom of past good health and easy circumstances. 'Call no man happy', said Solon, 'until he is dead.'

Call no man saint until he has suffered.

The Pure in Heart, pp 124–5

People ask 'Why doesn't God intervene? Why doesn't He put out His hand and prevent these things . . .?' Let us . . . remind ourselves of certain principles which our answer must respect.

1. God rules His universe by law. He does so for our good. No knowledge would be possible at all in an erratic world.

All science depends on the principle that the same cause gives the same effect. If quinine killed the malaria parasites on one occasion and killed the patient on another, no medical service would be possible. If God answered every prayer in the way the petitioner asked, the world would be chaos. A farmer pleads for rain on the same day that a child on holiday asks for a fine day. . . . Imperial Airways will not delay the departure of a liner a single hour to include the most distinguished passenger . . . the duty of the directors is to maintain the system.

2. God respects our freedom. If His heart of love could have been content with marionettes and not men, He could have had a sinless and perfect world. . . . No parent would desire that his child remain infantile all his days, even to receive unquestioning obedience. God made us free . . . and He respects our freedom still.

3. God's kingdom is of the heart . . . His chief aim is character, and in most people character is not best built by an unalloyed compound of health, comfort, prosperity, leisure and recreation. Other elements are needed to nerve our faint endeavours—sterner, rougher things. . . . Suffering taken to God begets a wonderful tenderness. Let it be kept in mind that God's aim is the most precious thing in the universe—character.

Providence, pp 11–13

Let me conclude with a personal testimony. The one desolating doubt I have had in my adult religious life was on this question [Is Christ really God?]. It was midnight in my soul, but I emerged more sure than ever and the passing years deepen my conviction. I am quite sure now. Christ was incarnate God. He is utterly trustworthy. Travel with Him and travel with confidence. (Forgive me if I sound presumptuous, but I have tested Him, and been tested, in many ways.) I am in no doubt that God spoke through the Hebrew prophets and the Eastern sages, but His fullest final Word was Christ. All men must come to Him at the last. He has the answer to the problems of our private lives, our families, our business, our civic and national affairs. Apart from His triumph, I see no hopeful prospect for our race. He is our rightful Lord and God.

I offer Him to you again this morning.

He can't rule the world till He rules you.

For some of you it could be *now*, but—if it can't be now—God speed the day when you can get down beside Thomas and say with utter sincerity: 'My Lord and my God.'

Westminster Sermons (vol. i), pp 46–7

Don't think that God can make you holy for ever in one stroke. The willingness to have it so may come in one moment, and a complete revolution of thought in a moment, too. . . . But it is better to think of life in Christ under the metaphor of breathing, rather than of surgical operations aiming to eradicate sin by one deft use of the knife. It is a moment-by-moment life in God: an in-breathing of the spirit; an out-breathing of the breath devitalized by use or tainted by a subconsciousness not yet completely interpenetrated by the Spirit of God.

The open secret of it all is in prayer. The place of discipline is not in working up holiness in oneself, and never to think on it as a toilsome process of self-effort, but in unhurried daily waiting upon God who gives according to our faith. A simple hymn of other days says: 'Take time to be holy, speak oft with thy Lord.' If the art of meditation and mental prayer is understood in this 'taking time', there is no more advice to be given. It is all there. If men and women knew what prayer could do for others and for themselves, no trouble would be too much to secure it. They would rise early and stay up late. No novel or newspaper could hold them from it. Like one hopelessly in love, they would scheme for every extra moment with the Beloved. They would actually enjoy being kept waiting in the ordinary commerce of life (that fuming experience for those who do not know this secret) because to be kept waiting would all be extra and unexpected moments for the mind to fly away to its Lord.

Holiness (Pharos Paper), pp 6–7

We are appalled to realize how few of the 960 waking minutes of every day are *really* given to Him.

We have our work to do and we realize that the degree of our concentration must vary with the hours of the day.

But we know that even when our minds are necessarily concentrated on the most material things, our work can all be offered to Christ and the background of our thinking be still of Him.

We know, also, that there must be no strain about this.

But why should we be strained? It isn't as though we were really doing it. We look to Him. We think of Him. We walk and talk and sing with Him. But *He* it is who does things. He chose the apostles that 'they might be with Him' and unconsciously they grew like him. So may we!

To our morning quiet-time (Bible study and prayer) we are adding this exciting venture. We are going to see how much of the day we can think about Him. There will be solemn moments, of course, but many more gay ones because He is such a Gay Companion. . . . As He comes into us, other people will be drawn to us because He is literally the most attractive Being in the universe.

And we will seek by His help so to make this companionship second nature that the day will come when we shall really understand what Paul meant when he said: 'I live, yet no longer I, but Christ liveth in me.'

How to Live in Christ, p 8

Wherever any brave soul faces the God-denying look of things, and still trusts God even in the shadows, there the examples of Jesus, who trusted His Father even when He seemed deserted on the Cross, is gloriously emulated.

I have recently had a letter from the relatives of some of my friends who are missionaries in New Guinea. . . . Their house had been burned to the ground, and all their possessions stolen. Nine years of hard work in translating the Scriptures, and in shaping a dictionary, had all been wasted . . . the papers had perished. The missionary himself was afflicted with a terrible skin disease, and had some trouble with his kidneys, due to long exposure in the sodden bush. His wife was ill also. And I had written to ask 'What is the state of mind of these people who have suffered so much and seem deserted by their God, who have seen the things to which they gave themselves broken, their own health gone, the future all unknown? Tell me, what is their testimony now?'

The letter I received the other day from their relatives was the reply. It just said 'Their faith is unshaken. They assert that God is good'. Just that. Just like the Saviour hanging transfixed upon the Cross and saying, 'God is love'; illustrating it by His dying; showing us, in a moment of time, what God is through all eternity.

God be praised that there are these ministries open to us still: that we can carry the Cross for Jesus; moisten His lips; share His shame; prove, by our own devotion, the potency of His dying.

They Met at Calvary, pp 75–6

Many people live all their lives in a state of resentment. Sometimes the resentment is vague and diffused—against God, or the world, or just 'things'—and sometimes it is focused on persons. I met a man once who proclaimed himself an atheist, but had, none the less, a most bitter feud against the God whose existence he denied! It is well known that people born illegitimate, or maimed, or facially disfigured, or halt, or odd in any way, have a harder battle often in their minds than in their bodies. They may burn with resentment against God, or the 'luck', or the 'fate' which dealt them what they judge to be this heavy blow.

The saints soar above this. Alexander Whyte knew of the shadow on his birth but (as he hinted to the students at New College, Edinburgh) it only made him feel all the more akin to all who were not of Norman blood. Paul was no Adonis, and had some recurrent and prostrating malady, but he came to believe that God could use even that. Bishop Lightfoot had a most unprepossessing appearance. One of his most devoted students said that 'he was startlingly ugly: a stout little man with grotesque features and a squint, but also the greatest, the best man I have ever encountered, and I say this deliberately after the experience of many years. In a day or two his face appeared the most beautiful and lovable thing imaginable.' Resentment cannot live in the hearts of those who deeply believe that Infinite Wisdom and Infinite Love watch over them all the time.

The Pure in Heart, p 126

196

When I first went to the old Belgian town of Bruges, I went with the set purpose of seeing the Memling Art Gallery, one of the most famous of all the smaller art galleries in the world. The guide book told me that it was near the church of Notre Dame, but I searched for the art gallery a long while in vain. The only buildings of any consequence quite near to the church were the Mansion of the family of Van der Gruuthuus and the Hospital of St John. Finally I found a policeman and asked him in my halting Flemish where the Memling Gallery was. And he said —'There!—there in the Hospital'—and I found it there, all housed in one small room of the hospital and adjacent to the beds of the sick and the dying. There was the world-renowned casket of St Ursula within sound of the consumptives' racking cough. And the marriage of St Catherine and the Entomb-ment and the Epiphany—all there, where the sick and weary come and go, and where the tear-drenched cheeks of the mourner are no unfamiliar sight.

I had not expected to find such beauty there. I had supposed such pictures would be hung in a magnificent hall, built for the purpose, and separate from the ways of common men. But that experience became for me a parable of the love and beauty of God. I am not to look for His love and beauty in some cloistered retreat, far from the cry of our suffering humanity, and kept pure because it is kept apart. I am to seek Him in the busy press of normal life, where men toil and women weep; where hearts break and hopes are buried till their resurrection morn. . . . And that is where I expect to find Him now—not simply shining in glory so as to be untroubled by our way. That isn't Jesus—but sharing it, bearing it, and transforming it into the sterling of eternity.

Why Jesus Never Wrote a Book, pp 77–8

If you had a friend who was ill, you would gladly give an hour to visiting him. But he might live too far away to do that. Even if he lived near, he might be too ill to have visitors, or too tired to maintain prolonged talk. Why not give the whole hour to prayer? Does the idea strike you as absurd? A whole hour?—to one friend? But you would have given him more than an hour (with the journey) to visit him. It can't be the time you begrudge. Is it more important to talk to him than to talk to God about him? What wonderful things have you got to say to your sick friend which can compare with what God might say to him? Sometimes a visit is just right. But what modest mortal can really believe that his help can compare to the help of the Holy God?

Forbes Robinson . . . once said to a friend that in his younger days he had taken every opportunity of personally appealing to men to come to Christ, and then he added this: 'As I grow older I become more diffident, and now often, when I desire the Truth to come home to any man, I say to myself "If I have him here he will spend half an hour with me. Instead I will spend half an hour in prayer for him" . . .'

Don't dream that this is a criticism of all sick visitation. God is using that lovely ministry every day. But it isn't always possible and it isn't always best. Prayer is always possible, and nothing can surpass it in worth.

(*continued on page* 199)

Let us suppose that you have put the hour or half-hour aside. What will you do?

Get alone. Go to your room and shut the door. 'Pray to the Father in secret' said Jesus. Compose yourself in God's presence. Be quiet, and quite unhurried within. Feel like a person with 'all the time there is'.

Think on God. The way to think on God, of course, is to think on Him as revealed by Jesus—loving, loving the people whether they have been good or not, forgiving and full of compassion, always meeting penitence with pardon. See Him responsive to the cry for help at all times—moving out in healing to the sick.

Then think on your sick friend. Be careful not to dwell on the symptoms of his sickness so vividly that imaginatively you reproduce them in yourself. See him well, happy, buoyant. Compassion will grow in your heart. This compassion is most important. It gives 'lift' and power to prayer in a way which duty can't do. Let your mind move from God to your friend, and from your friend to God, while this compassion gets deeper and deeper. It doesn't matter if twenty-five out of your thirty minutes goes in this way (or fifty-five out of your sixty). The moment will come when you seem able to hold together in the crucible of your longing heart the readiness of God to bless and the readiness of your friend to receive, and all your plea can go into the minutes which remain.

You may later hear of the effect of your prayer, or you may not. It doesn't matter. Don't fidget for the day-to-day confirmation. Such praying can't fail to bless.

The Pattern of Prayer, pp 92–4

If envy spoils friendship, what havoc it has been known to create in the branches of a family. . . . One brother succeeds; another will hew wood and draw water till he dies. A touch of patronage on one side and a bit of envy on the other, and the old fellowship has gone. Somehow it seems to foster our sense of inferiority when one in the family circle, begotten of the same parents and enjoying no greater advantages than we had ourselves, wins through to conspicuous success. No loophole seems left for the grudging spirit that would explain the triumph away on other grounds, and it seems to force us to face some inferiority in ourselves.

Oscar Wilde used to tell a fable. . . . The Devil was once crossing the Libyan Desert when he came upon a group of small fiends who were tempting a holy hermit. They tried him with the seductions of the flesh; they sought to sow his mind with doubts and fears; they told him that all his austerities were nothing worth. But it was of no avail. The holy man was impeccable. Then the Devil stepped forward. Addressing the imps he said, 'Your methods are too crude. Permit me for one moment. This is what I would recommend.' Going up to the hermit he said, 'Have you heard the news? Your brother has been made Bishop of Alexandria.' The fable says 'A scowl of malignant jealousy clouded the serene face of the holy man.'

. . . Who can cure this evil thing? How shall jealousy be done away? Who is able? Christ is able! He can uproot this rank weed in human hearts and plant the lowly flower of magnanimity in its place.

He is Able, pp 68–9

Turn your mind at once to Him. If you wake slowly let each step to wakefulness be a step toward Him. Address to Him your first words of the day. Say in your heart: 'I am here, Lord, and eager for another day.'

Cultivate the custom of linking your Lord and yourself with 'We'. 'What are *we* going to do together today, Lord?' If it seems too familiar at first, remember that He encourages such intimacy. It is beyond our understanding why He should want to live in our soiled hearts . . . but He *does*. . . . *Say 'We'*.

Glance ahead at the day. 'We are going to do everything together today, Lord.' See yourself going through the day with Him. Meet every known duty in thought with Him before you meet it (still with Him) in reality. 'We must make the most of that opportunity, Lord.' 'We must be particularly watchful there, Lord.'

Then rise with zest and begin your day. These are the first steps of the indwelt life. Murmur the prayer:

> *Come nearer, Lord, than near me*
> *My succour to begin:*
> *Usurp the heart that craves Thee!*
> *O come and dwell within.*

How to Live in Christ, p 9

When Thomas Carlyle read in the papers of an amazing act of heroism in a Cornish mine, and of how one miner had thrust his friend to safety at the sacrifice of himself and gladly opened his own arms to death, he was so moved by the story that he made inquiries, first as to the facts, and then as to the explanation. The facts he fully confirmed. The explanation I give in Carlyle's own words. He says of the miner that he was 'an honest, ignorant, good man, entirely given up to Methodism . . . perfect in the faith of assurance'. We live in a world made grey by the atomic bomb. Is there anything that would more, and better, publicize the faith than life lived with joy and assurance—the gay abandonment of those who live to better all things but who know . . . that if the worse comes to the worst they need not fear those who kill the body and afterwards have no more that they can do? The world is hungry for that kind of assurance . . . I was in Sils-Maria in the Upper Engadine the week before last. I noticed the house near the Post Office where Nietzsche lived for seven years and wrote his chief works. I remembered the time when he felt the appeal of our faith, and set himself to study it in the lives of some Christians he knew, and I remembered the acuteness of his disappointment in their joyless natures, and how he said 'These Christians will have to look more redeemed before I can believe in them'. . . . The American members of this Conference will hear without surprise . . . that the wealth of America is sometimes a cause of envy in other lands . . . but we have been surprised to learn, from the reports of your publishers, that the best-sellers are books on how to be happy. . . . Is that, then, what people really want. . . . Don't they plainly need Christ and the assurance of His salvation?

Proceedings of the Eighth Ecumenical Methodist Conference,
1951, p 75

The fruit of the Spirit is longsuffering. It is the courage which *endures*. They go on when everything seems knocked out of them and the cause itself quite lost. In their early days, many of the saints were in a hurry, but, when they learned that God is not in a hurry, they learned patience. The things they longed for were coming as fast as God could bring them, and they learned patience with the patience of God. Perhaps nothing helped them more than the recollection of God's long patience with their own unsanctified souls.

Someone has said that the secret of patience is 'doing something else in the meantime'. The 'something else' the saints do is to dwell on the use God can make even now of the trials which beset them. 'Let me receive this with patient meekness', they seem to say, 'and perhaps by this means God will polish His jewel.'

At his first employment, St Gerard Majella was placed under a foreman who was nothing less than a cruel brute to all the apprentices. He had a special spite for Majella. Even in embryo, a saint can draw persecution. There is that in him which unconsciously convicts sin and makes it savage. Through all the fiery trial, the saint-to-be never gave way to impatience or ill-humour. . . . Jeremiah said out of much tribulation that 'it is good that a man should both hope and quietly wait for the salvation of the Lord'. Both hope and quietly wait! Some rush on with their work for God, and, meeting disappointment, get discouraged. . . . The saint both hopes and quietly waits. Not all he has to endure robs him of the patience of hope, for he knows that God will have His way in the end.

The Pure in Heart, pp 129–30

. . . We ought to keep prayer-lists. I don't know how any person serious in intercession can avoid it. I am blessed with a good memory myself, but to leave the objects of our intercession to the half-casual recollections of prayer-time itself will almost certainly issue in a lack of . . . particularity . . . and the omission of many who justly claim a place in our prayers.

Making a prayer-list is a means of grace in itself. Some people make a list to cover a month; others work on the week as a unit; nearly all these serious intercessors have a 'priority' list, which is constantly changing, of people in the most urgent need and for whom (during their period of acute necessity) they pray *every* day. Even so holy an occupation as prayer . . . *can* tend towards self-centredness. Confession, thanksgiving, dedication, and the plea for guidance, keep the self very much in mind. As one glorious by-product of this secret intercession with God for others we have this lovely *un*self-centredness, and prove once more that we never do anything for others which does not bless ourselves.

. . . Certainly we cannot use a prayer-list as though it were a telephone directory, and just run our eye down a list of names. Nor is it much better, I think, to speak the names aloud, if it is all done at speed. There is more in it than that. Wait before God in the quietness. Recollect His presence, His power and His love. Wait. . . .

Teach us to Pray, p 28

Emotion cannot be cut out of life. No intelligent person desires it. To unpick human personality and remove all deep feeling is an impossible occupation, and if it could succeed would leave life sterile indeed. Imagine life without the warm overtones of love; conceive a family where every one acted only from a cold sense of duty; suppose a youth to ask a maiden to marry him, having carefully explained to her first that he had no feelings for her. . . . Life cannot be filleted this way. . . . And carry the same enquiry over into religion. Require that the herald of God announces the offer of his King, freely to pardon and fully to bless, but firmly forbid that any transport of joy should accompany either the announcement of the news or its glad reception . . . and you ask the impossible.

The dread of emotion in religious expression has gone to extreme lengths, and some critics appear to suspect any conversion which does not take place in a refrigerator! No doubt there have been dangers in emotionalism. The evangelism which attacks the heart without any appeal to the mind, and snatches pathetic 'decisions' from folk gale-swept by feeling, but quite unaware of what they are doing, is unworthy and dishonouring to God.

But that doesn't cut out emotion. The man who screams at a football or baseball match, but is distressed when he hears of a sinner weeping at the Cross, and murmurs something about 'the dangers of emotionalism', hardly merits intelligent respect.

Let me Commend, pp 46–7

How calm and private that blessed sepulchre must have been after all the dreadful and shameful publicity of the Crucifixion. How quiet and still! How blessedly secluded. Jesus loved solitude and He had no solitude between Gethsemane and the sepulchre. Working out the time is difficult, but it seems that eight hours after His arrest He was on the Cross. Eight awful hours! In the brief space of six hours He was examined five times by four different tribunals. In all the haste of their fiendish cruelty they rushed Him from Annas— to Caiaphas—to Pilate—to Herod and back to Pilate again— and then to the Cross. Oh! having driven in the nails and done their devilest, why couldn't they let Him die in quietness and the company of His dear ones? But no! The cup must be drunk to the dregs and the ghastly publicity of it was part of the bitterness of the Cross.

So as He hangs there—the noise, the dust, the pain, the thirst—and perhaps the incessant noise was not the least of His pangs, the crowds, the jeers, the curses, the sobbing women —and He hangs . . . between earth and heaven.

O for quietness; for solitude; only to be alone. Through His swimming eyes He sees His mother's face. It brings Nazareth back to Him. Childhood and the fields of Galilee. And John is there. Dear John! 'Woman, behold thy son; Son, behold thy mother.' And still the noise . . . raucous laughter and bitter sobbing . . . until the blessed numbness steals over His outworn frame, and the . . . 'It is finished! Father, into Thy hands I commend my spirit.' And then the sepulchre. Do you think of a tomb as eerie and cold? No! no! It is quiet, and calm, and our crucified God rests for hours and hours on a cool bed of rock.

Westminster Sermons (vol. ii), pp 79–80

Was it not Erskine of Linlathen who said that of all the waste in the world nothing was so wasteful as a wasted sorrow? Fancy going through some great grief and not learning the lesson that tears had to teach! Fancy entertaining Sorrow in the home and not finding the gift she always brings in her hand! The saints believe that no sorrow met in God is sterile of good. Suffering buys something, they believe, worthy of the price which pain has paid. Woe never need be wasted. Their thought of God will not allow the saints to trifle with the idea that His tender heart is indifferent to their longsuffering. Good will come of it. Love will find a way.

And there is more courage in that faith than the inexperienced know. One of the sternest tests God allows to fall upon His saints is to permit them to suffer apparently for nothing; not to see the fruits of their pains. His Son passed out of sight of men unvindicated. The sun set in blood and there was darkness over all the earth. Many a saint endures and sees no fruit to it. . . . One discerning writer says 'God has a further step that He must ask of saints of George Herbert's calibre. There comes in the lives of most saints a strange hiatus, when it seems as if the sacrifice that they have made is of no value, and leads nowhere; a pause that looks like complete frustration.' Endure that! See your sacrifice in the eyes of the world, not as the splendid deed of a noble soul but as the quixotic aberration of a fool. In the dark, these brave souls hold still to the skirts of God. . . . With this longsuffering, they confidently believe that He will purchase something worthy of the price which pain has paid.

The Pure in Heart, pp 130–1

It is in the intervals of our day that weakening and self-obsessed thoughts can take possession of us. It is when we have no need to be concentrated, and thought can dart where it will that it often darts to fear, fret and self-absorption.

Going to work is such a time. There is no need to concentrate on the journey. You know it so well. Go to work in Jesus. Talk with Him as you go.

Pray for the people you pass in the street and sit by in the bus or the train. How sad so many people seem when their faces are in repose! What secret cares are gnawing at them? Turn the widest stream of God's love on them that can channel its way through your narrow but broadening heart. . . .

Enter your place of business with your Lord. See the people you work with through the eyes of the Saviour. You have brought Christ with you to work, and your colleagues (though all unaware) are going to work with the Saviour. How long before they find out? How long, at least, till they know there is something strangely different about you? How long before they ask themselves: 'What's he got that I haven't got?'

Some people are not easy to work with. Am I easy to work with? If the fault is in them, how would Jesus look at them? How much allowance would He make for the secret hurts and disappointments which have made them what they are? One thing is certain: He wouldn't allow their brusqueness or ill-manners to make Him ill-mannered too. He would still look on them with His Father's love.

How to Live in Christ, p 11

. . . Benjamin Hellier, yet another exponent of Wesley's teaching, and one who 'adorned the doctrine'. Classical Tutor in the mid-years of the last century at Richmond College, Surrey, then Governor of Headingley College, Leeds, he made the paths of holiness winsome by a piety which was irrepressibly gay. Dr Moulton bore witness to it, and Dr Sugden, and Dr G. G. Findlay. Dr Findlay said that he never knew 'a saint more blameless and unworldly, yet more pleasant and conversable'. Benjamin Hellier's children said 'He did not within our knowledge ever profess to have attained entire sanctification, and yet no one would have more readily accepted such a statement than the members of his family'. And he himself records that he enjoyed 'constant victory over inward and outward sin, perfect freedom from anxious care and implicit trust in God'.

The high quality of life seems almost to have been left as a 'legacy' in his family. It was of his brother, J. B. Hellier, that Edgar Wallace, the writer of detective fiction, said 'J. B. Hellier was a perfect man . . . I believe that much of the good which is within me came because I knew him. He is an everlasting barrier between me and atheism'.

. . . Sanctity is not the monopoly of any one community, but its origin and growth are of vital interest wherever it is found. Many of the world's 'great' men were very little men. It is the saint who stands by the throne in the Court of the King of Kings. Some we can name, but far more 'there be which have no memorial' the fragrance of whose lives God has used to sweeten His world.

The Path to Perfection, pp 200–1

Thy life was given for me;
What have I given for Thee?

Teresa was over forty and a very practical person. She was no adolescent girl. She had been in the convent for years before the great experience came to her, and when it came, it came unheralded. Going into her private oratory one day, she noticed a picture of Our Lord being scourged. She must have seen it hundreds of time before but, in that moment of revelation, she saw it as she had *never* seen it before. She saw God suffering —suffering for love and suffering for her. It struck her to her knees, sobbing in pain and wonder, and, when she arose, she arose a new soul. . . . This was the great divide of her life. *She* knew it, and none of her biographers have questioned it. Before this experience she was one woman, and, after it, she was another. . . . She said that she arose with 'a sense of unpayable debt'. Those who would understand all the labours of the subsequent years, all the testings and all the triumphs, all the courage and all the certainty, will find the clue to most of the mystery in 'the sense of unpayable debt'.

Is it possible to understand a little more perfectly what comes to these elect souls in those moments of revelation? They know themselves loved: loved deeply and loved personally. They know themselves loved *for* nothing: just for themselves. They see as in a flash that there are 'no strings' to God's love. He is not loving them *if* they will do this, or *if* they will do that. He loves them for themselves alone. . . . The poverty of their own love comes over them at that moment. The love they have offered others has often been conditional love. . . . None of this is love like the love of God. The saint knows himself loved for himself alone. Not being loved *for* anything, he knows that no failure can rob him of that love.

The Pure in Heart, pp 240–1

Almost all people who are intimate with God delight in the joys of corporate worship. The form their worship takes may vary according to their temperament and training . . . but, howsoever the worship may express itself, the wonder and privilege of it are known to almost all who are known to God. Attending church may seem the essence of boredom to the uninitiate, but to those with inside knowledge—ah! nor tongue nor pen can show.

At one period in his ministry, Dr George Morrison suffered a breakdown in health and was unable to attend public worship for twelve months. All the while he longed to be there. When the hour actually came he was allowed to join with a wee Highland congregation; it was too much for him. Strong man that he was, he almost broke down and wept.

It is the realization of the preciousness of public worship which makes men and women who are spiritually sensitive aware of the awful loss this deprivation involves for others. There are people nursing the bed-ridden who are never able to get to church. There are invalids whose invalidism could be overcome, to some extent, if only a friend would push a bathchair. There are blind people dependent upon a pilot, and mothers of young children tied at home. Some of them ache for 'the courts of the Lord', but duty or incapacity firmly forbid. . . . They want to be in church; among God's people, joined with Him and them in the rapture of worship. They know that God visits the soul in its separateness (for they have lived this way, maybe for many years) but they know also that this can never take the place of corporate communion. How can it be? . . . Their only hope lies in this: that in their circle of friends, there may be some . . . who . . . dedicate themselves to this obscure but splendid kindness, to give the . . . prisoners of the home the joy of the house of the Lord.

(*continued on page* 212)

... They delight in God's house.... Yet they are willing and, indeed, eager to give it up that others may have occasionally what they can have at any time. They are ready to sit with the invalid, or mind the babies, and they do it with such a gentle ease that no sense of burden rests upon the bed-ridden, nor yet upon the grateful soul whose watch is thus relieved.... I knew a nurse whose irregular hours of work made her attendance at worship irregular at any time, but who got such good when she came that she was always eager to release those who were nursing the bed-ridden in their own homes. Her professional qualifications gave extra confidence to the people she wanted to help, but, even so, she always made a point of getting to know the patient socially beforehand, and establishing relations of friendship so that *everybody* was happy about the arrangement.

And I think also of a fine woman I knew in middle life, denied the joys of maternity herself but fond of children and very skilful with them, whose particular pleasure it was to relieve young mothers and give them the happiness of going to worship with their husbands. She undertook the task with such thoroughness that she always visited the home two or three times before taking on duty, in order to win the confidence and affection of the children first.

'It would never do', she explained to me, 'to have a little child suddenly wake up in fear, and find no one but a comparative stranger in the house.' We may say of ... these obscure disciples ... what Leigh Hunt said of Abou ben Adhem— 'may their tribe increase'.

Methodist Magazine, 1947, pp 294–5

Kindness . . . for some folk . . . is not thought of as a fruit of
the Holy Spirit, or as requiring any divine inspiration, sanction
or buttress. . . . People have come to believe that we can have
that kindness . . . without any Holy Spirit at all. And just as all
talk of the brotherhood of man hangs in air, and has no basis
in reality without the Fatherhood of God, so does kindness,
divorced from the Holy Spirit, degenerate into sentimentality
and become a travesty of the real thing.

Kindness recovers all its apostolic quality in [the saints]. In
the saint it is never sentimental: never divorced from reality:
never undisciplined: never evasive. On the other hand, it is
ever-present: never excluded by their concern for God's holiness: never driven away by any pride in their own virtue. . . . He
shows it grounded in the nature of God. It flows directly from
his faith. It is supernatural love disclosing itself in costly
affection towards his fellow-men. That is why it does not cease
when it is snubbed, injured and lied about. That is why it has a
robustness and pertinacity unknown in the sentimental kindness of the world. The man whose kindness is an appetite for
praise and gratitude gives up when praise and gratitude do not
come. He gives up still more quickly if the objects of his bounty
begin to wonder aloud what he is 'getting out of it' himself.

The saint never gives up.

The Pure in Heart, pp 133, 136

... It may be felt ... that no room has been left in the scheme of things for any 'special' Providence at all. It will appear to some that if we are not the pawns of chance we are the prisoners of law, and they will wonder if half our petitions are not a waste of time.

Yet that would be a sad and false conclusion, and one unwarranted by the facts. If the relationship between God and His human children is best conceived as that of Father and child, it may safely be assumed that God has not so made the world that He cannot make a Father's response to a child's plea.

Moreover, it needs to be borne in mind that laws can be respected and yet adapted to an astonishing degree. It is a law of nature that iron will neither float in water, nor air, yet we have immense liners floating on every ocean in the world, and aeroplanes sailing through the air from continent to continent. The law has not been broken; it has been adapted.

If *men* can do this, it would be childish folly to put a meagre limit to what *God* can do, or even to suppose that we have a complete knowledge of all the laws in operation. We are not prisoners of law: God can maintain His system and sustain His needy children too. . . .

It is clear also that His providence finds increasing opportunity as men grow more sensitive to His guidance. . . . How much easier must be the task of God, in all His providential dealing with His children, if they cultivate the listening ear and learn (as they may learn) to disentangle the Divine voice from the murmurs of self-will.

Providence, pp 13–14

The normal housewife does not *go* to work. She gets up in the morning and the work is all round her!

But no work surpasses hers in importance. Christian homes are our great need.

How would Christ run a home? What would He have more than good meals, cleanliness and modest comfort? How would He take the milk in? How would He shop?

The housewife, whose longing desire it is to have Christ living within her, has advantages and disadvantages. So much of her work is mechanical. The preparation of meals, the making of beds, cleaning the room, washing-up . . . the same thing over and over again.

When one is busy with habitual work which takes only a tenth of the mind, the rest of the mind . . . wanders off on its own: to fears of sickness, failure, loss of love . . . or to day-dreams of sudden wealth, ample leisure, greater charm. . . .

The battle for those who would live in Christ is set here. Hours of all our lives—though especially the housewife's— are subject to this fantasy thinking. Don't let thought wander to fear and fret and self and sin. Gently draw it to Him. School yourself to the point where every thought released from necessary concentration darts back at once to the Beloved.

Talk to Him as you work. Sing to Him. The deep hymns— and the not-so-deep—either will do so long as they centre in Him.

How to Live in Christ, p 12

215

Every man and woman must come, sooner or later, to the Cross. The meaning, and the power, and the preciousness of it will elude us unless we see that we were involved in it too. . . . Yet that is the hard part of the Cross to multitudes . . . how to get 'me' into it, how to see that it matters to them personally, enormously, eternally. Fifty-seven generations separate us from those who stood on that first Good Friday by the green hill outside the city wall . . . I wasn't thought of then . . . and neither were you; the slow unfolding of many ages was to elapse before the opportunity of life should be mine or yours. How, then, can it be said with truth that 'He loved me, and gave Himself for me'?

And yet the Cross is powerless without that personal note in it. If I honestly cannot see its reference to me . . . then it is just an event of ancient history, like the fall of Babylon, or the march of the Ten Thousand, or the death of Socrates, which are of interest to the historian but cannot truly be said to matter much today and much to me. How can I get the 'me' into the Crucifixion? How can I say with sincerity that 'He loved *me*, and gave Himself up for *me*'?

. . . I will go and sit before the Cross. I will *attend* to it. I will be concentrated, and unhurried, and let it speak to me.

> *I take, O Cross, Thy shadow,*
> *For my abiding place . . .*

Yes, I must *abide* here. Here is cleansing, security and renewal. Here the past is dealt with, and the future secured, and all the present—peace. Here I take strength for service, patience in waiting and healing for any wounds that may come. I rest my whole weight on the Saviour. I no longer care about myself. I do not need to. What freedom to be free of that fretting self-concern! In any case, *He* cares for me.

They Met at Calvary, pp 77–8, 99

. . . Because these critics found it hard to believe in God, they transferred their faith to man. They invented (in the middle years of the last century) that strange creed of positivism—the worship of humanity . . . 'Glory to man in the highest'. 'The difference between the old artists and me', Walt Whitman said, 'is this. They painted one head with a halo of gold-coloured light about it, but I give a halo to all.' The years went by and this worship of our human nature grew popular because it fed our conceit. It was nice to be told that there . . . was no sin at all—just a bit of selfishness which time would correct; that the Golden Age was inevitable and that, by gradual steps, man would move unaided to perfection. . . . And then we woke up! First in 1914, and then again in 1939, we found ourselves in hellish war. The mid-years of the century find us still unsure of peace. This, then, is the perfect world we had been promised by the men who sneered at original sin; a world of atomic submarines, air-raid shelters, gas-masks for babies, guided missiles, and hydrogen bombs. A world of television, plastics, possible trips to the moon—but also the possibility of radiation poisoning and mass death! The incredible folly of it; the ignorant conceit; the puffed-up egotism!

Is it not obvious now to everyone that unredeemed man, neglectful of his Maker, takes the path to the pit and would make this fair earth a gory hell?

Westminster Sermons (vol. ii), p 3

You cannot make joy. She is a coquette: follow her and she eludes you; turn from her and interest yourself in something else and you may win her. Set out with the specific intention of finding joy and you are doomed to failure: forget yourself— and all your wants in some disinterested service of others, and joy will come home to you and nestle in your bosom. There is no escaping this: it is a law of our very being; psychology and the New Testament are at one here, and the experience of millions confirms their findings. . . . Do you enjoy a game of golf or tennis? Then your pleasure is strictly proportioned to the degree in which you lose yourself in the game. While it lasts it must absorb you: your whole mind should be on the game. If you stop in the midst of it and ask yourself precisely what degree of pleasure you are deriving from this particular stroke the pleasure will evaporate and you will begin to feel rather foolish in following a wee white ball over a mile or two of turf. To *get* the pleasure you must *forget* it. . . . And so it is with peace. The Apostle says 'Let the peace of God rule in your hearts'. Oh, that word 'let'! The whole of my message is contained in that. The Apostle does not say 'Make the peace of God'. He is too keen a student of the human heart for that. He knows you cannot make it; the very effort to do so defeats its own end; many people are missing it just because they are trying to make it, and you must *let* the peace of God rule in your hearts. Note that the Apostle says 'in your hearts' not in your circumstances.

Why Jesus Never Wrote a Book, pp 81–2

We live in grey times. The darkness which followed the blinding flash of the atomic bomb when it burst above Hiroshima on 6th August 1945 has crept like an impalpable shadow across the world. . . . Truly our future is all unknown and the hearts of men fail because of fear. It is not surprising . . . that many Christians, not normally or deeply interested in apocalyptics, should catch themselves wondering whether some catastrophic consummation is at hand and listen with something more than amused contempt to the people who specialize in discerning 'the signs of the times' and assert that the end of all things is at hand. In some ways, it doesn't matter if it is.

> *Sleep after toil, port after stormy seas,*
> *Ease after war, death after life, does greatly please.*

. . . Most Christians are still of opinion that God does not even yet despair of our race, and that the prayer . . . 'Thy will be done in earth as it is in heaven'—will have a glorious fulfilment. . . . It is fortunate that this variation of view makes no difference to the Christian's plain duty from day to day. The clamant task is evangelism either way. . . . It should not be one whit more imperative for those who are preparing to sing *Dies irae* than for those who see the slow unfolding of future centuries and the gradual triumph . . . of the things of God. Using whatsoever gifts we have . . . we must bend our strength to the supreme task we have been given to do. 'Go ye therefore and make disciples of all the nations. . . .' This is our commission. We have seen our Lord permanently change individuals . . . we believe He could do no less for cities and communities; we hold that He could save the world. He sweeps His sceptre over every area of life.

Methodism: Her Unfinished Task, pp 118–20

If you don't feel like praying, prepare your mind by reading a favourite passage of scripture or even a favourite hymn. When desire rises, think first on

ADORATION. Everything depends upon God at the last. Adore Him. He is like Jesus. He is infinitely loving, infinitely wise. Every breath we draw, we draw by His permission. He lends the atheist breath to deny Him. Think how awful it would be if there were no God—or a devil was Lord. Think of God as revealed by Jesus, and just adore Him in your heart.

THANKSGIVING. What a lot you have to be thankful for! Go over your blessings in your mind. Health? (Some health at least.) Love? Home? No great money worries (you make ends meet, don't you?). Children? Grandchildren? Good books? Flowers? Friends . . .?

Heap them together. Most days bring something extra too. Note it for thanksgiving.

DEDICATION. Solemnly give yourself afresh to God every day.

GUIDANCE. Go through your whole day (so far as you can foresee it) slowly with God. (This, that . . . this, that . . .) Meet each foreseeable experience with God before you meet it in reality. You may (with passing time) get little warnings or 'alerts'. Increase your own sensitivity to God's will for you. You do it by exposing yourself more and more to His presence.

INTERCESSION. Don't leave them to the casual recollection of the moment. Have lists. What better use for the back pages of your diary?

PETITION. Is there something you want for yourself? Here is the place for it. Last and least.

The Pattern of Prayer, pp 100–1

* See p 239

No man remains envious who really sets his whole heart on the approval of heaven because that secures an independence of the praise and blame of earth. The simplest servant of the kingdom, quietly confident that he is doing his best, may feel the smile of God upon him. There is no richer reward in store for anyone. . . . Being sure of God's approval no man need envy the praise of earth.

'The Master praises; what are men?'

And when Christ does rule in a heart what marvels of magnanimity He can effect. Henry Melvill Gwatkin was lecturer in ecclesiastical history at Cambridge in 1884 when it was decided to endow a chair in that subject. Most of his friends were confident that Gwatkin would be appointed and he was strong in hope himself. But when the decision was made, the choice fell upon Mandell Creighton . . . and the keenness of Gwatkin's disappointment can be imagined. He had been doing the work for twelve years. It would not have been surprising if some bitterness had crept into his heart when he heard that the honour had gone to another. But next day he wrote to Creighton and his letter is a glorious example of the Christian's triumph over jealousy. He said:

'For myself I am ready to work under you and to support you loyally in all that falls to me to do. So far as I know my own heart, no jealousy of yesterday shall ever rise on my side to mar the harmony and friendship in which I ask and hope to live with the first Professor of Ecclesiastical History in Cambridge.'

When he succeeded Creighton in the chair in 1891, the promise of his letter had been kept in spirit and in truth.

He is Able, pp 71–2

The first duty of the Christian at work is to be a good workman; not to persuade others to go to church, or 'to give up the drink', or to get converted . . . but to be a good workman. And this applies whether you are in the office or on the factory floor.

While there are parts of all people's work which are half-habitual, and can be done with the mind on something else (or on Someone else) the more highly skilled the work the more concentration it requires. The Christian's duty at such work is to put his *whole* mind to it. The operation is in progress . . . the experiment is on the way . . . the speech is being made. Nothing less than the whole mind is engaged.

Living with Christ does not militate against that concentration. It adds to it. Work approached after prayer (and done with Him) is more concentrated, more complete and more effective than any work done on our own. The increased sense of effectiveness is enormous and can only be imagined by those who have not experienced it.

. . . To that complete sense of concentration is added an exhilarating sense of colleagueship. One *knows* one is not alone. 'My hand is held by Another. . . . Another is thinking in me. . . . Somebody else is looking through my eyes. . . .' The sense of aid increases with the gravity of the work . . . and as soon as the need for absorbed concentration is over, one turns one's whole mind again to intimate talk with the Beloved Colleague and whispers: 'We did that well, Lord, and we did it together' and (though we have contributed but a thousandth part of the whole) He smiles and says: '*We* did!'

How to Live in Christ, p 13

It is any time between 1841 and 1873 in the heart of Africa. A white man is pushing through the jungle alone—alone but for the company of a few black friends. He is fighting the slave trade . . . at its source. He will not rest until this wicked thing is done away. He pushes on. Constantly racked with fever, he spreads the message of God's love as he goes. He heals the sick, starts a school, plans a church. He steels himself against all the glad endearments of home. He makes himself strange to his own fellows if only he can pay one particle of restitution as a white man for all the wickedness his race has inflicted on the black. But, most of all, he longs to end the slave-trade. He never retires. Dying on duty and on his knees, his body is carried to the coast and identified by the teeth-marks of a lion which had once chewed him; and when his body is laid in Westminster Abbey, Mr Punch doffs his jester's cap and stands in reverence at the grave to say

> Let marble crumble
> This is *Living*stone.

The kindness of the saints, who can measure? Think of the fount of them, the number and the cost and the duration of them! Think also of the sweep of them: not directed only or chiefly to those with whom they had affinity and who were humanly appealing, but to the unlovely and the repellent. Nothing so much as the kindness of God's servants could interpret His own tender heart to those . . . generations, or witness to them, as they suffered without hope on earth, that there was still hope in heaven.

The Pure in Heart, pp 138–9

Perceiving, as other mortals have not perceived, the burning love of God, the saint gives God love for love. He cannot help it. . . . Having seen the love of God, his own love leaps in response. His heart is drawn out of him and lost in God's immensity.

No mortal can love as God loves, but the saint loves with all that there is of him. . . . With passing time, all his life is love. Every fruit of the Spirit . . . is related to love. . . . The miracles which God works in Him, He works by the alchemy of love.

It is by love that the saint becomes free—free of that awful self-centredness which is the mark of most mortals. Not only is he free to accept or reject the love which God offers him (and which will not be withdrawn though he spurn it), but the love which leaps out of him in free response to the love of God is the very means by which he can escape the bondage of pride, of passion, and of self. Passion enslaves us: the love which God gives sets us free. Passion blinds us to the defects of the loved one: this love sees the defects in other mortals, but loves just the same. Passion is demanding, hungry, exclusive: this love is generous, releasing, eager to be shared. Passion can turn to sudden anger and destroy the object of its fierce desire; this love is never ungovernable and always creative. It is by love that man comes to freedom, and there is no other way.

The Pure in Heart, pp 242–3

If a minister ruefully remembers that the people who support him expect him to do many more things than save souls, let him solemnly recall that they are not to be his judges at the last. His Judge is the One so intent to redeem that He 'came . . . to give his life a ransom for many'. The outcome of such a meditation is sure. The emphasis will fall again in that man's work on evangelism. . . . Full, therefore, of the preciousness of his gospel, let him seek guidance from God concerning one other with whom . . . he should share his burning experience of the Saviour and his longing that his church should be known, above everything else, as a centre of evangelism. . . . Let him pray and witness until at least one other shares his hot concern, and shares it enough to go (by God's guidance) to a third member of the church, while the minister goes to a fourth.

A fellowship is born that way. It begins at a depth. It starts as 'one with one'. It depends upon people being willing to give themselves away to one another. . . . Let the minister draw these new-born and re-born souls into closer fellowship with one another and with himself. Let the 'sharing' be deep. . . . Week by week, they will knit into each other's life. . . . Now let the minister put into the group all the teaching that he can. Too many members of the Protestant Churches are uninstructed in their faith. . . . Let him relate their experience to Christian doctrine and Bible teaching. . . .

Observe how much has already happened in the Church. The minister has, at the centre of his flock, a group of people who know what they believe (and experience!). . . . It is no closed circle. All may enter it on the same terms. 'Are you ready for Christ to deal radically with you? Will you seek until you find? Are you willing to team in with others that still more may be drawn into this Way of Life?'

Let me Commend, pp 75–7

Forty days divided the Resurrection and the Ascension. What a wonderful forty days they must have been for the Apostles! There was first the almost intolerable ache of joy in their hearts as the wonderful truth slowly mastered the lifelong conviction that dead men do not live again. There was, also, the delirious hope every morning, that, at any moment, Christ might appear to them, and another proof be added to the accumulating evidence that He was, indeed, alive for evermore. Most of all there were the actual appearances themselves, the teaching and the reminders; the promises and the admonitions.

I think—had I been one of them—that what would have impressed me most would have been my own incredible dullness in the days before Calvary. Again and again I fancy, it would have risen in my bewildered memory: 'Yes, He did say that. "The Son of Man must be delivered into the hands of sinful men and be crucified, and after three days rise from the dead." It comes back to me now. How could I have been so dull? I must have been thinking of something else—what I was going to get out of it when He was made King—and in my selfishness I let Him go to His death misunderstood and alone....'

What a wonderful forty days they must have been for the Apostles!

Westminster Sermons (vol. ii), p 81

[Goodness] is perhaps the hardest fruit of all to define. It is so obvious. Of course a saint is good. But he is good in a peculiar way. The word 'good' is used so freely and, even in its ethical employment, so widely, that it can mean anything and nearly nothing. A man is regarded as good in some circles if he keeps out of the hands of the police, and anyone who is 'highly respectable' is judged to be good.

The goodness of the saint is a peculiar goodness. It flames with the numinous. It is a goodness which unconsciously proclaims itself. One feels it as an aura around its possessor. It is incandescent. It is *essential* goodness: goodness 'in the inward parts' it is white with a whiteness 'no fuller on earth can whiten'.

It is spiritually discerned. Yet its radiations are so powerful that it may be doubted whether anyone could be near it and quite unaware of it. . . . An evil man might be angered and made more hateful by it. . . . The saint is unconscious of it himself. Blissfully unaware of the impression he makes, he moves on his way *reminding people of Jesus Christ*. Men cannot know him and be cheerful in unbelief. He seems to convict people of their poverty if they are living without invisible means of support. Many have doubted the existence of holiness until they have met it in a saint, but they have not doubted again. This is different! It speaks! An untravelled Roman Catholic met John Keble and said, 'I never knew before of holiness outside my own Church'. But he knew it then, and he knew it at once.

The Pure in Heart, pp 140–1

The word 'decent' is vague. Some people use it of anyone who keeps out of the hands of the police. But let us use it now in the best sense we can . . . of people who are kindly, neighbourly, good citizens . . . but who have no use for religion.

All human nature is self-centred—even the nature of 'nice' or 'decent' people. Education makes no difference to this self-centredness—except to put a veneer over it and make it less obvious. . . . Here is a nice grandmother with a pack of her grandchildren's snaps. She can bore you for an hour with them—and be weary in five minutes if you take out your own pack! 'How is your boy?' a nice and cultured gentleman said to me one day. 'Let me tell you about mine.' And he did, for thirty-five minutes!

The thing that is deeply wrong with human nature is not that some people commit adultery, and some steal, but that *all* of us are self-centred—the decent and the indecent, the nice and the nasty. Manners, polish, refinement, and culture only cover that disease . . . they can't affect the deadly disease underneath.

To be saved is to be saved from that disease. We all have it; therefore we all need to be saved. Some who claim to be saved have still got it and unconsciously bring religion into contempt. . . . When Christ saves us, self is no longer at the centre; *He* is at the centre. And when He is at the centre, life is transformed.

Of course decent people need saving.

Give God a Chance, p 50

As the day comes to its close and you are composing your mind for sleep, run back over the day with your Lord. Yes! *With* Him. Remember, the aim is everything together!

. . . Roughly assess how much He has been in your mind during the day. There will be much to be happy about . . . and even more with passing time. As you build this technique into the very structure of your days it will become more and more habitual—and all the better for that. The bits you do on your own will be fewer. Far as you may be from all you desire, you will draw daily nearer the identified life.

'We took *that* opportunity, Lord!' 'We helped *them*!' 'We got *that* sorted out!' 'We know the next steps *there*. . . .' Again and again, the heart will swell with thanksgiving as the certainty of His companionship fills the mind again.

But there will be other moments in the review too; embarrassing, humbling, even scorching moments. We shall remember the things He had no part in. Hurtful things we said: un-Christlike deeds and thoughts. . . . Sometimes we will be dumb with shame or find ourselves faintly whispering '*I* did that alone'.

Claim His forgiveness. We can all slip *but we must not wallow*. When you can do so, lift yourself up. And do so as soon as you can. Then go on living the indwelt life—humbler, less assertive, and more Christ-centred than ever.

How to Live in Christ, p 16

Young men and women in this country under twenty-three
. . . and convicted in the courts of crime, are usually sent to a
Borstal institution. . . . The sentence is usually for three years,
but the convicted youth . . . may be out on licence [within] nine
months . . . under the eye of a . . . supervisor. Now this period
on licence is the critical period if the youth, already seriously
astray, is to be won back to good citizenship again.

We may be thankful that the work of the Probation Officer
. . . attracts a fine type of men and women. . . . Now what these
workers need is colleagueship in their service; Christian people
who are willing to undertake a complementary ministry of
friendship with wayward youth. It would be foolish to foster
false ideas about the work. It is hard. It has no glamour. It
often seems unproductive in the end. To make friends of folk
who don't really want your friendship (however much they
may *need* it), and whose range of conversation is largely limited
to films and the other sex, is not an undertaking for those who
are expecting some excitement out of it themselves.

. . . This is a task only for the tough—but for those who come
within that category, and can snatch exhilaration from the
difficult, nothing can exceed the challenge of this herculean toil.
There are cruel disappointments in it. One feels at times that
nothing one can do can overcome a will chronically weak, or
unpick a personality into which heredity has woven a dreadful
bias to evil. . . . But God is mighty, and the resources of grace
are limitless. . . . Make contact with a Probation Officer, or
Borstal Associate, or an After-Care Supervisor. . . or ask your
minister to do so for you . . . interpret it as God's leading, and
go forward in bold hope.

Methodist Magazine, 1947, pp 341–3

[The saints] say in effect: 'Don't go in search of peace directly. Don't probe yourself and get morbid with introspection. Just recognize the fact that you haven't got peace and then bring every thought in concentration upon God. Dwell not upon your poverty but His riches: not upon your impotence but upon His power. Fill your whole mind, not with negative, enervating thoughts about yourself, but positive and bracing contemplation of God.' Soon you will find yourself saying in the language of the twentieth century what Paul said in the language of the first: 'O the depth of the riches both of the wisdom and of the knowledge of God!' Your mind will be stayed upon Him. Then give yourself in service to others: every needy soul is an opportunity: seize every self-pitying thought in its early stages and direct it in pity to somebody else. Have no time to moan your own lot: be too full with giving a hand to someone else: be so absorbed that self is forgotten and pray for power to exclude every known sin. Then the miracle will happen. Peace will come to you. You have not made it: you were not trying to make it: it just came as a by-product of the process, or better still, as a gift of God. Not a gift made in any arbitrary fashion: given where it could be given: given to those whose mind is stayed on Him and who have lost self in the service of others.

Why Jesus Never Wrote a Book, pp 83–4

The life of the saint is all Christ-centred.

. . . This, more than anything else, makes him a saint. The fruit of the spirit only appears in him in perfection because the whole centre of his life has been shifted from self to Christ. He might hesitate to say with Paul, 'I am crucified with Christ, nevertheless, I live; yet not I, but Christ liveth in me', but others would say it for him. . . .

Occasionally the saint will speak of this secret death. Normally, he does not speak much of himself, but, under the pressure of the Holy Spirit, and to aid a seeking soul, he will tell of it.

George Müller did. . . . His *Autobiography* gives little idea of the power, and indeed, the charm of the man to whom God gave thousands of orphans and more than a million pounds. But, hard-pressed on one occasion to tell his secret, George Müller said: 'There was a day when I died; utterly died . . . died to George Müller, his opinions, preferences, tastes and will; died to the world, its approval or censure; died to the approval or blame even of my brethren and friends and, since then, I have studied only to show myself approved to God.'

It is in the enormous difference made by that secret death that the uniqueness of the saint lies. The old man being crucified, the Christ-man rises in his stead, and the power of the saints to appeal to the highest in others, and to challenge their conscience and haunt their memory, is all here. God never gets nearer to an unsurrendered man than when He calls to him in a saint.

The Pure in Heart, pp 141–2

Sometimes a man suffers in his professional advancement because he has identified himself with the Christian cause.

I could give many better instances, but perhaps you would forgive a simple personal reminiscence.

In my Army days I had great ambitions—forgive my confessing so much—to get on the educational staff of my battalion. I was an auxiliary lecturer for a long time, and I had a comfortable understanding in my own mind (and other people had too) that when a vacancy fell due I would get it. The vacancy fell due . . . and I didn't get it. I will not deny that I was inwardly grieved and wondered why.

A friend of mine, already on the staff, enlightened me. He said, 'The officer in charge wouldn't have you. You finished yourself off with him that night, months and months ago, when you came and borrowed the education tent for a weekly meeting of prayer and Christian fellowship.

'You should have heard what he said when you'd gone. He's the kind of man who carries picture-postcards of nude women in his pocket. He has a mind like a cess-pool. I've heard him say more than once, referring to you, "Whatever happens here, we won't have that Holy Joe on the staff". '

Westminster Sermons (vol. i), pp 50–1

We have known something of the wine of sporting honours, and of the plaudits that are reserved for those who are first. Is any thrill quite like the thrill at the end of a long and stern race? Can you recall it? Unconsciously, as one enters the last lap, every reserve of wind and nerve and muscle are called up. It is all out now. With the tongue like a piece of leather in the mouth and one's breath coming in great gasps, one strains forward with all one's being compact of just this thought—to be first! The shouting increases: the faces in the stand seem to run into long white streaks: things get misty: dimly one feels that one may be fainting, but it doesn't matter: nothing matters because the tape is round one's breast and the race is won. First! And it's not for one's self. No! But the school, the college, the team!

These are great moments. . . . But I have known greater moments than that. There was no press of spectators: no shouting crowd: no medal: no points: no handshakes. It was all quiet and private: a matter of one's inmost being. It was the moment when I knew that with God's help I had at last got my heel on some old weakness. It was that moment, solemn and happy for ever, when I knew for certain that I had taken some old temptation in both hands and thrown it under the table. It was that hour, past description and too grand for anything but silence when I knew that the great God had deigned to enter my mean heart: and come to live with me. There was nothing fantastic about it: nothing unreal: it was just as natural as sunrise: as simple as putting your hand in a friend's. These are the greatest moments of all and the real milestones on the march of life.

Why Jesus Never Wrote a Book, pp 123–4

It is in the enormous difference made by that secret death that the uniqueness of the saint lies. . . . If we keep this central truth in mind, we can pick our path from those other paths which appear to resemble it but are not, in truth, the King's Highway. Many people have equated sanctity with keeping an ethical code, but the ethical code is only a consequence of the Christ-centred life, and if the path of ethical achievement is deliberately chosen, and a man comes to have pride in his achievement, we are back at the sin of Pharasaism again. They keep the code by their own taut wills and lapse into the sin of supposing that they have done it themselves. Some of these moral athletes seem to keep a more rigid code than the saints themselves, who remain, in most ways, so sweetly human, but it does not prove that they are more advanced in sanctity. . . . The same error is commonly made by plain people who often protest their indifference to all religion and offer themselves as ready for any judgement that may come, on the ground that they have been doing 'good turns' all their lives. It is the sin of Pharasaism in overalls. It is still trying to work one's passage to heaven by what one has done. Self is still at the centre. It is tainted, not because the things are evil (they might be the best things conceivable) but because the self-regarding principle animates them and *I* am doing them in *my* way for *my* ends. How deep this disease runs is only clear to us when we realize how firm a grip it has on good people—and on ourselves. To see it is essential to its cure, and essential to the recognition that the goodness which is a fruit of the Spirit is different in kind from the goodness we have striven for and rejoiced in achieving.

The Pure in Heart, p 142

To be saved (in the New Testament sense) is to be re-made in Christ, or to be in process of that great change. That is why the Bible sometimes speaks of the converted as *being* saved (Acts 2⁴⁷). When the Holy Spirit is within us and the transformation has begun, God anticipates the perfection of His work and says that we *are* saved.

The signs are not to be mistaken. Life has a new centre—Christ and not self. The fruit of the Spirit appears: love, even to the unloved; joy, which fills the heart and lights the eyes; peace, seeping into every crevice of our being; patience, kindness, goodness, integrity, humility and self-control (Gal. 5 ²²,²³). These things can't be overlooked when they appear in anyone. *And they grow*.

What bliss there is in personal salvation—to know oneself clean and fully forgiven, to be sure of God and certain that life has purpose, to have the fear of the future and of death all taken away, to be convinced of heaven and of meeting our dear ones again . . .!

How can one help but thrill to the rapture of it. Saved! Assured! Tracing no part of our salvation to our own deservings, but believing it completely on the pledged word of God!

In the exuberance of their gladness some Christians have said that no shadow falls on their happiness at all.

How Much are you Saved?, p 4

Augustine, seeking peace, plunged into the wilderness expecting to find it in the solitude and quiet. In the desert he found calm tranquillity, everywhere *but* in his heart, and when peace found him he was in the strenuous life of old Milan. Wesley had this peace though he travelled more than five thousand miles a year on horseback and preached half a dozen times a day. Fitzgerald, the translator of the *Rubáiyát* of Omar Khayyám, seems to have missed it, though he lived the life of a recluse and kept doves. It is not dependent upon circumstances. We have seen it in the face of the old-age pensioner and missed it in the gaze of the rich. We have marked its presence in people standing beside the open grave of their dead, and missed it in others who had no obvious care in the world. It is not to your circumstances but to your hearts that the Apostle prays the peace of God may gain admission.

Have you ever met a soul in whom the peace of God fully dwells? You have not forgotten the meeting. Life has few things to show more beautiful than this. They are poised: it is not in the power of circumstances to force them from their balance. . . . They display that 'toil unsevered from tranquillity' that Matthew Arnold praised: a hundred duties claim their notice but are powerless to dislodge that central calm: the surface waters swirl and foam, but the hidden depths are still and tranquil. They are not irritable or impatient: they neither boast of themselves nor complain about life . . . and if you ask their secret they smile and say 'He keeps them in perfect peace whose mind is stayed on Him'.

Why Jesus Never Wrote a Book, pp 82–3

Saints often strike their observers with their simplicity. They live simply. They are unpretentious and uncomplicated. Worldly people have sometimes thought them fools.

In a worldly sense, they often are fools. The wisdom of this world is foolishness with God. The 'imprudent' things done by saints would fill many volumes. Their indifference to money and to their own reputations (to mention only two things) have amazed and amused people through many centuries.

But the explanation of their simplicity is what interests us now—and it is not far to seek. The circumstances in which they accept life give it a sovereign simplicity. Life *is* complicated for people consumed with earthly ambitions. How can they help but constantly and feverishly calculate their chances of achieving what they are after? —winning that position, those honours, or some high renown? Is this rival forging ahead in common esteem? How do I play my cards to keep abreast of this one . . . and that one? Can I placate X without antagonizing Y? So the necessary manoeuvrings go round and round in the mind, ever-changing because the manoeuvrings of others are changing too, but leaving no leisure for interior peace, or that harmony which comes to a life integrated in something outside of itself.

In contrast to this, life for the saint is simple. Its centre has shifted . . . from the self to Christ. He has but one ambition: to do his Master's will. . . . So he greets each new way with child-like wonder, knowing himself dearly regarded by Infinite Wisdom and Infinite Love.

The Pure in Heart, pp 145–6

Guard against coming to your evening prayers too tired. It affronts the majesty of Heaven to fall asleep over them. Prepare for the closing devotions of the day by getting a quiet mind and thinking of God. A Bible reading often brings you right into His conscious presence.

Now—beginning just where you are—go back, in thought, over your day. . . . Picture Christ at your side. . . . Look at your day together. There will be much to be thankful for—strength for work, warning of dangers, fellowship with friends, your senses, flowers, fun, home, dear ones. . . . There may be some things to be sad about—warnings ignored, impatience, nasty and wounding words, coldness to someone who had a right to expect warmth, showing-off, neglected duties . . .

CONFESSION. Examine your sins in confession. Use no portmanteaux phrases (e.g., 'forgive me all my sins'). Say what sins. (If God tells you to apologize or make some restitution, note it and get it done as soon as you can.) Wait for His word of forgiveness. *Wait* . . .

THANKSGIVING. Now let your tongue caper. What a loving Heavenly Father you have! . . . Thank Him. Pour it out—for this and that—and this and that. Of the special and divine origin of many of His blessings you were totally unaware, so you had best include a word of gratitude for them also.

INTERCESSION. The serious intercession of the day has been offered earlier, but on most days there are one or two urgent needs you feel you must mention again; mention them now.

BEFORE SLEEPING. Our last thoughts often affect our dreams—and sometimes are our first on waking. Choose them therefore. . . . Feed the right thought to the brain. . . . A couplet from a hymn. . . . Or a picture lifted from the gospels of Jesus, healing, blessing, teaching. . . .

A good day tomorrow.

The Pattern of Prayer, pp 101–2

*See p 220

Gossip is vaporous and so easily made, but it is deadly. One is never sure that one has it all, or has it firm. Somebody knows somebody who says that somebody saw . . .!

How can this evil thing be destroyed? By what discipline of heart and tongue can Jesus secure His servants from this common and malign sin? Surely in ways like these. He deepens our love of *all* people. So many folk have told me that the surrender of their heart to Christ has this immediate consequence, that I now expect to hear every new disciple say so. Many men and women have resentments against society, and feel that they are compassed about with those who plan their hurt. . . . The entry of Jesus into the heart vastly widens the scope of love. In place of suspicion and a bias to believe the worst of others, there come the most compassionate thoughts and a readiness to believe the best. Evil gossip cannot live with this love. . . . The heart swells with a desire to help and all the nobler possibilities of human nature are in view.

Love is like that . . . 'always eager to believe the best'. When our neighbour's child is cross and peevish, we are tempted to complain about the nasty temper and ill-training of the child. When our own child is cross and peevish, we say that he is unwell or over-tired. That is the ingenuity of love. When Christ widens the love in us to include all for whom He died, gossip is killed. Our bias is to believe the best. Even when we cannot close our eyes to the evil of others, it is still possible to close our mouths.

He is Able, pp 78–9

... Are we failing this age ... in not bringing that passion to religion which it surely requires? [Methodists] offer the world nothing new in doctrine. ... Our *raison d'être* wasn't in novelty of doctrine, but in the conviction and passion we brought to its proclamation. *Religion in earnest!* What has happened to that awful earnestness which fired Wesley and Asbury; John Nelson and Caleb Pedicord; Peter Jaco and Freeborn Garretson; Alexander Mather and Jesse Lee? ... On and on they went. They seemed to live in the saddle. If Asbury had a slogan it was this. 'I must ride or I *will* die.' Do you remember the day when they thought he *was* dying, and called a doctor to that mighty man? ... One glance at him and the doctor said 'If you ride, you will die' and even in his pain and utter weariness the St Francis of the Western world replied, 'No, Doctor. You have it wrong. If I do *not* ride, I will die.'

Think again of that youth rally two weeks ago in Berlin.* A million and a half, and all young. From almost every country in the world ... Oh yes! There was an International Boy Scouts' Rally at the same time in Australia. By no means so large. Hardly as meaningful. What has happened to our Christian youth organizations? Do we keep our young people young too long? Would a million and a half youth make a long journey anywhere to march for the United Nations? How is it that that God-denying creed can beget a devotion greater than that of those who pursue the Christ Himself? A passionate pursuit of the evil—or half-evil—can only be matched by a passionate pursuit of the good.

Proceedings of the Eighth Ecumenical Methodist Conference,
1951, pp 75–6

I knew a young, unmarried man who fell out of work during the long trade depression between the wars. He was a skilled workman and a fine Christian, but how he lived during those lean years I hardly know. His joy when, at last, he got a job in a wireless factory it would be difficult to describe.

There was, however, a fly in the ointment. He soon found that the men with whom he was working regularly used the most filthy language and it was impossible all the time to close his ears to their obscenities. He was a gentle soul . . . and yet bold with the boldness of those who belong to our 'royal priesthood'. He could not feel that it was right to make no protest. . . . At the beginning of his second week he told a few of them gently, affectionately, but plainly, how he felt. A word, he hoped, would be enough. It was a vain hope. They laughed till they cried and blasphemed the more. So he got a . . . collecting box from the local infirmary—and put a penny in whenever they swore. . . . When they first realized what he was doing, they swore the harder. . . . They said that it was their first opportunity to curse for the cure of the sick. After being out of work for years, that poor, brave, obscure disciple put, by his own act, nearly all his first week's wages in that box.

But he broke them. When they saw what he had done, something happened. The Spirit of God used the simple artifice of it. They saw how much it hurt him and the blasphemy . . . died down. . . . In the passing of time, when it happened, it happened only by accident, and it was followed immediately by an apology, and the offender himself paid the 'fine'. He was a plain working man, speaking with a provincial accent, but he belonged to the royal priesthood. . . .

Methodism: Her Unfinished Task, pp 110–11

Evangelical Christians are not indifferent to the needs of other people. They long that men and women everywhere may share their experience of new life and be re-made in Christ. Their missionary labours at home and abroad are not excelled in any branch of Christendom.

Where some of them have failed is in their inability to see how people's social and economic circumstances can affect their soul's health and make it easier or harder for them to believe in the love of Christ. If devout Christians won't let a man come into their church because he is black, if Christian nations steal their country from primitive people (and give them the Bible in exchange!) if the professing followers of Christ are more concerned to maintain their own standard of living (four meals a day, cars, TV, etc.) than to secure a second meal a day for the hungry multitudes of the East . . . how hard it is for despised and suffering people to believe in Christianity at all. Talk of 'abundant life' sounds like a cruel joke, and the offer of 'salvation' smells of hypocrisy.

Unless Christianity works itself out in deeds, how hollow it seems; how hollow it *is*. Those who are really saved are filled with divine love, and divine love in a human heart has no way of expression but in service to other people, for those who claim to love God and hate (or neglect) their fellow men are liars (1 John 4[20]).

How Much are you Saved?, p 6

243

Every kind of suffering has fallen upon [the saints]: physical, mental, and spiritual. They have endured it all. Simply to read, slowly and imaginatively, Paul's bare catalogue of his experiences, is to be lost in wonder, love and praise.* Toils, imprisonments, beatings, stonings, shipwrecks, treachery, hunger, thirst, cold and nakedness—he knew them all: and thrown on the top of all this was a daily anxiety for the churches.

How do the saints endure? By what divine strategy do they maintain their faith? They believe that God is in their sufferings all the time! They do not see events as happening apart from God, nor put an undue stress on the difference between what God does and what God permits. They find God even in what He *allows*. Because the Universe is God's at the last, they see Him as taking ultimate responsibility for *whatever* happens. If it were possible to conceive of anything utterly sterile of good, God, they believe, would not permit it. Anything that happens, rightly met with God, is fecund of good. Therefore, they find God even in suffering; even in suffering prolonged, undeserved and bitter.

The Pure in Heart, p 150

* 2 Cor. 11²³⁻⁹

If one lived on *facts*, and not on feelings, even the feelings would respond in time to the facts. These are the facts!

God is on the throne. Behind those rain-heavy clouds the sun is shining, and, behind the God-denying look of this mad world, God is always there: the Father of Jesus, whose love is as great as His power.

This is the day that He has made. I will rejoice and be glad in it. I will think on His light, His joy, His power . . . and myself as His beloved child. I will *run* on His errands—still *His*, though so ordinary and so same. Done for Him they will be *extra*-ordinary. I will make them as perfect as possible.

And, as I meditate, though it be but for five or seven un-hurried minutes in the morning, it will bless me in the moment, and sink down into my subconscious to bless me a hundredfold when it rises again in an hour of special need.

Fancy having a subconscious stored with treasure like that, richly accumulating from a daily deposit! Fancy being ready to turn the mind over to meditation whenever one is kept waiting: not fuming and fretting for the bus which doesn't come (and getting worse for doing it!) but dwelling on the peace which will seep into me at any moment by the turning of a thought. Holi-ness, freedom, power, peace, light, joy, beauty, wisdom, love . . . all are key words for meditation, all are attributes of the living God, and all of them, as I dwell on them in Him, rest in my own soul too. Prayer and meditation! these are the ways to intimacy with Jesus.

Teach us to Pray, pp 31–2

1. Live at the centre yourself.

Fail here and you have nothing to give. Fail here and (if you go on talking) you will get the sweetest thing in heaven and earth a bad name. Talk about religion when it is plainly contradicted by the speaker's life is a wound in the body of God. But live at the centre yourself; guard your periods of unhurried quiet with God, and all your work is made easy. You will not have constantly to *make* contact with others; people will often make contact with you . . . I no longer wonder at the ability of the Curè of Ars to read souls. I have had enough experience myself of mystic help in sensing hidden problems to guess how much more of that help a man truly intimate with God might enjoy.

2. Don't try to do people good; love them.

Tagore said: 'He who tries to do people good stands knocking at the door, but he who loves finds the door open.'

We know, ourselves, how much we resent being stalked by someone intent to do us 'good'. 'Who is he', we unreasonably ask, 'to think that he could do *me* good? I might do him a little . . .'

But few people can resist genuine love.

So love them—with supernatural love: the love which does not run on lines of mere affinity, but loves even where it cannot like.

It is a gift, of course—a gift from God; freely given to importunate prayer.

Let me Commend, pp 94–5

246

. . . Dr R. F. Horton, the eminent Minister of Lyndhurst Road Church in Hampstead for half a century. There was some of the saint in R. F. Horton. His people loved him, but they said 'You could never *give* him anything'. Whenever their love expressed itself in a gift, he gave it at once to Overseas Missions.

So they tried again. 'We want to give you something,' they said, 'but please don't give it this time to Overseas Missions.' He promised to think and pray about it. The guidance came. He told the somewhat disappointed deacons that in his travels round the country he had found many earnest but lonely ministers and he would like his church to do something for them. 'Let us invite them for three or four days into retreat at Lyndhurst Road', he said. 'You can pay their fares and our people will entertain them and, under the blessing of God, they will go back to their work refreshed and eager again.'

And so it was done! It wasn't quite the personal gift the church wanted, but what can you do with a saint? When the ministers gathered from all over the country. Horton was asked to take the chair, but he begged them to leave the chair empty. 'I want our Lord to preside over us', he said. 'I will sit at His side and say such things as need saying, but let Him take the chair.' Dr J. H. Jowett, who tells the story, said: 'It sounds nothing, but the effect of the moment was almost overwhelming, and if, at any of the meetings, any man was tempted to let fall any word that was unworthy, the sight of the empty chair froze the word upon his lips, so that it could not get itself said.'

Westminster Sermons (vol. ii), pp 89–90

Christians never seem to be able to plumb the depth of meaning in the Cross. It is no wonder that it has become the most sacred symbol of the faith in every branch of the Church. That God should suffer men to nail him on two pieces of wood staggers the minds of Christ's followers whenever they strip away their familiarity with it and look at it afresh. But here are a few of the things which make it unspeakably dear to them—

It shows how bad men are. Men don't like to admit their badness. Most of them think they are quite nice fellows and in no need of a Saviour. But Christ, the noblest soul who ever walked this earth, was crucified by men—not peculiarly *bad* men, not the 'criminal types'; He was done to death by some of the 'best' people of His day. Nothing like the Cross reveals the basic evil in men and shows the vile depths to which our nature can sink. . . .

It shows how loving God is. Christ came to save. He meant to fight wickedness with love, and beat it. By mere power He could have blasted His enemies, but He let them murder Him, and prayed for them as they did it.

The Cross shows the supreme power of God to transform evil into good. In some senses, the Cross was the worst thing our race ever did. But God made it, at the same time, the best disclosure of His love to men. . . . How can we help but wonder at times what God is like? If we really want to know, we must go to the Cross. The answer is clearest there. He loves like that.

The Cross shows . . . Christians . . . how they must live. Self-assertion must be cancelled out. . . . And all this is but the fringe. However much Christians make of the Cross, they can never make enough of it.

Give God a Chance, p 51

Job never took his sufferings from the Sabeans, nor the Chaldeans, nor from 'natural causes'. He took them from God via Satan. 'The Lord gave and the Lord hath taken away. Blessed be the name of the Lord.' Or was it the psalmist who taught [the saints] this truth? When the storm smote the psalmist, he refused to accept it just as a storm. He must find God in it! With mighty faith he plants God in its heart and, as that icy green water engulfs him, he cries: 'All THY waves and THY billows are gone over me'. Somewhere, at the heart of this awful experience, he holds that there is a loving purpose of God. They are God's waves and God's billows.

Or was it from the Saviour Himself that the saint learned this secret transformation of suffering? Every saint knows Gethsemane. He has overheard his Lord say 'Father, if it be possible, let this cup pass from me', and has overheard Him also say later: 'The cup which my Father hath given me, shall I not drink it?' One can transform the contents of a cup if one can change the hand from which one takes it. It is as though the Lord said: 'If I must drink it, I will not take it from Judas, Pilate, Caiaphas, or the people. I will take it only from my Father. . . .' The saint always takes the cup from his Father. He recks little of secondary causes. Half the secret of his triumph over suffering is there.

Here, too, you have the secret of Etienne Mattier reeling beneath an awful blow and crying, 'No questions, Lord! No questions! *Only Amens!*' Here also we understand St Francis de Sales's beloved phrase: 'Yes, Father. Yes!—*and always Yes!*' By this means, I learned to understand the repetitive word of a little saint of my own acquaintance. . . . 'Have it your own way, Father.'

The Pure in Heart, pp 150–1

Some notable reformers and revolutionaries have not been Christians; indeed, some of them have been avowed anti-Christians.

The Christian recognizes and admires courage and high purpose wherever he sees them, and is sometimes shamed by the readiness to sacrifice which is found in those who don't know Christ.

But—surveying the centuries and thanking God for all good men everywhere—the Christian is convinced that the world can only be saved by Christ at work in His devoted disciples.

Those who do not own Christ as Lord are not equal to it. Some have their heart broken by the ingratitude of men and give up. Some revolutionaries—not having Christ's nature within—turn into tyrants. Most become careerists, elbowing for office and covetous for titles and honours. How many who have offered themselves as champions of the poor have 'made a good thing' of it for themselves!

Christ's work in the world can only be adequately done by Christ's men and women. It is so hard at times that only those crucified with Christ can endure it. To love those who hate you, to go on serving those who are not only ungrateful but wonder what you are getting out of it yourself, to see others get the credit for what you have done and not mind it so long as Christ is exalted, to die unknown and unappreciated but humbly grateful to have been used by Him at all—it is not in unredeemed human nature to attain this quality of living; this is possible only to those re-made by Christ Himself. The world cannot save itself, but Christ can save it—and He alone.

How Much are you Saved?, pp 7–8

Aged people are too often neglected. They do 'not strive nor cry' to draw attention to themselves. . . . Many of them are the survivors of their generation, and every year the number of those who know them gets smaller and smaller. In other days they may have been great servants of the Church and the community . . . but a generation has arisen that knows not Joseph —and still less his quiet old widow—and she lives now with her memories, practically forgotten on earth, and foolishly tempted in her depressions to believe that she is half-forgotten in heaven, too. We have a duty to these dear old people—an obligation so rewarding that it isn't hard to lose the duty in the joy.

We want an intensified ministry to the thousands of old people who are living alone. . . . Not much heed will be taken on earth of this lovely service. . . . It doesn't matter. It is noticed in Heaven. Our God—who lives to give rewards—will not fail to mark and bless this careful tending of His ageing servants.

. . . I know a lady who regularly gives immense pleasure— and derives even more—by having groups of old people to tea as guests in her garden whenever the weather allows. 'They don't want any entertaining', she protests. 'It's as simple as anything. . . . Just get it into their minds that you are truly glad to have them and proud to call them friends . . . and it's all done. If you let them know ahead, they enjoy looking forward to it for weeks, and back upon it, with gratitude for months. It is the easiest way of giving happiness I've ever discovered.'

Fine! Perhaps others will discover it, too.

Methodist Magazine, 1947, pp 485–7

As a Christian, you will never sever fellowship with other people if you can avoid it.

Imagine a young fellow, a member of a set of gay sparks whose whole idea of life in their twenties is to enjoy themselves, and this young man is arrested by the Holy Spirit and drawn by God into His way of life. Some Christians would tell him to sever his fellowship with his old friends at once. 'Forsake them', they would say. 'Cut them off! Finish with them!' I say quite the contrary: 'Don't forsake them. Hold on to Christ first, but hold on to them too. You may be God's supreme opportunity in their life. If the fellowship is to end, let *them* break it.' If your fellowship with them is a peril to your soul, God would warn you and tell you what to do, but if Christians are always going to withdraw themselves from the world, where will it get us? There is a deal of good in plain ordinary people. There is indeed, a divine spark in them, and God might use you to fan it into a flame. We shall be living little segregated lives, with less and less influence on the modern world, if we are continually 'withdrawing' from all these social contacts. If we believe in individual salvation, but have no interest in society, we shall be like men arriving at a great fire, willing to rescue a person here and there from the holocaust, but quite unwilling to assist the authorities in putting out the blaze.

Westminster Sermons (vol. i), pp 54–5

I lay down my life . . . No one taketh it away from me, but I lay it down of myself. John 10[17,18]

Those devils and weaklings who met at Calvary would have said, 'We did it'. He cries from His Cross: 'I did it! It is finished!' If they were right, the Cross would be a gibbet, a symbol of shame, something to hide and speak of only by compulsion and with bated breath. In point of fact, we placard it to all the world. No steeple so high that it will not bear it; no point of earth but is honoured to be the stump of His Cross: it lies in a cache on the summit of Everest. It is His message, not theirs, which it bears at the last.

That free and evil men sought and secured His death cannot alter the fact that He knew what they were doing—and let them do it. You cannot martyr *God*. . . . Hold in mind . . . *who* it was who hung and suffered there, and you will not think of it as martyrdom.

If He was man, it was murder; if He was God, it was an offering.

If He was man, it was martyrdom; if He was God, it was sacrifice.

If He was man, they took His life from Him; if He was God, He laid it down of himself.

If He was man, we are called to admiration; if He was God, we are called to adoration.

If He was man, we must stand up and take our hats off; if He was God, we must fall down and give Him our hearts.

They Met at Calvary, pp 82–3

The Psalmist says (Ps. 40[8]) 'I delight to do Thy will, O my God' and the emphasis falls on the word 'delight'. . . . It is as though the Psalmist had heard somebody say, 'Oh, it is hard to work for God' and he had turned to the Lord in surprised denial. It was no toilsome task to him; it was no burden grievous to be borne; it was his pleasure, his happiness, his source of perennial joy. . . . If it were possible for us to stand and watch the pedestrians upon the path of virtue go by, we should discover that many of them are kept in the pathway by meaner reasons than that of delight. We should notice . . . the almost effortless (and nearly aimless) walking of the man who is good simply because his friends are good . . . the spiritless walk of the man who is good because he is afraid of the consequences of evil . . . the man whose life has duty for a motive. How splendid he seems in comparison with those others. What steady progress he makes. His jaw is set; his eye looks straight ahead; he has but one purpose. Up the flinty way he comes. He passes the craven and the invertebrate. He is on that path because it is right to be on that path. He doesn't claim to enjoy it. 'Enjoyment' is a word he doesn't often use. He braces himself at the thought of duty and steadily but joylessly . . . he passes by. Finally, we see the comrade of our Psalmist; the man who is on the path because he loves it. He comes along at a swinging gait. There is a spring in his step. He barely notices the paths that lead aside. His whole bearing suggests a joyous adventure and not a perilous pilgrimage. . . . I wonder to which of these types we belong? . . . Is it just our 'set' that keeps us there? . . . Is it fear that builds a wall . . . fear of the consequences if we did wrong? Is it duty? . . . or are we impelled by love, glad to serve, happy to do His will?

Why Jesus Never Wrote a Book, pp 85–7

The heavens—and His other gifts—*declare*
the glory of God

There are certain times and places which make meditation easier than others and which (if cultivated) can be one of the richest extras for those who are eager for communion with God.

Half an hour quietly sitting in a garden can be wonderful. No, don't read. Look—and think on God. Brother Lawrence . . . was converted looking at a tree. Just look. There are some ugly things in nature, of course, but look now at the flowers. 'The hand which made these flowers cannot be unkind.' Think of the cycle of the seasons. Think of growth. Think of God's annual revival in nature. . . .

Music is a medium of God to many people and would be to more if they'd take the trouble to listen. The music needs selecting, of course. . . . But half an hour listening to the right music and thinking on God can open Heaven to a reverent mind.

Do you love maps? I do. They fascinate me. I often have a session of prayer with maps. When I was praying, for instance, for the Easter Evangelical Campaigns of our college students, I did most of it with a map. I had a list of the places and the men. I put my finger on the spot on the map, pictured the situation from the information I possessed, thought of the men and the deaconesses, and prayed a blessing on all their enterprise.

Do you ever pray with the stars? Some night, when you are not too tired, turn out the light before getting into bed, and look at the stars. What an awe there is in the night sky! No wonder Kant found his way back to God by 'the moral law within and the starry heavens without'. . . .

These are just some of the ways. Find your own, but be sure you find them.

The Pattern of Prayer, pp 106–7

The heart of this grave sin [of pride] is just here; that a man or woman thrust himself, or herself, right into the centre of the picture and make themselves the test and standard, and measure of all things. It is rather odd that it is necessary to state it, but man's place in the universe is that of a creature. The discerning and truthful mind says 'It is God that hath made us and not we ourselves; we are His people and the sheep of His pasture'. But that is only the person of discernment. The pride of man rebels against his place in the universe. Protagoras cries 'Man is the measure of all things', and Henley bawls out in his blatant way:

> *I am the master of my fate,*
> *I am the captain of my soul.*

Now that is the real germ of this soul disease. It puts self in the centre. It struts, and shouts, and brags. It strikes an attitude. It says 'I . . . I . . . I . . .' It dethrones the Creator in the heart of man. It makes the puffed-up little ego the pole of all things. It blackens this fair earth from end to end. If men only knew the thousand sins which pride begets, they would hate it for the devilish thing it is . . . it builds barriers between the social classes; it builds barriers between the nations; it prevents reconciliation; it . . . poisons the virtues; it doubles the viciousness of the vices: in short, it is hell to have self in the centre and not God.

Who can deliver us from pride, the outer rind and the endless inner casings? . . . Christ is able. Only Christ.

He is Able, pp 80–1

. . . How does that burning, bleeding love reach the generations of sinning, suffering people, and shame them from their
wickedness and save them from themselves?

Christ does it through His truly devoted servants—those
who will suffer a spiritual crucifixion with Him and (having died
to self) allow Him to live in their hearts. No others are really
equal to it. Unless our self-engrossed, aggressive and demanding nature is subdued, how near-to-useless we are in the service
of the Kingdom.

But how few—even among those who profess to love Him
—is the number of those ready for the inner crucifixion and
eager to have their nature changed into His. They revere the
sacred symbol of the Cross but shrink from the spiritual
crucifixion which it symbolizes; they take the symbolic bread
and wine, yet are not ready for their bodies to be broken in the
service of others, or their blood poured out for people who spit
on them while they are doing it.

And while this remains true, Christ is hindered in saving the
world. To point to His Cross and insist that He has saved it
already, obscures the truth. Has He fully saved *us* if we can be
indifferent to the needs of others? Can He save the world if—
impeded by their own sin and disappointed in what they see in
professing Christians—men and women will not turn to Him
and live?

How Much are you Saved?, p 9

Some devout souls seem never to have a serious doubt in their lives. . . . With others, the doubting is mild, forcing them to reflection but not robbing them of sleep. Some young people even ape doubt as a sign of mental maturity. But the real thing is terrible beyond all description. The religious man whose doubting has never got beyond the authorship of a book of the Bible, or the authenticity of a miracle . . . is in the kindergarten of doubt. It is when you doubt the sense of the Universe itself: the existence of God: the validity of your own thinking: the distinction between right and wrong: your own separateness and significance as a person . . . that is doubt! And it is not doubt when it remains speculative and fleeting. It is only doubt when it grips you, and holds you prisoner for weeks . . . months. . . . Then the foundation of all things opens at your feet, and the sun goes out, and there is gross darkness over all the earth, and only death seems a friend.

Not all the saints . . . walk this way, but many do. Sometimes they have had to toil in circumstances which only God could alter, and which contradicted all that they have taught of Him, but they have had to go on working though He gave no sign. Think of David Hill in the awful scenes and sufferings of the Shansi famine. . . . The man who came to proclaim that God is love watched them dying. . . . Most saints have a breadth and depth of mind as well as a sensitivity of heart, and they have looked on the sufferings of the world with seeing eyes. Doubt has assaulted them and been defeated. Perhaps no one rises to the rapture and truth of the Christian religion who has not first felt its incredibility, impossibility. . . . And then faith grasps it. It is true! Glory! Hallelujah!

The Pure in Heart, pp 153–4

On my way to preach one day in Portsmouth I stood in a doorway because of the heavy rain. Another man sheltered too. I remarked on the weather, but as the conversation proceeded I told him of the errand I was on. He knew, it seemed, next to nothing about churches, but quite willingly accepted an invitation to come. He decided for Christ that night. It was all very simple and very sweet.

But one thing he never seems to get over. 'Fancy standing up out of the rain', he says, 'and all your life being changed because of that.' Yet if the challenge had not been put, he could have come and gone in no way seriously different.

As a small boy, a little fearful of my stern father, I sometimes hesitated to ask him things I dearly wished, and would confide my hopes to mother instead. Always—or nearly always—she said, '*Ask* him'. She knew the character of his heart better than I did, and she believed also in the direct approach.

I have remembered the advice through the years, both in my dealings with God and man. When foolish hesitations have hampered my commerce with heaven and with my fellows, I have remembered that loving admonition *Ask Him*. So I have asked God for men and men for God. It has usually been easier than I feared. Times without number tremulous souls have as much as admitted that they were *waiting* to be asked. I dread to think how many I have failed in that way.

Let me Commend, pp 101–2

He came from Nazareth and was called Jesus. The fishermen of Capernaum noticed nothing peculiar about His dress or His accent, but His words, and His power, and the impress of His whole personality were almost beyond belief. He was a carpenter by trade and had had no more formal schooling than they had had themselves, but 'never man so spake'. He held the lake-shore crowds in the hollow of His hands and spoke with such authority that He compelled them to hear.

He had supernatural powers too. He could heal the sick with a touch or a word. On His first Sabbath in Capernaum He seemed to be healing all day, and others besides the fishermen felt that the Kingdom of Heaven had come. When He said to some of these men who earned their living in boats, 'Follow Me', they couldn't resist Him. . . . Altogether, He chose twelve companions and they lived closely with Him for two or three years; saw Him at all hours of day and night; when He was tired and hungry . . . when He was on the crest of the wave and thousands were wanting to make Him King. . . . He never became small, petty, revengeful, personally ambitious. . . . He seemed more wonderful with passing time. He was strangely different from anyone else they had ever known.

Women were not 'chattels' to Him. . . . He could keep company with notorious evil-doers and remain unstained. The winds obeyed Him, and mental disease defeated Him as little as physical. Three of them once saw Him positively transfigured and overheard Him in conversation with people from another plane of being . . . the conviction grew in them that He was the Christ, the Messiah, the promised deliverer of their people. . . . 'This is He', they said, and one day Peter spoke it aloud in the face of their Master. 'Thou art the Christ', he said, 'the Son of the Living God.'

Westminster Sermons (vol. ii), pp 114–15

Most certainly—if we are careful of the sense in which we can use the word 'believe'.

There are sixty-six 'books' or 'writings' bound up in the Bible. It is, indeed, a little library all in itself. Its composition covered hundreds of years and it was originally written in Hebrew and Greek. Most forms of literature are included: history, allegory, poetry, prophecy, letters, laws, proverbs and parables.

Now, if we use the word 'believe' to mean a factual or scientific accuracy in every phrase, we shall go astray. How could you read any poetry that way? Most history, too, is written from 'a point of view'. And the details of parables are usually deliberately made up, for the truth does not lie on the surface; people listen because all people like a story, and it is only afterwards that the truth is seen, not in the narrative, but in the deeper meaning. Most people know the Parable of the Prodigal Son. Almost certainly, Jesus made the story up. . . . But who cares about that? The deep divine truth of the parable, the precious unalterable fact that should mean everything to all the teeming millions of men and women in the world, is that God is like that father. . . . Now that is the kind of truth to seek in the Bible. We shall not find it if we get bogged down in endless arguments about whether a man can live in the belly of a whale, or whether the sun ever 'stood still', but only if we ask what this book is telling us about God.

And what this book—understood as a growing revelation—tells us about God we can most surely believe.

Give God a Chance, p 58

All progress is progress in humility, and Paul's progress may be measured by the fact that in his First Epistle to the Corinthians he says 'I am the least of the Apostles'* and writing later to the Ephesians he says that he is '*less* than the least'—not now of the Apostles—but '*of all the saints*'† (with 'saints' used here as descriptive of all believers) and writing to Timothy later still, he says 'that Christ Jesus came into the world to save sinners *of whom I am chief*'.‡

We see it in the Curè D'Ars. He was a humble man and no doubt his fellow-clerics in the diocese, who took no pains to conceal their dislike of him, would have said that he had a great deal to be humble about! Aware of his lack of learning, they wrote him letters saying that he disgraced the cloth, and that it was in their mind to petition the Bishop to have him removed, and he replied to all but the anonymous ones with gratitude, begging the prayers of his correspondents that 'I may do less harm and more good'.

Finally, the petition was ready and signed but, either from bravado or remorse, one of the priests who had signed it sent it to the Curè D'Ars himself, who carefully and tearfully signed it, agreeing with all that it said about his ignorance and incompetence, and when it arrived on the Bishop's desk, his own signature had been appended also. 'He united himself with his accusers to gain a disgrace which he agreed with them in thinking he deserved.'§

The Pure in Heart, pp 160–1

* 1 Cor. 15⁹.
† Eph. 3⁸.
‡ 1 Tim. 1¹⁵.
§ Ghéon, *The Secret of the Curè D'Ars*, p 129.

When the tide of reproach is rolling over you; when for
Christ's sake you are made an object of reviling—'rejoice and
be exceeding glad, for great is your reward in heaven; for so
persecuted they the prophets which were before you'.

In the late seventies of the last century there was a girl living
in Lisburn near Belfast, named Priscilla Livingstone Stewart.
She was lovely to look upon; blue eyes, bright colour, golden
hair, Irish gaiety. . . . All the boys in the neighbourhood thought
she was grand. Her admirers queued up for a smile!

Then she met Christ. Having been heartily opposed to religion before, she became an ardent disciple now, and, soon
after, the Salvation Army came to those parts. It was altogether characteristic of her that she should throw in her lot for
a while with that despised people, and she chose to walk in their
procession in days when they were pelted with old boots, bad
oranges and worse eggs. Now, notice this! I give you the exact
words of her reminiscences. She said, 'None of my friends
recognized me in the street, and all the young men who were
fond of me walked on the other side.'

I have no doubt that, being a normal girl, there was something of pain for her in that, but she felt that she had gained
infinitely more than she had lost, and truth to tell, God had
other things in store for her. She went as a missionary to
China and became the wife of that extraordinary missionary,
C. T. Studd.

Westminster Sermons (vol. i), pp 56–7

. . . Our Lord . . . is not content to save us in our solitariness but means to save us in our relationships as well. How little is left of a man if we ignore what he is as a son, brother, husband, father, worker, citizen and friend! Salvation is for the whole man.

With men and women experiencing this kind of 'full salvation' Christ is seeking to invade the world. It is *His* world!— the place of His incarnation, the scene of His Cross, and holding still His borrowed and discarded tomb. His followers are not to sneak through the world teaching it as little as they can; but *claiming* it, *asserting* His Kingship over it, challenging evil wherever they meet it, and admitting no segment of life as alien to His rule. Art, science, politics, commerce—all are His.

The view long held by some Evangelical Christians that politics are poison may have some excuse, but if it leads to a deliberate neglect of politics it is a deep disloyalty to the purposes of the Kingdom.

So much of our life is social (in the family, workshop, community and nation) and our social life is so knit into our private life, that if our Lord is to be excluded from these areas, how can He save, rule, reign . . .?

Let us face it. There is only one gospel, but it is as wide as life, and some earnest evangelicals have failed their Lord by refusing to see the gospel's social nature and have unconsciously hindered the One they sincerely love.

How Much are you Saved?, p 10

Go back to the Cross! When we were looking just now at the Cross and considering the sins that Jesus put there, you recognized, I think, that they were *your* sins. . . . The Cross revealed it to you. . . . That is the kind of person you are. Don't shrink from it. Don't say you are not. Don't announce again 'I have never done anyone a bad turn'. I don't believe it. I *do* believe that you have not realized how bad a turn you have been doing people. But by your selfishness (which is inbred in you and me) . . . by many other things you know and God knows, you are really shot through with sin; you are dyed in it. . . .

The Cross has opened your eyes to it. It has shown you what you are—and you can do nothing about it. You cannot, yourself, wash out the past, and you cannot, with confidence, expect to overcome in the future. That is where you are, and I say reverently 'God help you' because nobody else can.

What are you going to do about it? What are you going to do about the past which you cannot undo, and the future in which, without supernatural help, you will commit the same sin again and again?

Do you think you can make up your little mind never to be selfish again, and keep that resolution all on your own? You cannot do it. That is why I advise, 'Go to the Cross'. There is nowhere else for helpless sinners to go. Go to the Cross. . . . Don't defend yourself. The cause is lost if you do that. Don't base your plea on justice. Plead for mercy. Ask God, for Christ's sake, to forgive you your sins.

They Met at Calvary, pp 83–4

I turn to those who are virtuous out of a sense of duty;
because it's right. These command our admiration. They are
full of the soldierly virtues. . . . 'Is it right?' they say, and, being
right, they do it. It would almost seem an impertinence to find
fault with men like these. . . . If a man trudges steadily along
the path of virtue because it is right to do so, isn't that enough?
Is it just, or sensible, to ask for anything more? Yes! It is
enough. In some senses it is the very highest motive of all.
There are, however, certain limitations. . . . A life that is dominated merely by duty and not tempered by love is apt to become mechanical, hard and unyielding. It is observant of the
letter, but may be neglectful of the spirit. It will go the mile of
compulsion but will not go the extra mile of regard. . . . Rules
are not enough for the religion of Jesus. You can play a game
of chess on the rules, but you want more than rules to write
a poem. Duty will make a soldier, but it takes more than duty
to make an apostle. Duty is cold: love is warm. Duty measures
its giving: love gives with prodigality. Duty will make a good
man: love of Jesus will make a good man a winsome man as
well.

Duty alone may produce the type of character that is cold
and unattractive, the sort of man of whom we say, 'Yes, he is a
good man—undoubtedly a good man, but I don't want to be
like him'.

Why Jesus Never Wrote a Book, p 90

. . . All human experience goes to show the folly of playing with these deep desires. In certain natures they are not easily kept in check even by a strong will and divine help, and without either . . . the way to sin is alarmingly short.

Christ in heart and mind is the safeguard. To Him supremely the prayer may be offered:

> *Breathe through the heats of our desire*
> *Thy coolness and Thy balm . . .*

Nor is it hard to understand the simple psychology of it. If a man builds within himself a strong picture of Jesus: if a regular part of his leisure is consecrated to such reading, meditation and prayer as will make Christ clearer to his mind and dearer to his heart: if he develops a keen ear for the personal words of his Master and directs his life accordingly; if Christ becomes to him a living personality whose encouragements he covets and whose disapproval he dreads, it is not hard to see what help that man will have in any moment of swift temptation. The minute the thought comes to his mind and is recognized, he looks to his Lord.

Evil thoughts are not driven out by dwelling on them, even guiltily or prayerfully. It is bad tactics to direct sustained attention to them even in penitence, or as one plans improvement. The longer they are in the focus of attention, the deeper they are burned on the memory, and the more mental associations they make. They must be outwitted by swiftly directing the mind to some other absorbing theme. Hence the wisdom of knowing Jesus as a personal Friend, and turning the mind at once to Him.

He is Able, pp 90–1

There is a suspicion among people—and who among us will say that it is groundless?—that, whatever men undertake, self-interest is really the driving motive. In king or commissar. In president or bishop. In minister or layman. Get down to the base of things, they suspect, and it is always self. Inevitably, this has spread a certain cynicism through the community. The ache which all normal men and women feel for the highest is mocked by doubts as to the purity of motive in those who lead.

It is hard to believe that our pioneers suffered that suspicion. Their poverty, their sufferings, their toil, their virtual homelessness, the scorn with which they were so often treated, the absence of material rewards, must have had its slow part in convincing people of the sincerity of their motives, and that they were, indeed moved 'by the pure flame of love'. . . .

We can face this disillusioned age and offer them perfection in Christ. The sheer audacity of it will startle them, if nothing else does.

> *He wills that I should holy be;*
> *That holiness I long to feel.*

All men must press on to perfection.

. . . If we want power with the people—and with youth especially—this is the way to it. God forbid that we should despise learning, but . . . it is not great learning which subdues men but great goodness. . . . And—by grace—sanctity is a gift we may all aspire to. A body of believers, living right at the Christ-centre of things in this evil world, would be the grandest contribution we could make . . . to this present age.

Proceedings of the Eighth Ecumenical Conference, 1951,
pp 76–7

In the early nineties an evangelist was holding a mission in York of set purpose to call the sinners home. One night, in response to his appeal, a number of needy souls came forward and among them, an elderly man who knelt in penitence before the Saviour. . . . The evangelist counselled each in turn and the elderly penitent among them, who meekly answered the questions put to him and then went his way. Later, the evangelist learned that the penitent was none other than David Hill the missionary and saint on furlough from China. . . . He sought him out and made some halting apology for having treated him as a beginner in the holy life. David Hill brushed his embarrassments aside. 'I thought it would do me good to kneel among the penitents', he said. It was an evangelist, too, who . . . holding a mission in Edinburgh . . . fell to criticizing the resident ministers in the city, and, among them, Dr James Hood Wilson of the Barclay Church. A man who heard the criticisms called next day on Dr Alexander Whyte. 'I went to hear the evangelist last night . . .' he began. . . . 'He said that Dr Hood Wilson . . . was not a converted man.' Alexander Whyte leapt from his chair in anger. His fine face went dark with indignation. 'The rascal!' he said, 'the rascal. Dr Wilson not a converted man.'

The visitor was amazed to see a saint so furious. So he went on. 'That wasn't all he said, Dr Whyte', he continued. 'He said that *you* were not a converted man either!' Dr Whyte stopped in his stride. All the fire went out of him. Sinking into his chair, he put his face in his hands, and for a full long minute he did not speak. Then, looking up, he said to his visitor with awful earnestness: 'Leave me, friend; leave me! I must examine my heart.'

The Pure in Heart, pp 161–2

You will remember that at the close of Paul's Epistle to the Philippians, a letter which he wrote from Rome, he says 'All the saints salute you, chiefly they that are of Caesar's household'. Then there were some in Rome who did not do as Rome did! Who was that Caesar? Who was that imperial prince in whose palace these saints lived out their noble lives? Nero! He was the reigning Caesar. Nero! Believed by some historians to be the most inhuman monster that ever filled a gilded throne. He is said to have compassed the death both of his mother and his wife. In his reign Rome was deluged with the blood of her noblest. He is said to have instituted one of the fiercest persecutions against the Christians and to have had them torn to pieces by dogs and burnt to death in his palace grounds. And he was sunk as far in debauchery as he was sunk in blood. Yet there were saints in his household. Not only in Rome but in the central cesspool of that decadent city. Saints! They were in Rome and they had not done as Rome did. What hardy saints they must have been! What strenuous, sinewy sons of virtue! Praise God for the saints in Caesar's household who, though they dwell in Rome itself, carry the red cross unsullied on the white shield.

Why Jesus Never Wrote a Book, p 43

The Faith at work in society and the world has another consequence also. . . . It is a constant pain and bewilderment to those re-made in Christ that when they bear honest witness to all that Christ has done for them (and to their possession of love, joy and peace) others do not turn at once and accept the Saviour.

But it is not only the sin in men which prevents them accepting the Christian message. They are hindered also by an honest doubt of its ability to meet the world situation. Deep in the heart of many a decent but Church-neglecting people is a longing for a new order, a recognition of the insanity of so much international life, a conviction that there must be a way to a better world.

But where?

Occasionally these people take a wistful look at the Church. With some remembrance of God in their soul, they wonder if He really exists or whether their hazy sense of Him is a delusion. Is the Church His instrument? Can this hoary, feeble institution be the 'Body of Christ', and His means to a perfect world?

What evidence is there of it? The vital members are not numerous. Some are lovely and clearly enjoy a radiant life. Others are quite unimpressive. But, radiant or glum, what do they do in the present world situation? If ten and twenty million more were converted and could talk sincerely of their 'love, joy and peace' how would it affect in a large way the life of the nation and the world? A church boldly challenging this present social order, and giving visible evidence of our Lord's power to reshape it nearer to His own desire, would open to evangelism millions of people to whom the offer of changed feelings seems a well-intentioned but pitiful irrelevance.

How Much are you Saved?, p 11

271

Rare as saints now are, they could (in the New Testament sense) be common. Nothing but our faithlessness and indiscipline prevents us joining this high company.

The Bible *commands* it and the Bible never commands the impossible (Lev. 9^2; Matt. 5^{48}).

The Bible *promises* it. (2 Cor. 7^1; Titus 2^{14}; 1 John 1^9; 2 Peter 1^4).

The Bible *illustrates* it. The Bible is full of people enjoying this quality of life. Indeed, in the New Testament this quality of life is regarded as *normal* for Christians. Stephen might be taken as a typical example. He was filled with the Holy Spirit and Christ was being formed afresh in him. In his lustred life, his courage when on trial, and his sublime forgiveness of his murderers when dying, you see a clear reflection of his Lord. Nor was he singular. In the early Church (with all its faults) saints were common.

The Church *exults* in it. Every bona-fide Communion in the Church of God has its saints. Some of them have come to fame. Most of them are obscure. Only God can make a saint and only God can know for sure when he is made. And God wants nothing but faith and discipline to work this miracle.

Why not *you?*

Lord! Lord!!

You Can be a Saint, pp 8–9

He begins by convincing the people who think they don't need to be saved that they do. Millions of men deny their need of a Saviour. 'What's wrong with me?' they say. 'I don't do anybody any harm. I'm always doing good turns.' So they say, and so they sincerely believe.

When these men meet Christ—that is, when they get a clear picture of Him as given in the Bible and feel themselves in His presence—they know themselves unclean. Nobody need tell them so. They know it themselves, and they know at once that they need saving.

Nobody has the power to do this like Christ. Men are seldom convinced by argument that they are sinners. Most argument on this point is waste of breath. Just get them to see what Christ is like and introduce them to Him. They feel dirty at once. And because nobody wants to be saved until he knows he is lost, that is the first thing which must happen.

Then Christ goes to work. To a man who knows he is unclean and wants help, Christ says, 'I can change your nature if you will let me'. If a man will take Christ into his life, his soiled past can be forgiven, and he will be given sound judgement and moral power in every day as it comes. He will cease to be the man he was and become another—the same personality but transformed. He is changed as a son, brother, husband, father, friend, workman, citizen.... Consequently, his personal change affects society, too. His home is different, his club, workshop ... even his town and country to some extent, and ... this influence begins to affect the world. Christ's power to save is unlimited. He hacks down the barrier of class, race and colour ...

Give God a Chance, p 49

I was reading a while ago of the early history of the white settlements in South Africa, and I came across some strange eccentric characters.

One of them was called Ikey Sonnenburg. Ikey ran a store catering for the needs of the Boers, many of whom were simple and pious men whom Ikey did not find it hard to deceive.

One day a Boer was selling his wool to Ikey. The wool-bales were weighed and the price was fixed at 3d per pound. Ikey made a rapid calculation and announced that the total amounted to £153.

The farmer consulted his ready-reckoner, and said, 'No; according to my reckoner the total is £173 4s. 3d.'. Whereupon Ikey seized the Boer's ready-reckoner rapidly examined it, and exclaimed, 'Good heavens, you're using last year's ready-reckoner. It's worthless *this* year!'

The old Boer meekly received the correction and was content to accept the amount that Ikey was eager to pay.

Ikey caught the Boer. He wouldn't have caught you. You would have said that a ready-reckoner does not vary from year to year. You would have said that what is true in mathematics now will be true in mathematics tomorrow.

And with great confidence you may say 'What is true in the law of God now, and what was true in the moral law of God in the dim dawn on Bible history, will be true in the law of God for all the generations which may succeed us'. Our apprehensions of His will may vary; our obedience most certainly does. But *the law of the Lord* does not change.

Westminster Sermons (vol. i), pp 66–7

It belongs to the nature of sin to blind as it grows; the more you have of it, the less you see of it. That is why people who disbelieve in God and ignore His Church are always the first to protest that they are not sinners. 'What is wrong with me?' they ask, and patter again about their 'good turns'. Nothing so illustrates the lost condition of man as his intimation (overt or covert) that he has no awareness of sin.

But the pre-requisite of all repentance is a recognition of one's sin. One cannot *prepare* to repent unless one sees sin for what it is, and how can a sin-blinded man even *see* the thing for what it is? And if he cannot recognize the sin, how can he repent it?

. . . In my army days in the First World War, I remember a camp on the top of a hill near Boulogne. The Medical Officer's Room was on the top of another hill some distance away. Any man 'reporting sick' was required to leave the camp and present himself with full pack and in marching order to the Medical Officer on the top of the other hill. We often smiled at the grim humour or the insanity of it. Only a man fighting fit could have reported 'sick' at all. No man really ill was capable of marching up the hill with all his kit upon him. It is a picture of our human dilemma. Only the holy can see sin for what it is, but if one cannot see sin for what it is, how can one repent it? So our race drifted to destruction, beaten by a problem beyond all human cure.

They Met at Calvary, pp 87–8

There are many who complain that life has never given them a chance . . . and that if they fail completely the blame belongs not to them but to the conditions under which they were born. The circumstances of which they complain are many and various . . . it may be something purely physical—some bodily malformation that rankles in the heart and creates a crippling sense of inferiority. One thinks of the withered hand of the Kaiser, or the club-foot of Lord Byron, or the limp of Sir Walter Scott. Only those who bear such a disability know how much it can depress the spirit as well as the flesh.

Ah yes! Many are the dark thoughts and awkward circumstances of life—how many and how dark perhaps only a faithful minister of souls knows. The sombre knowledge that one was born out of wedlock; the terrifying recollection that there is a streak of mental instability in the family . . . the denial of a good education when one could really have profited by it. . . . How often the less valiant souls give up the fight and seek refuge in excuses. . . . I want to convince you . . . that God has taken upon Himself the heaped-up disabilities of our race and that however unfriendly the world may seem, still—

> *There is no place where earth's sorrows*
> *Are more felt than up in Heaven . . .*

None the less, I shall leave you in no ignorance . . . that these comforts and helps are for the adventurous. God is no refuge for the cowardly, cringing soul. He is the goal and the sustainer of those who dare. . . . Come, then, let us get our backs beneath it, whatever it is. Our God demands courage! May He observe that courage in us all!

Why Jesus Never Wrote a Book, pp 93–4

I have found in many minds a latent *condition* in all their dealings with God. Beneath all their praying—and a seeker is often the most earnest in prayer—there is an unexpressed condition. Every promise they make to God—and some of their promises are most fervent—are really hypotheticals. 'If this . . . then that.' It is surprising that such a condition could be half-unconscious, and yet it often is.

Here is a young man, who has been ill four years—very ill. Before his sickness, he loved all sports and played several outdoor games keenly and well. Then he was laid on his back, and has been on his back most of the time since. Hope and despair of recovery have alternated in his mind. Brief periods of sitting out in the garden; longer periods on his back in bed. He had prayed to God, and God, he felt, had ignored him. Faith had all but gone and cynicism was taking its place.

In the quietness, one memorable day, after much thought and prayer, God showed us why his normal praying was unreal. A big condition lay beneath all his promises to God; a natural one, certainly, but God does not brook conditions. The only purpose of his praying, even when he did not mention it, was for health. Unexpressed he was saying all the time 'If you make me better, Lord. . . .' 'If I can have my health again. . . .' 'If I can be as fit as my brother. . . .' Tenderly, I told him where the flaw was, and nobly did he respond. Very moving was his prayer of dedication: 'Lord I have always come to you with "ifs": now I come to you with no "ifs" at all.' He does not *suffer* his sickness now; he uses it. And God has gloriously used him.

He is Able, p 96

Christians will not suppose, as they move more resolutely into social and public life, that they have a simple and ready answer to the problems which await them.

It is easy to denounce war and bombs, poverty and disease, social distinctions and racial inequalities. You can even get a 'kick' out of hearty denunciation and suppose that you have done something. Some people spend their lives denouncing. . . .

But where are the answers?

When war is so obviously insane, why isn't it abolished? Whence comes this awful honest fear which pours out the world's wealth on armaments? How can people be taught mutual trust?

When the surplus potatoes were thrown in the rivers during the depression in America, and the dumped oranges sprayed with kerosene, and the pigs which couldn't be sold were killed and made to rot, and the starving people looked on but were not allowed to touch the food (because no one had made a profit on it) it was appalling wickedness; but it was not *intended* wickedness. Men were boxed up in their own economic laws. The dreadful truth is that it takes more than goodwill to give things away, and that fact confronts us still when we think of the hungry people of the East.

Add the problems of an ever-increasing world population (and increasing most rapidly where there is most need) and no one will think the answers to our problems easy. It takes more than amiability to meet the world's needs: it takes high ability also. Much prayer and thought are required in those who would serve the world in this dark hour.

How Much are you Saved?, p 12

The saints see God. The blessing promised to the pure in heart is theirs. They see God. . . . Not even the saints see the full glory of God. But the shadows cast by His face bring them to the dust. Most men and women catch a gleam of God's glory at some point of their earthly pilgrimage. But the cares of this world, and our fatal preoccupation with ourselves, keep our eyes cast downwards. We neither watch, nor long, nor expect to see it again. The saint watches, longs and expects. He watches unto prayer, longs with a growing intensity, has patience in the dark, and faith to believe that his eyes will behold it. The vision of God begets humility in his soul as naturally as our eyes blink when we step into strong sunshine.

Not only is humility a necessary consequence of seeing God. The saint learns that the more humility he has, the more of God he will have also. The primal sin is the assertion of self against God. Pride, therefore, heads any well-drawn category of the deadly sins and humility is its opposite. This explains why, though love is the first fruit of the Spirit and the basis of all the rest, discerning souls have often pointed to humility as the first of the graces. They do so because pride is the deadliest of the deadly sins and humility is its plain contradiction. The more humility, the less pride. The less pride, the more of God. The vision of God begets humility in the soul, and the more humility the clearer one's eyes become to see Him as He is.

The Pure in Heart, pp 164–5

Inevitably . . . the society of God's intention will have a democratic mould, but to equate it with democracy as we understand the term today is inexact and cannot pass without comment. It may be . . . that almost every social order, which has proved valuable among men, may have its place . . . in the final society. Monarchy—because it is a *Kingdom*. Aristocracy —because its leaders will be the *best*. Democracy—because it will be composed of *equals*. Communism—though the communism will be *voluntary*. Certainly the Kingdom of God will not be democracy as we know it today. Democracy as understood in this God-denying modern world is not a subject for uncritical praise. For all the adulation lavished upon it, the ballot-box is an insensitive instrument. It can count, but it cannot weigh. It says 'One here' and 'One there', but it has no ability to say 'This is a better one than that one'. The judgement of the keenest, clearest thinker can be cancelled out at the ballot-box by any fuddled, drink-besotted moron who staggers to the booth and puts his cross. If it is asked 'Doesn't Christianity believe, then, in the common man?' the answer is plainly this, 'Whom do you mean by the "common man"?' If, by the 'common man' is meant the man who seldom thinks at all, buys his opinion . . . in a newspaper; spends most of his leisure in the bar of a pub . . . we do *not*.

The common man, in whom the evangelist deeply believes, is the man, in any walk of life, who has been touched by the finger of God, and has responded to Him. . . . A democracy composed of such men and women is the social aim of the evangelist. It is theocracy looked at from the human side. It arises, inevitably, from the family ideal.

Let me Commend, pp 120–1

I met a depressed man one day who told me that he had
nothing to be thankful for, so I said: 'Well, I'm going visiting;
come with me.' I was going to the Institution for the poor aged
sick. In the town where I then ministered it was an old-fashioned
building, and its management left much to be desired; but
the man came with me. It was not a public visiting day, but I
got him in . . . round the wards with me. From bed to bed we
went, seeing a great many of these pitiable old people. Some
were dim of sight, and some were *quite* blind. Some were hard
of hearing and some were *quite* deaf. Some were imbecile, and
in some their reason was *partly* impaired. . . . I didn't say anything much to my companion. I had come to visit the poor souls
themselves; he just followed me round. When we were outside
again I did not rub in the moral. I just shook hands with him,
because I had other duties to do, and he parted from me saying:
'I don't think I'll ever grumble again.'

It was a simple device; just showing him people less fortunate
than himself. He went away saying (I think) under his breath,
'I can see. . . . I can hear. . . . I have my reason unimpaired. I
can think and plan and pray. I am not well off, but I have
enough . . .'.

. . . Thank God for the common blessings commonly overlooked. Don't wait till you lose them to be grateful. . . .
Thank God for common blessings; for the harvest fully
gathered in and the great harvest moon rising above; for the
sudden smile of a friend met unexpectedly in a place where you
did not expect to meet anyone you knew; thank God for home,
for birthday anniversaries . . . for all ordinary things, taken for
granted when they ought to be taken with gratitude: Thank
God! Thank God!

Westminster Sermons (vol. ii), pp 141–2

Our reading of any book is affected by the state of mind in which we undertake it. If a man comes to the Bible believing that the Old Testament is largely unimportant Jewish history and Jewish law, and the New Testament a story (largely legendary) about Jesus Christ and the early Church, he will not profit much by his reading. His mind is barricaded against the deeper wisdom the Bible has to give. But if he comes to it impressed by the fact that it has fed the souls of millions of people of all types through many hundreds of years, he will treat it reverently, and with a sense of honest quest. If, moreover, he has the humble desire in his heart for any supernatural aid which may be available in his study, it will soon begin to show him hidden treasure. . . .

The Bible is not an easy book for beginners. It is best read under the direction of one who knows the inwardness of it, or by the aid of those fellowships and unions which publish notes on selected passages. There are parts of it which are very dull to all but experts. Yet there is no book which more repays the right kind of persistence, and in the end, to those who read it as it is meant to be read, it becomes the Book of all books and life's greatest treasure.

That should not surprise us. The book which tells of God's dealings with the most spiritually sensitive people of ancient times, the book which alone contains the record of His Son's life on earth, the book which records the founding of the Christian Church must ever be a book apart. . . . Hurriedly to leaf the Book over at random is to court confusion. To penetrate to its heart is to understand why people call it 'The Word of God'.

Give God a Chance, p 60

Tersteegen said: 'Self-denial makes prayer easy and prayer again lightens self-denial. The more the flesh is under restraint, the more liberty and delight is experienced by the spirit, in living with God in its true element. . . .' The great gain to the questing soul from this fruit of the Spirit is that it offers to God an ordered and obedient personality, not cloyed by comfort nor sluggish from indulgence, but sensitive to guidance and ready for all His perfect will.

What perplexes beginners in the holy life concerning the discipline of the saints, is that it covers so many *good* things. They expected the sword of the Spirit to flash out against evil, but it surprises them that those advanced in sanctity are so severe *with themselves* about many things which are either innocuous or unmistakably wholesome. They do not see with John Wesley that a thing can be innocent in itself and yet increase the authority of the body over the mind. They do not realize that one can hardly leave the kindergarten of the School of Sanctity until one has seen that the battle is not only against evil but also against the lesser good. Nobody, so far as I know, has claimed sanctity for Jenny Lind, but she was a devout and aspiring soul, and her great renunciation illustrates her clear recognition that the good can be the enemy of the best. Asked by a friend why—still young, and at the height of her fame— she had withdrawn from the operatic stage, she answered, as she picked up her Bible: 'Because I found it left me so little time for this and'—pointing to the sunset—'none for that.' The saints want God. God above all things. All things in God. Nothing is really a sacrifice that gives them more of God. They put down the penny to pick up the pound.

The Pure in Heart, pp 171–2

. . . A friend of mine—a coal miner, in County Durham, a man in middle life now, before his conversion, was a drunken sot. He was a cheat as well. Playing once in a dominoes competition, he covered a dot with a bit of chewing gum and cleared the 'kitty' of £29.

He had a good mother and a good wife, and he came near to breaking the heart of both of them. One day his mother said to his wife, 'Leave him, Nellie. Leave him! He'll drag you to hell!'

But Nellie didn't leave him, nor ceased to pray, and one wonderful Sunday evening she had the answer to her prayers. Spent up and miserably sober, he yielded to her pleading and went with her to evening worship, where a friend of mine was preaching his characteristically powerful evangelical word. When at the end of the sermon, my friend made an appeal, Jack stumbled forward and asked God to forgive him.

What an hour! I think he only ever glanced back once . . . and it was but a glance! He was transformed in the astonished gaze of all the neighbourhood. In the passing of only a few years, the Holy Spirit wiped from his face all the marks of dissipation and made him radiant with an unearthly light.

When I first knew him, I had been ordained twice as long as he had been converted and there are some things I can do, I suppose, that he can't do. But oh! there are many more important things that *he* can do which I can't do. It is wonderful to hear him talk to men who have missed their way; such love, such incisiveness, such skill with sinners, I know he has travelled the road of Christian discipleship faster than I have ever done.

Westminster Sermons (vol. i), pp 69–70

. . . Yet fully committed Christians enter the field of social service with very large equipment. If Christ rules in their hearts they have the gift of supernatural love, and that is the key to all things.

Love has been the key to the social work the Christian Church has done through all the centuries. Hospitals, schools, orphanages, homes for unmarried mothers—it has suckled them all. Love will guide it in the high constructive tasks it has yet to do.

Conversion does not make disciples into geniuses, but it quickens every aspect of their personality. They see things in the light of God. With a view unbefogged by self-interest, they are sensitive to guidance from above.

They hold in indissoluble unity the twin principles of *involvement* and *detachment*. They will not withdraw from the world. Salvation, as they understand it, is bound up with social concern. They will never deny their relationship, even when their brothers are prodigal. They will hold to them for nothing but love—the love Christ had for them and plants in their hearts for others.

But they will be detached also—as saints have understood the word. They will want nothing for themselves. They will be careless of earthly gain or widespread fame, and take a smile from God as their whole reward.

So equipped they will go to work, and the gates of hell shall not prevail against them.

How Much are you Saved?, p 13

The central and most glorious truth of the Christian Gospel is that God, in the person of Jesus Christ, bent to man's dilemma and did for him what he could not do for himself. It was, indeed, a problem for God alone. Horace, in his *Ars Poetica*, laying down the rules for young dramatists, warned them against the too ready use of a device employed by playwrights in that period. When their characters were entangled in difficult situations, a god would be introduced to extricate the hero or elucidate the plot. The young playwrights overdid it. Horace laid it down that, in tragedy, a god should never be introduced save to untie a knot which baffled all human skill.

That describes our human situation; it was a knot which baffled all human skill. But Christ bent to our need. He was born among us, lived our life, was tempted in all points, like as we are, suffered at the hands of sinners, and offered, as Man, a perfect repentance for our race. He exposed sin, accepted God's righteous judgement which makes punishment its consequence, sacrificed Himself in willing acceptance of the price, in some mysterious way bore the entail on our behalf. And it was *God* who did it. . . . It was not a pathetic, beaten figure who cried from the Cross: 'It is finished!' It was God's own Son, Royal, and Priestly, and Sovereign. He alone could do it. No one else could see sin for what it was. No one else could bear the heaped-up wickedness of our race.

They Met at Calvary, p 88

More than 1900 years ago a child was born in a stable at Bethlehem. . . . The child was born in the stable by reason of the overcrowding of the local inn, consequent upon a census that was being taken. The circumstances of the birth were peculiar in all ways. The supposed parents of the child were not married and the tongue of scandal was soon busy. Scandalmongers are found among all people and in all ages. When Mary returned to Nazareth we cannot doubt that she returned to the head-shakings and the muttered and scornful undertones of evil-minded women. The evil-minded always delight to direct their darts against those who have a reputation for purity and none could have had a higher reputation than the Mother of Jesus. The agony which culminated for her at the Cross began when she first brought her lovely baby home. She made no attempt to defend herself. Nobody would have believed her, the evil-minded least of all. . . . 'So', says Luke, 'so . . . she hid these things in her heart.' Does it require a wealth of imagination to glimpse the life at Nazareth in the years that followed? The baby growing up into a sturdy and lovely boy, swift in obedience to His Mother's will: going at her bidding with a child's water-pot to the well and as He draws the water some gossiping creature notices Him and tells the ugly and lying story once again. So, as He turns towards the carpenter's shop again . . . they use of Him a tainted name. Is there anybody who complains that they are cursed with a tainted name? Without justification your Lord has borne that shame. The slander followed Him through life . . . and His enemies have poisoned their tongues with it in many ages since. Oh! Surely . . . 'Surely . . . He hath borne our griefs, and carried our sorrows'.

Why Jesus Never Wrote a Book, pp 94–5

. . . It would seem at first that anybody who had a resentment in their heart, would realize that that would be a barrier to God's indwelling, but experience shows that it is not quickly recognized as such, especially when the resentment has a just cause.

In the days when I was more immature in this work than I am now, I spent many valuable hours trying to help a man to a vivid awareness of God, and never mentioned the possibility of resentment to him. That I finally did so, I owe (as I believe) to the guidance of God. As I waited on God in the quietness, a sense of the character of this man's need came to me, and the moment I touched the spot he winced. . . . He brought me a bundle of anonymous letters and asked me to read them—foul things, full of libel on himself and on a dear one. Nor was he ignorant of their author. The chain of evidence was all but complete; he had taken advice from a solicitor, and he was just waiting . . . waiting . . . for revenge. He seemed to gloat on the letters, and said that they were worth more to him than the £200 which he had saved. . . . So we went to work. I showed him that, however just the resentment might be, it was a poison at the heart of his life, and no peace could come till the passion for revenge had gone. He saw it all when we looked at the Cross. If resentment was ever justified it would have been justified in Jesus. But He did not look down from the Cross upon the howling mob who had not the common decency to let Him die in quietness, and say 'Are these the brutes for whom I am dying?' He said, rather, 'Father, forgive them, they know not what they do.'

So he went home, burnt the letters before he went to bed, and has been busy ever since trying to win the one who slandered him. It was a wonderful night when I saw them sitting together in Church.

He is Able, pp 98–9

They discipline themselves in *food*. Fasting, as taught in the New Testament, is common with them. To set down a list of the saints who were firmly disciplined in eating and drinking would simply be to transcribe the holy calendar. . . . Bishop Ken lived on one modest meal a day. William Law was inflexible in his fasting habits. He said that almost every ill-temper, every hindrance to virtue, every clog in our way of piety and the strength of every temptation, chiefly arose from the state of our bodies. Gerhard Tersteegen denied himself both tea and coffee, ate only the coarsest food and little of that. John Wesley fasted, at one time, every Wednesday and Friday until after three in the afternoon. John Fletcher ate sparingly at all times, confining himself largely to bread and fruit. John Woolman was abstemious to the point of asceticism. . . . His abstinence from sugar had a double purpose in his mind: he wanted to deny himself and he did not want to support West Indian slavery.

The saints discipline themselves in *sleep* also. It borders on the unbelievable that men and women could sleep so little and do so much. The modern notion that everybody needs seven or eight hours' sleep a night is made to appear nonsense in the lives of the saints. John Wesley did his herculean work on six hours' sleep a night; he retired always at 10 p.m. and rose at 4 a.m. Yet he was indulgent in comparison with his friend John Fletcher, who trained himself to sleep only when he could not keep awake, and yet carried an alert mind to multifarious duties, and prayed and meditated through two whole nights a week.

The Pure in Heart, pp 172–3

At the hearthside all the children are equal. No true parent has a favourite child. Nature is markedly unequal in the placing of her gifts, and even in the same family one girl may be pretty and her sister plain; one boy may be brilliant and his brother bovine; one child may grow up to find music in everything, and another be all but tone-deaf; yet none of these differences can make any difference to true parental love. All are equal at home. Kisses and smiles are evenly shared among the children. Neither mother nor father feeds the inferiority of one child, nor the superiority of another. The table symbolizes the equality. The family sits down to a meal, and all the children are peers.

The world makes differences in families. When the children grow up and leave the old home, some succeed, according to the standards of the world, and others, according to the same standards, fail. But all this makes no difference at home. The family re-union brings children together again and, in the old homestead, where kisses and smiles were always equally shared, the successes of one are forgotten with the failures of the other, and all are equal . . . because it's home!

And God holds us all in an equal love; black and white; red and brown; male and female. The evangelist peers through the ages and longs for the day when all will sing:

One family we dwell in Him.

Let me Commend, pp 121-2

There are fine things in the Moslem faith. The Moslem faith has its saints. Mohammed himself was, in his age, a great reformer. There are fine things in the philosophy of Hinduism. There is noble, ethical teaching in the writing of Confucius. There are things in Buddhism beautiful indeed. Christianity recognizes these fine things and blesses God for them, but Christianity says (if I may adapt the opening words of *Hebrews*) 'God, who at sundry times and in divers manners spake in time past unto the fathers and by the prophets (and by these Eastern sages), hath, in these last days, spoken unto by His Son'.

That is our claim. Not that other world religions contain in them nothing of value. God forbid! But that they were not God's last word to His people. Christianity is not one religion among others. It is in a category by itself. . . . No other world faith even claims that its great teacher was God incarnate. We claim for Christ that—as God—He meets every human need. . . . His call is to all humanity. He abides no barriers of race, class or colour. It seems, to the devotees of other faiths, intolerant on the part of Christians to refuse to allow Jesus to go into a pantheon. How can they? Believing what they do about Him, they cannot concede even by implication that there are any 'gods' or prophets equal to Him. He is unique in His Person, in His Mission, and in His finished work.

Christianity is not a Western religion forced on the East. It is, in its origin, an Eastern religion, but in its nature it is a world faith. It is no more mine and yours than China's, India's, Africa's. It is God's provision for man, as man, and knows no barrier at all.

Westminster Sermons (vol. ii), pp 1567–

It is a bitter experience for decent parents (at any social level) when their children go wrong. I remember seeking to comfort a father in those circumstances years ago. His boy had broken his father's heart; broken his own heart as well. Socially, morally and spiritually, the lad had made a mess of things, and ended by taking his own life. 'I can't make it out', said the distraught father. 'I never denied him anything. I even sent him to church. . . .'

Those last phrases have long echoed in my mind. . . . Is it a good thing not to be denied anything? Doesn't our stubborn nature require at times the discipline of denial? Is part of the reason why the sons of successful men often disappoint their fathers, the fact that they have had it too easy? Can you give people things so readily that you take away something more precious than you give: independence, the necessity of effort, the satisfaction of having done something 'by myself'?

And he'd *sent* him to church! As a *boy*, of course. He'd not *taken* him. He'd been too busy to spare an hour a week for worship. Yet he shared the common idea that Sunday School and church are good for children, and he sent the boy to church. When the lad was twelve, he insisted no more. After all, he had to attend chapel at his public school. During holidays, the lad could please himself. . . .

There is an enormous difference between *sending* a child to church and *taking* him. If you go with him, he realizes (even as a small boy) that it means something to you. If you never go yourself, he comes to think that church is just 'kid's stuff', and takes it as a sign of maturity when he is allowed to give it up. We don't go to church primarily to be made moral. We go to worship God. But sincere worship has glorious consequences.

The Little Book of Sermons, pp 40–1

God made men and women for fellowship with Himself. He made us (the Bible says) 'in His own image', and however vastly greater God must be than anyone whom He has made, we can at least catch a glimpse, in the thought, feeling and will which blend in our own nature, of the mighty Being who is behind all things.

In making us for virtue and for loving fellowship with Himself, God made us free. He *had* to. Only the free can be good, and love is acceptable only when it is freely given. It is of course a *limited* freedom; we cannot pluck the sun from the sky, or change the order of the seasons. . . . But within its limited orbit, our freedom is real. We can withhold our love. We can do evil and not good. . . . For the purpose God had in mind he had to make us free.

Robots cannot love. Puppets are not persons. The great God could have filled His world with machine-like creatures who would always have reacted in precise ways to precise conditions, but they could not love and they could not be good. Hence He took the risk of evil, and the evil came. . . . Some believe that it has tainted our nature. To call this evil . . . just 'the survival of the beast' in us is too shallow and is unjust to the beasts. No animal is guilty of the evil of men. . . . Men argue sometimes that we are not free, that whatever we do is the result of 'pressures' upon us; but no one has ever been able to prove this point. Certainly the awareness of all sane men is against them. We *feel* free . . . at the last we *choose*. 'I couldn't help it!' is a weakling's cry. (Nor do the people who say that we are not free to act on their own conviction. If their house is broken into, they prosecute the burglar as soon as anyone else!)

Give God a Chance, p 75

He is the soul and centre of our *thoughts*. We revel in the Gospel records. Imagination comes to the aid of faith and we jostle with the crowds that stood around Him in the days of His flesh. Indeed, the Holy Book becomes autobiographical. We are ourselves the leper He cleansed; the demoniac out of whom He cast the fiends of hell; the paralytic He bade rise and sin no more. Whenever our minds relax from the concentration of daily tasks, they turn to feasting in thought on Him. He is the blessed background of our minds when the cares of the world are most absorbing, and, when these cares no longer call for concentration, our minds turn to the full enjoyment of thinking on Him as lovers think of the one beloved.

Clearly, then, He is the soul and centre of our *affections* also. As knowledge increases, love deepens, and, as love deepens, the eagerness for still more knowledge increases also. Our hearts run out to Him with an ever-increasing love. . . . He burns with love—love pure and personal. He died for me— the shameful death of the cross. If I were the only sinner in the world, His love would still have led Him to die for me. How then can I help but love Him in return?

Love leads to imitation—conscious and unconscious. I aim to be like Him, and, when I am *not* aiming, my love sets my disposition that way. Consequently, He becomes the centre and soul of our *actions* too. Steadily, the Holy Spirit aims to beget in us the Lord Jesus—in some sublime spiritual counterpart of the way He once formed in the womb of the Virgin the flesh and blood of Him who was to be the Saviour of the World.

The Pure in Heart, p 192

The voice of expediency says to us sometimes 'It is wise not to see things' or 'It is wise not to hear some things'. . . . Far be it from me to suggest that a little blindness or a little deafness may not sometimes serve a good cause. Think of Nelson at Copenhagen. But so often this counsel is given to us in the most questionable circumstances, and we are asked to repeat Nelson's trick without Nelson's excuse. This is the moment to be watchful; that is the time to be on guard. You may feign not to see something that is questionable and your indifference will be interpreted as consent. . . . In my Army days I was in charge of a billet that the troops used as a centre for gambling, and I was much exercised in my own mind. . . . And the RSM gave me this advice. He said 'Don't notice it. It is wise not to see things'. So I took his advice. I feigned not to notice it. But the men knew that I knew, and I knew that they knew that I knew, and one day one of them came to me in great distress. He wanted to borrow some money. He was in debt. It must be paid at once. He had lost heavily at gambling, and when I spoke to him of the blind and stupid folly of the whole silly business, he said, 'Well! you knew that it was going on and you didn't object'. . . . I'd been *too* smart. I'd followed the dictates of policy and not of principle and this was the result. Be on your guard against this! . . . Be sure that you are not yielding to the fear of facing up to an awkward situation and really seeking an easy way out. It will take all the heroism of your soul to stand up to the powers of evil—and still stand.

Why Jesus Never Wrote a Book, pp 44–5

I am writing this deep in a Swiss valley. A cable car swings on a thin wire overhead. It carries thirty-two people and is moving over an awful abyss at a height of 5,000 feet. I doubt if one person in that car knows how it works, how thirty-two people can be conveyed in a box of metal and glass over a great ravine on one steel wire. Does the wire move, or only the car? But how can the car go steeply upwards with no rack and pinion principle involved at all? They do not know. They do not care. Soon they will land on the mountain peak and enjoy the most heavenly views. It will avail for them, though none of them understands. Yes, but somebody understands. The genius who conceived it—he understood. The artificer who made it—he understood. The engineers who maintain it—they understand. Heaven help those poor souls in the car if somebody does not understand!

. . . So it is with the Cross. It can avail for those who do not understand it so long as they trust themselves to it. But somebody must understand! If the theologian cannot understand fully (and what electrical engineer fully understands electricity?) he must understand more than the simple believers on whom the burden of thought is not laid. For the teachers of the faith to abandon the quest of understanding would be fatal. A spiritual fact, like the saving Cross, would cease to be a fact if no explanation were possible. Doubt would invade the mind. . . . It would be ignored by one generation, declared unnecessary by the next, and denied by the third. Passengers would cease to travel by the cable car. The rumour would spread abroad that the engineers had lost faith in the thing, and nobody would land on the lofty peak to enjoy those heavenly views. Few things are more nourishing to our Christian religion than a grasp of its principles.

They Met at Calvary, pp 90–1

. . . Do you complain that you have lost a parent early in life, and that real education was denied you, and that you were saddled with the care of younger children? Consider the circumstances of your Lord! There is an ancient . . . tradition in the Church that Joseph died while Jesus was still a youth, and the care of the household devolved in large upon Him. There were four younger brothers and at least two younger sisters and He had to take Joseph's place. Can you deny that He understands your difficulties? The only formal education He received was the teaching of the Synagogue school. . . . He never went to a scribal college: He never sat at the feet of the Rabbis. The best that His land and age offered in education passed Him by. He was busy at the bench toiling for His widowed Mother and brothers and sisters: turning out yoke for the oxen, a plough for the farmer, and the wooden bowls and platters that served the men of those days for crockery. He was thirty before His public ministry could begin. You might have turned a deaf ear to me if I were describing the life of some young prince in a palace, but you dare not turn away from this toiling, sacrificing carpenter of Nazareth. . . . All our difficulties are known to Him. . . . Is He not worthy to be your example? Does He not justly demand that you kill those self-pitying thoughts that invade your soul? Courage! Don't moan! Don't get sorry for yourself! Never say again that you've never had a chance! It isn't true. You've had difficulties certainly . . . but some of those difficulties could have been used for your triumph. Look into the face of Jesus Christ. . . and see if those excuses do not die on your lips and make you feel already half ashamed.

Why Jesus Never Wrote a Book, pp 96–7

And scarcely can we turn aside
For one brief hour of prayer

The obstacles to prayer are many, though some are mere excuses, and would quickly yield to a resolute act of will. There is the difficulty about *time*. People complain that their busy lives give them no time for prayer, but it is usually a shallow evasion because they clearly find time for less important things —the newspaper and amusements. No one deeply in love would fail to find time for a daily word with the loved one, if the loved one lived at hand. Christ stole time from His sleep to pray. Wesley rose every morning at four for the same purpose. Francis Asbury was astir at five. The first thing in the morning is the best time for prayer, but if peculiar circumstances really make that impossible, the keen mind will find time before the day is old. One of the busiest women I have ever known, a working-class woman with a large family, keeps her tryst with God in the early afternoon when the last member of the family has returned from the mid-day meal. Before beginning again, she reads the book of God and spends time in unhurried prayer. 'Then', she says, 'I wire in again.' It is not always possible for a will to find a way, but it *is* possible in the matter of prayer. Time *can* be found. One could begin with a minimum rule of fifteen minutes each day. Even so slight an investment of well-used time would bring a vast and precious gain.

He is Able, p 102

There was nothing haphazard about it. 'In the fulness of time' God came to earth in Jesus Christ. *Just* when it was right. When Christ came to earth, love came to earth. As they saw Him, and heard of Him, men had the chance to know what God is like.

Only a human life could reveal God at all adequately, and even that could not reveal Him perfectly; but all that was possible appeared in Jesus. Not all people recognized that this was love, for men . . . have muddled thoughts on love.

Love as revealed by Jesus wasn't sentimental, or indulgent, or concerned only with feeling. Indeed, there were some people who felt that Jesus had a rough side to His tongue, but even His warnings and denunciations were the judgements of love. He was against whatever obscured the love of His Father, and it was love, also, for those who obscured it which made His warnings so sharp.

What tenderness He had for the sinners, the sufferers, the bereaved, the poor, the hungry; what patient persistence, what selflessness. . . .

And he never gave up. When wickedness triumphed and hammered Him on the wood, love achieved a greater triumph. The wickedness couldn't hammer the love out of Him. . . .

The Greatest of These, p 7

. . . In this adoring contemplation of God, we come to the heart of anything that can be called 'the secret of the saints'. They are not weighing, probing, seeking, asking. . . . They are not even trying to understand. They are just looking in love and longing on God as revealed in Jesus. They only want to

> *. . . gaze transported at the sight*
> *Through all eternity.*

All their holiness is a by-product of this. They look at God, and He looks at them. They grow in holiness as they grow in the steadiness and fixity of their gazing. Though the most mature saints complain at times of mind-wandering in adoration, their self-accusations must be understood only by their own high standards. Normally, they lose all sense of time in their holy attending. Hours slip away as moments. Even the most egocentric person, reducing all prayer to personal petition, grows weary of saying 'Give me . . . Give me' for thirty minutes. But who that sees God—however dimly—could grow weary of gazing on Him? At times, the saint is in a coma of contemplation; rapture and ecstasy may come to him and transport him into 'the third heaven'. He may indeed, with Paul, hear 'unspeakable words which it is not lawful for a man to utter'.

And, all the time, by the blessed agency of the Holy Spirit, and all unaware of it himself, that dedicated mortal is being made a saint. He asks for nothing. He only looks on God in Jesus. But it is enough! God uses his steady gazing and gives him Himself. The Holy Spirit effects that blessed by-product and a saint is made.

The Pure in Heart, pp 199–200

Think of our problems. Who are we? Why are we? What is this human life? What is the *meaning* of it? Where is it leading to? . . . That is the dilemma of the humanist. He doesn't really know what to make of this strange human creature. . . .

Nor are we better off if we turn with the same question to a modern philosopher like Bertrand Russell. . . . He has no other answer than this: 'You are an eddying speck of dust; a harassed, driven leaf.' If you seek from him and his kind the meaning of life, they say 'The *meaning* of life? There is none really. No doubt we could make our brief existence a little better if we tried.' Or if you ask for light on what follows when this life is past, they say, with Sir Arthur Keith, 'Nothing follows. Life goes out like a guttering candle.'

They walk in darkness, and they do not see a great light. So I turn to Jesus and the apostles, my hot, impetuous questions falling from my lips. I will ask *them* who I am, and what is the meaning of life, and what comes after this, and there is an answer for every question. 'You want to know who you are?' says Jesus. 'You are dear to God, and dear enough for me to shed my blood.' 'I can tell you', says Paul. 'You were bought with a price.' And John breaks in: 'Beloved, now are we children of God, and it doth not yet appear what we shall be.' 'What is the meaning of life, Lord?' I ask. 'What am I in the world *for*?' Plainly He answers: 'To seek, first, God's kingdom and His righteousness.' 'And, Lord, when the fever of this life is over?' . . . He smiles and says: 'In my Father's house are many mansions . . . I go to prepare a place for you.'

There it is. Plain dealing with plain questions. Light in darkness. The fruit of His coming. Is it any wonder that we . . . say from our hearts: 'Come, Thou long-expected Jesus. . . .'

Westminster Sermons (vol. ii), pp 4–6

If a man loved Christ as the Son of God, if he conducted his life on the example which Christ gave, if he, also, 'went about doing good', no one would want to deny that he was a Christian when he claimed the title himself. . . . Yet . . . it would be a limited Christian life that he would enjoy if he were not a member of the *visible* Church. He would not be acknowledging his debt to the Church in time past. It was through the Church (under God) that he got the Bible. The Church has carried the faith to him through the long centuries. It is hard to see how he could ever have become a Christian at all but for the existence and fidelity of the Church.

He would be failing, also, in many of his Christian duties in the present time. The Church has to give a corporate witness to the Christian life in the nation—and he would have no part in that. The Church has a concern over social justice at home and missionary endeavour abroad, but what orphanage could he open *alone*, and how many missionaries could *he* send overseas? . . . He would be limiting, moreover, his own Christian growth. He would be cut off from the grace which comes through the sacraments, worship, and Christian fellowship. God has as many avenues to a man's mind as the man has friends who are friends of God: but, if he is trying to be a Christian in isolation, he makes it more difficult for God to help him. Men who have been imprisoned have maintained their faith in solitary confinement by prayer alone; but almost always they were in the Church in their heart and intention, and usually the Church was aware of their need and was holding them up. In some watered-down sense . . . a man could be a 'Christian' and not a member of the visible Church, but why have skimmed milk when you could have full cream?

Give God a Chance, p 85

302

Perhaps no picture puts it more clearly than a metaphor of St Paul. He speaks of reflecting as a mirror the glory of the Lord. That is what the saint does. Gazing on his Lord, he becomes a mirror in which the likeness of Jesus is more and more clearly seen. Yet it is more than *reflection*. Under the necessity of truth, St Paul mixes his metaphors and says that it is a *transformation*, as though the mirror were changed by the reflection that falls on it. The saint is transformed into the same image. He has held himself steadily where his Lord's reflection could fall. That has been his one concern. All his mind has been given to Jesus. He has practised His presence, studied and copied His deeds, and kept His living image before his eyes. And the reflection has become a transformation. They said of St Francis of Assisi that he was 'The Mirror of Perfection' and —allowing for the idiosyncrasy of personality in all the saints —something similar could be said of them all. They *reflect* perfection.

Not that the saints are aware how clearly they reflect their Lord. The mirror cannot see the lovely image on its surface. The whole task of the mirror is to keep still before its object. Keeping still before the Lord is half, at least, of the secret of the saints. They keep still in adoring worship before the 'Great Object of their growing love'—the Holy Spirit does the rest.

The Pure in Heart, p 200

There is no favouritism on God's part. He shows favour, true; but it is what the world's greatest hymn-writer calls 'an undistinguishing regard'. His favours move to all.

And if you still ask me 'Then *why* have these people received more grace than I have received?' I will tell you. . . . First, they knew that this grace was there to be had. They had dwelt on this and similar texts: an 'abundance of grace'.

They didn't think that God's dealings with them were over when they first surrendered to Him. Some Christians do. They seem to feel that God's only concern is to get us on the pilgrim way. You can tell this from their conversation. Their religious talk is only of their conversion. They seem totally unaware that God's supreme concern is not to call them 'saints', but *make* them saints; not just to cancel the sin, but break its power in them; not merely to *impute* righteousness, but to *impart* it also.

But not these pace-makers we are considering now! They see their committal, not as a completion, but as a commencement; not as something rounded-off but as something just begun.

God has more to give! Of that they are sure, and they keep it in mind all the time. It saves them from self-complacency. Always there is a sense of expectation in them. 'There is more to have!'

Westminster Sermons (vol. i), pp 71–2

The ordinary people under democracy can have whatever they want. . . . But they must want it passionately enough. Their passion must weld them into unity, and gird them with courage, and toughen them to a terrible persistence.

So far as effective action is concerned, to be neutral or indifferent on a moral issue is indistinguishable from a vote against it. That is how a handful of vigilant, passionate zealots can capture and run a vast trade union, made up for the most part by men who are against the ultimate aims of the zealots, but whose laziness and indifference open the door to the dynamism and subtlety of the people who manage the machine.

I am in no doubt that the mass of ordinary people, who had seen Jesus work wonders and who loved Him well, were unspeakably distressed by His crucifixion; but when the deed was done they were in bed. His enemies worked swiftly in the early hours of that solemn day which divides all history. When the ordinary folk were astir and about, He was already on the Cross. Many of them, no doubt, were shocked. They could have protested, with a good deal of cogency, that they were not to blame.

It is hard to blame people for not being vigilant, harder still for not being heroes. But that is how wickedness wins its way in this world. It counts on the sleepiness and comfort-loving character of the good—and it wins.

They Met at Calvary, pp 46–7

Not only do the saints nourish the faith of simple believers, but they speak to the world's need, and they often speak with startling relevance to the times.

Man's chief problem is with himself. Scaling the unscaled mountain, feeding the hungry multitudes of the Far East, finding the cure of cancer, are all small beside the problems which centre in man's chronic selfishness, his erratic will, and his lustful nature.

Can human nature be changed?

Many people outside the Church deny it, and not a few within the Church doubt it. There are theologians who argue that God can do nothing with sin but forgive it, and see the warfare of the Holy Spirit in the human soul as a long-drawn-out guerrilla struggle, never really ended by victory, but only by death. They do not doubt the *mercy* of God. . . . What they doubt is His ability or willingness to change human nature as we have it here. When the pessimism of the world expresses itself in uncertainty as to whether human nature can be changed, these believers cannot resolve the doubt. They doubt themselves.

The saints resolve the doubt. They do it less by argument than by example. Can human nature be changed? It has been done! Again and again. The worst made the best; the lowest lifted to the highest. Lust conquered; self dethroned; all life, a life of love. The question whether human nature can be changed will never be settled by argument. It demands another kind of proof.

The saints provide the proof.

The Pure in Heart, p xii

306

What is it, then, that makes the metaphor of the blood so precious and moves us even to tears?

> *His dying crimson like a robe*
> *Spreads o'er His Body on the tree;*
> *Then I am dead to all the globe*
> *And all the globe is dead to me.*

There is a deep conviction that the blood is the life. The Bible says so, and some sense of the truth of it is in the mind of natural man as well. No man has moved through the bloody horror of the battlefield or the air-raids, and seen people bleeding to death, without feeling as he watched in helplessness that the life pulsed out with the blood. . . . The ancient ritual of the Hebrew people made much of sacrifice and the outpoured blood. Is it any wonder that the first disciples (Jews to a man) saw Jesus as the very Paschal Lamb *offering Himself*, and caught up the symbolism of the centuries as they gazed on His streaming blood. . . . It is no wonder that being 'washed in the blood of Christ' has become so dear a phrase. See it as a solemn metaphor, and nothing dearer will ever come to mind. Put yourself in those pierced and bleeding hands, and know yourself for ever secure. A friend of mine had a comrade in the war who went into a shell-torn battle-field and brought back a wounded man . . . he was fatally wounded himself. He knew before he died that the man he had rescued would live. . . . At last (half in delirium) he kept murmuring 'I brought him through. . . .'

Look at the Cross. Look at the flowing wounds. He brought us through.

They Met at Calvary, pp 94–5

. . . Do you complain of your home? Home indeed! John Kitto would have been glad of a home of any sort. He was brought up in a workhouse, and through a life of continual vicissitude, during which he became stone-deaf through a fall, he kept alight the lamp of faith and became one of the greatest religious editors of his day. Or were the circumstances of your birth shadowed in shame? Is that the well-kept secret of your life? . . . Do you know that the greatest divine in Scotland of the generation just passed shared that crushing disability as well . . . Dr Alexander Whyte—he was a nameless child. . . . Or was some business failure the cause of all your trouble? . . . The career of Henry Edward Manning was broken from the start by the sudden and complete bankruptcy of his father. Just as he left Oxford, with every promise and probability of a great political career, his prospects were snatched away. Some would have spent their lives explaining to everybody who would listen why it was they had not made a success of things. Manning believed he heard the call of God in all this and rose to be a prince of the Church.

I do not expect you to be famous. I am not sure that I even wish it. I do desire that you be courageous; that you go forward in confidence and make the most of the opportunities God has put in your way.

Why Jesus Never Wrote a Book, p 98

Is Christ able to succour us in our loneliness? Can He enter deeply into a vacant life, and understand the full vacuity of days passed without a purpose? Is the Strong Son of God, on whom so much depended, able to meet the desires of those who feel that they have nothing to live for, and no one who needs them?

He is able!

He knew loneliness as no one knew it before or since. Greatness is always lonely. Great *men* have proved that. But who can conceive the awful loneliness of God incarnate among sinful men? So far as human understanding was concerned, He was lonely all His days. As a child He felt apart. He wist that He must be about His Father's business. When His ministry began it caused dissension and, finally, disruption in the home. . . . His brothers and sisters came to believe that He was deranged: His sweet Mother too. In what remained of His life, it was to His disciples that He looked for understanding, but He looked in vain. . . . It has been the comfort of martyrs at all times that somewhere in the world there were those who . . . understood the cause for which they died. Even this was denied Jesus. His sacrifice mystified the people who loved Him most. It mattered to all the world that He died for love, but no single soul in the world understood that He was doing it. . . .

No one understood Him. No one on earth approved. He was lonely with the awful loneliness of God. Can it be doubted that He can succour the lonely still?

He is Able, pp 37–8

Imagine a wireless operator listening on his first voyage across the wide Atlantic. What a riot of sound assails his ears as he moves the knobs upon his instruments! Any idea of the 'silent air and ocean' must seem laughably ludicrous to him now. How intently he must listen! All his brain reposes in his ears. Suddenly, he gets it. It is not as loud as other calls, but it is his signal. They are calling his ship. On that pin-point of sound, in all the babel of noises, he focuses the whole concentration of his listening, and, as he concentrates, it seems to get louder, clearer. . . . His pencil moves. The message has been received. The ship's whole course may be altered by that word.

That is a simple picture of the disciplined Christian listening to God. If an unbeliever says flatly 'I don't believe that God (if there is a God) speaks to men and women', that finishes the discussion for him. He has shut his mind on the issue. He won't even experiment and try this listening.

. . . It isn't any good Christians saying they believe in this if they never practise it, and, therefore, never experience it. Indeed, that is how a vague hypocrisy creeps into religion and that awful sense of unreality which can plague even a sincere Church member. It is personal experience of God, heaped up over the years and firmly based on the Christian revelation, which holds us in the times of life's tempest. . . . The way to learn to listen is to listen—and not to be surprised if interpretation takes a little time.

The Pattern of Prayer, p 21

It would be folly—and worse—to deny the selflessness of many lovely [non-Christian] lives spent prodigally in the service of others. It would be dishonouring to heaven to dissociate God from the beautiful work of those who . . . have poured out their lives for the love of humanity. God, doubtless, had more to do with their work than they knew, but it cannot be forgotten that some have served and suffered for their fellows without reward in this world, or any faith for it in a world hereafter.

Nevertheless, even of service . . . we may say . . . that worship 'disinfects us from egoism'. It cannot be without significance that our Lord always put the love of God before the love of our fellows and it is more than a priority. Moreover, seeing that it always belongs to our nature to identify ourselves with any cause we take up, the danger of the return of the self-regarding principle is always present where service and not worship is made the ideal. . . . One is insulated from that when worship is first. God is one's whole reward. He may direct His willing servant to many tasks in the service of others, but they are all subservient to God's will, and they are done for God's sake. If men are ungrateful for service rendered them at God's bidding, their ingratitude is a trifle. Certainly, it cannot tempt one to abandon a task which God has set. Experience would seem to show that for purity of motive, tenacity of purpose, indifference to reward and self-effacement in service, nothing equals those who serve their fellows as a consequence of their worship of God—much as we honour those who serve humanity for humanity alone.

The Pure in Heart, pp 202–3

The community of God's intention must be *classless*. Every kind of difference is possible in a family, except a difference of class. . . . If the brother who has succeeded is ever under temptation to disown one who has failed, the recollection of their common parentage will check him. . . . It was no good the elder brother in the parable spitting out his venom and calling the returned prodigal 'Your son' to his father's face. The father had only to reply 'Your *brother*'. So he was! And the Christian knows in his heart that the most drunken sot, the most vicious thug, the gangster and the grinder of the faces of the poor . . . are all his brothers.

Nothing is more absurd . . . than the survival of class-consciousness in modern society. . . . We fence ourselves off from our fellows, and make much of our fancied superiorities, but not one bit of it can survive examination. The only real hierarchy is that of the saints, and God has secured this hierarchy from the dirty sin of pride by designing that the more a man ascends in the order, the lower he sinks in self-esteem.

It is still a fact in England . . . that a man is usually judged in society, not at his real worth, but by his occupation. The first question anyone asks about a new acquaintance . . . is this 'What is he?' . . . The distinctions are not as sharp as once they were. . . . All alike defeat God's family idea.

Distinction of class cannot live in a family.

Let me Commend, pp 122–4

When Christ left the earth and His disciples saw Him no more, they were sharply aware of their own weakness. Their leader had three times denied the Master, and they had all deserted Him. What hope had they of carrying on the work?

But Christ had promised that God would come again in the Holy Spirit and that He would be with them for evermore. They waited in confident hope.

He came in the Holy Spirit at Pentecost and filled their souls. They never could explain the wonder of God within, though St John and St Paul (the two chief exponents of the gospel) tried very hard. John writes most of 'abiding' in God, and Paul of being 'in Christ' and having Christ 'in' him. They are describing the same experience.

Paul distinguishes nine fruits of the Spirit (Gal. 5^{20f}) with love as the first, and the basis of all the rest. He also has a hymn to love (1 Cor. 13) and he wants nothing so much as he wants his converts to be filled with this love. The nature of God, he says, can be in men and women. Indeed, the life of God in the soul of man is the very essence of salvation. Man can do more than *know* God: he can *have* God. Here is the central secret of the Faith—to have this pure unbounded love within. Have this and you have nothing left to long for. You have, indeed, the greatest thing in the world.

The Greatest of These . . ., p 9

Christ's coming gives us the truth about ourselves. I do not know how it is with you, but . . . when I meditate upon myself, I am brought very soon to depression.

There is such a contrast between the man I want to be and the man I am. So wide a gulf divides the ideal of holiness I carry in my heart and my meagre achievements. Even when my deeds pass scrutiny, my motives don't. How much have I ever done for the pure love of God? I come to the year's end and I look back over my past New Year resolutions, solemnly made, earnestly pursued, but O! so seldom achieved. I see that I am a strange being really, with something of largeness built into my nature, but more of littleness coming out; with longings to be clean through and through, but covered in stains.

I often wonder, as you must do: 'What is the truth about myself?' What—in the language of the theologians—is the real nature of man? And then I come to Bethlehem—and move to Nazareth, and to Capernaum, and follow Jesus through His lovely life. Here I see the man I ought to be.

So my longings after holiness are *not* an illusion! It happened once. A Man, who was tempted in all points like as I am, lived that life. It has been done. It shines through all the ages. Many who do not believe that He was God believe there was no man like this Man. Is this, then, the truth about myself.?

Westminster Sermons (vol. ii), pp 15–16

Isn't it best to leave children to form their own
ideas about Religion when they grow up?

People mean one of two things when they say this. Some mean that, while they will be careful to instruct their children in the Christian faith, and 'bed them down' . . . in some branch of the Christian Church, they will not . . . let them suppose that Christians in other branches of the Church are quite wrong. If, when they are grown, the children find their spiritual home in another section of the Christian family, they will not mind. . . . But it is not the usual one with people who ask this question. They mean to give their children no religious instruction at all. . . . All through the formative years of childhood—when children ask questions . . . they are put off with vague answers and grow up in a spiritual haze. The idea appears to be that, when they reach their teens, these uninstructed children will be able to line up in their minds the great . . . teachers of the world and say to the one they select '*I'll* have you'. As if (not being deeply impressed with the importance of these things) they will even want to! Children have a right to the best we have learned in every branch of life; in art, music, science, civics—and in religion too. The best this world knows in religion centres in Jesus Christ. To deprive children of instruction in His life and teaching is to rob them of something enormously precious. . . .

And don't deceive yourself that, if you are careful not to give the children any 'spiritual' ideas, they won't get any. They may make their own—or borrow bad ones! They may think the world exists just for their enjoyment, and the deep selfishness which is in us all may make them quite repulsive and impossible to live with.

Give God a Chance, p 92

The British people used to believe that they had a special and high destiny in the world. Some aspects of the idea were a little silly. The British Empire and the Kingdom of God got confused in their minds. Old memorial tablets in churches to generals and admirals leave the impression that whoever resisted British arms resisted heaven.

Most of that imperial pride has gone. God has a purpose for all peoples. The doctrine of the essential superiority of one race over others is false. . . . No nation can count on tomorrow which does not aim to bring its purposes into harmony with the purposes of the Almighty. Yet Britain could do that more swiftly than most peoples. She has a longer history and experience of self-government than any other large nation on the face of the globe. Her long enjoyment of civil and political and religious liberty has given her a maturity of judgement . . . which is still rare. . . . Vast changes have come in Britain but no civil war for nearly 300 years. Tolerance, fair-play and a freedom from frenzy mark this people. For all the spiritual disappointments of the times this nation has never deliberately turned its back upon God. The mass of Englishmen may neglect the Church, but they still want it there, and they want what it stands for in their soul.

If some forms of greatness have passed from Britain for ever, others remain. She can teach the family of men tolerance, fair-play, civil and religious liberty. She can teach how these may be achieved without war. . . . Britain has a high destiny still. Perhaps she could guide our race . . . to make humanity rather than nationality the important thing, to wipe away all that is evil in class and caste and colour and creed. . . . But only a new tide of religion would give the vision this crusade requires.

Revival: the Need and the Way, pp 7–8

You have all heard the name of Fletcher of Madeley—that great friend of John Wesley; the man whom Wesley designated as his successor in the leadership of the Methodist people, though (as it happened) Fletcher died before John Wesley and never came to the succession. Fletcher's biographer says of him 'He was more than Christian; he was Christlike'. Wesley said that he was the finest man he had ever met. When he had the solemn duty of preaching Fletcher's funeral sermon, he took a text from the Psalms: 'Mark the perfect man.'

Fletcher once made an important public utterance on a question which was agitating the country at the time, and rendered a signal service to the Government of the day. He didn't do it *for* that reason. He was—as ever—speaking what he believed to be true, but it had that consequence and the ministers of the Crown noticed it. . . . It occurred to the Lord Chancellor that, in return for this service . . . some preferment should be offered him; 'some promotion' as plain people would say. . . . When the official despatched by the Lord Chancellor called on the seraphic Fletcher at Madeley, he was at some pains delicately to hint at his errand, but the holy man was slow to take the hint. (Saints are terribly dull in some ways. Their wits are not sharpened by self-interest.) . . . The visitor asked if there was anything Mr Fletcher wanted? The Government would be very happy to . . . if . . . Mr Fletcher would understand. . . . And then perhaps some understanding *did* break on the mind of that good man and he said 'How kind! How *very* kind! But I want nothing . . . except more grace.'

Westminster Sermons (vol. i), pp 72–3

The Bible teaches that it was for the whole world that Christ died. 'God so loved the world. . . .' All the 'Comfortable words' of the Communion Service are universals. The unity and solidarity of the human race is a commonplace of modern thought. . . . From the shape of our nose to the idiosyncrasy of our temperament, we belong to others. . . . We are, in large part, the past. Even the future does not come from the front to meet us, but streams up over our head from the past. . . . Seeing that we gain so much by our place in the whole, we cannot complain too bitterly that we must bear the penalties of solidarity as well. Sin is the chief penalty. We come of tainted stock. . . . Many people today, interested in social righteousness . . . are deeply impressed with socialized sin. Sin inheres, they truly say, in the very system in which we live. . . . The 'world' which is condemned in the New Testament is the world organized apart from God. . . . Sin inheres in our whole system of life . . . sin infects *humanity*. . . . The problem is not a political theory, or a form of government, or what coloured rag blows over which bit of earth—but *sin*—sin which inheres in the whole race. Individuals illustrate the sublime outworking of the sacrifice, but it was offered for the *race*, and the sweep of this salvation encircles the whole world. A British soldier came across the body of a Japanese officer in the jungle, and buried it. Then he put a cross on the grave. . . . Later . . . he said 'I don't know what the padre would think, but he said once in a sermon that Christ died for all, so I don't see how I've done wrong. . . . I suppose Christ had a thought for that poor beggar too'.

They Met at Calvary, pp 95–8

Nor would I have you ignorant that the Day of Judgement is coming and you will be expected to give account. We do not know of what character the Judgement will be . . . but there can be no doubt of the fact. Nor is there any doubt as to the identity of the Judge. John tells us that all Judgement has been committed unto Jesus. How are you preparing for that Judgement? Are you polishing your excuses? Look at the face of your Judge! Remember what He suffered! Can you possibly offer that excuse to Him?

Will you plead a physical disability with Paul and Clifford and Helen Keller and Frances Ridley Havergal standing at His side? Will you say that it was your home with John Kitto standing there? Will you come up and whisper 'Illegitimate' with Alexander Whyte at His right hand? How can you?

. . . All these difficulties can be used for your own spiritual profit if you will come to them in the Spirit of God. There is a power with God, available to us all, that makes stumbling blocks into stepping-stones. I'm old enough to have learned this,* that the man who has every advantage is not the man to envy. The man who gets everything he wants, gets something he doesn't want: either an unsympathetic hardness of heart or a dangerous flaw in his will. Adversity is one of our greatest teachers. God polishes His jewels that way.

Why Jesus Never Wrote a Book, pp 98–9

* 1932.

I felt that Christ had given me birth
To brother every soul on earth

You find yourself loving people more—not just your relatives and friends, *all* people, even those whom by nature you don't like. You walk down the street and find love moving out from you even to the strangers you pass.

Your judgements are kinder. Though you are more sensitive to sin, you do not loathe the sinner. You feel rather a pity for him, though you may be yourself the object of his scorn and hate. Censoriousness goes, and even your occasional criticisms are guarded and loving.

Your vision seems keener. You see God more clearly in His creation, in people, trees, flowers, birds, stars. . . .

Your values change. Money seems less important. Above a modest level, you don't want it. You can give it away as God directs with ease and a sense of privilege. The little honours of life seem trifling. Office, position, titles, don't draw you. You can be sincerely happy with those whom these distinctions make happy, but you don't envy them.

Your attitude to death changes. Death remains awesome but not so terrible. It is only a doorway to the world where love has its perfect way. You do not clutch so fiercely at life as we have it here.

The Greatest of These . . ., p 11

Can Christ save us from self-pity? None better! One can comb the record of His days with scrupulous care and not find a trace of this unmanly vice. He suffered the cruellest treatment from His enemies, and from some He thought His friends, but his sensitive soul was never ensnared into self-pity. He saw all His problems in their true proportions because He saw them in the light of eternity, and neither faith nor courage wavered. How forgivable it would have been if, in the last few hours of His earthly life, betrayed, deserted, scourged and spat upon, His mighty heart had burst, and some great cry of compassion had fallen from his lips. But you will look for it in vain . . . there is no self-pity. Indeed, the selfless practice of His life is the whole motive of His death. His thought of others explains the death itself, and every detail of it. . . . In the High Priest's palace, and amid the raillery and abuse of the servants, He can turn to Peter, thrice-denying Peter, and save him with a look. His thought is so little of His sufferings that in the Praetorium, almost with an air of detachment, He can discuss with Pilate His mission in the world. . . . On the Cross itself He prays for His murderers, makes provision for His mourning mother, and grants pardon to a penitent thief. A heart so occupied with love for others is secure against self-pity. That is the great lesson which He is able to teach. Self-pity is begotten by selfishness out of sensitiveness. He can inspire unselfishness. Unselfishness and sensitiveness beget sympathy.

He is Able, pp 45–6

The saints obey God—utterly, instantly, gladly. . . . They make no assertion of themselves over against God. They seek only identity with Him. . . . they are not worried when they do not understand the reasons for His will. They obey it just the same. . . . Many saints come to look upon human reason (at its best) as an inadequate guide and (at its worst) a serious obstacle in obedience to God. The reason wants to know *why*. The saint only wants to know *what*. . . . 'Do not consult me', they say in effect. 'Command me!' . . . The only legitimate sphere they see for the use of human reason is, first (in times of perplexity) to make *sure* what God's will is and then, in how best to carry out the commands which He has given. . . . When tragedy overtakes them—or overtakes the community—they are assured that it is only blessing in disguise. . . . They are certain that God is on the throne of the universe. All things are in His loving hands. . . .

Now and then, brooding on the mystery of existence, the saint sometimes glimpses the Divine plan behind the seeming contradictions of earth . . . but when he *cannot* see it, the saint still trusts—and, trusting, he obeys. St Francis de Sales taught his people to greet God's will in all events—even the bitterest—with 'Yes, Father. Yes and always Yes' . . . and that glad cry was not, I need hardly say, a cry of stoical endurance. There are people who grimly boast in the face of calamity, 'I can take it', but that is not the spirit St Francis taught. He *welcomed* the will of God. He saw it always, as St Paul saw it, as 'the good and acceptable and perfect will of God'.

The Pure in Heart, pp 203–4

It is with the Church in its local life that the ordinary member has most to do. How can he make it nearer to the heart's desire? How can it best serve the interests of God's family on earth? It can serve the ideal best by illustrating and anticipating it. The local church must be a living, present-day illustration of what community life is like in Christ. . . . In every hamlet, town and village the local church must illustrate the social ideal of the faith. . . .

However simple the Church life may be [a man] should find himself in a fellowship which centres in the adoring worship of the Father-God. He should find the sweet equality of family life, with none of the world's distinctions obtruding in the sanctuary; no fawning upon wealth; no social superiorities and inferiorities; just the tacit admission that some have gone farther with God than others, and the quiet acceptance of the spiritual leadership of these strong souls who are gloriously unaware themselves that they belong to this aristocracy. . . . Bring the unbeliever into such a church. Let the man who says that human nature is so radically selfish that we can never have a wide family life on earth, sample fellowship of this quality. Keep him there till incredulity gives way to bewildered faith and he declares that 'if this were magnified to the size of the world it would be the Kingdom of God'.

What a task for the local church!—for *every* local church! . . . Is it not our plain duty—and one in which the humblest believer may have his share . . . that we show the world *now* —in microcosm—the society of our God's intention?

Let me Commend, pp 127–8

People who deny the existence of God, but feel the importance of morals, say that morality can be built into children's minds quite securely on their social instincts. We should teach them that all people have selfish instincts and social instincts, and that the art of life is to keep these instincts nicely balanced. When we are tempted to do wrong we should say to ourselves 'I must remember my social instincts. Other people must be considered too'. And then we shall do the right.

I sometimes wonder if these people know what real temptation is; whether they have ever been in a desperate jam, with careful lying as the only way out; or been in awful need of money, and had to fight night and day a neat little scheme which the subconscious mind has 'cooked-up'; or have ever known flaming lust, with fierce appetite and easy opportunity arriving together.

The idea of a tempted man in a desperate hour sitting down and saying to himself 'Now, now, I must remember my social instincts' borders on the ludicrous. . . . But if a man believes that the Ten Commandments were given by God, and that the Creator has all the right there is to lay down the rules of life, if that man can sense, moreover, behind the Commandments, the strong compassionate figure of Christ and hear Him say 'Let Me help you here', that man can win through. He may not do it, even then, without 'blood and sweat and toil and tears', but his chances are multiplied immeasurably. Those of us who know Christ know this; that the very *thought* of Him is cleansing, and to live with Him in our mind and heart is to have a steady victory over temptation.

Give God a Chance, p 93

By scientific standards of nutrition, one half of the world is hungry and a third of it is starving . . . and the cinema has penetrated to the jungle to portray the comparative opulence of Western life to the starving multitudes of the East. The uncounted millions of China and India want their place also at the feast . . . their half-empty stomachs lie behind the political and ideological ferment of the world. When people are hungry and so miserable that no situation could be worse, they are ready for revolution. . . . Meanwhile, most people in the Western World live on in the illusion that . . . the maintenance of their high standard of living is a sacred duty. Cars, radio sets, refrigerators and television seem more important to them than that their fellow-men should have a second meal a day. . . . Yet Christ died for all. His 'undistinguishing regard' moves out to all the children of men. In Him no racial superiorities and inferiorities can have any place. The prize He offers to the privileged is to share their privileges with those who are without them. Nor does He lack far-sighted servants who are seeking to work out His purposes in the most sacrificial ways, who are seeking the Christian answer to economic problems, who want to know how goods can be *given* without creating industrial chaos, who can prove the practical outworkings of Christian love. . . . Whoever so lives is moistening the lips of the Saviour, whether it be Albert Schweitzer living as a missionary-doctor in the steaming heat of the Gaboon, or Toyohiko Kagawa in the slums of Tokyo, or Frank Laubach fighting illiteracy. . . . There are thousands of others like them, unknown to fame. Christ knows them. They give Him a drink on the Cross.

They Met at Calvary, pp 73–5

Instant obedience to God does call for much passivity on the part of mortals. Charles Wesley sang:

> *Mould as Thou wilt Thy passive clay.*

But *active* obedience is called for also. Think of the massive *service* of the saints. Obedience to the will of God, even in the modern world, might lead in some lands to prison and to death. The deep answer to this question is in the saint's utter faith that God has all things in His hands. Loyalty to the will of God in any situation might lead the obedient servant to loss of property, limb, and life. This he quite understands and gladly accepts. Obedience to God might connect the saint—with all his passivity—in some widespreading revolution. He would not be seeking this deliberately, because all his deliberations in any moment are to do the will of God, but, if those consequences came, he would accept this also as God's will.

. . . The two basic principles of sanctity . . . attention and obedience. To those who were looking for something hidden and mysterious, they will seem simple to the point of absurdity. To those who say 'We knew it all the time' it will be enough to ask 'How are you getting on in the practice of them?'

> *The saint on his knees; his mind all adoration.*
> *The saint on his feet: his aim all obedience.*

It is as simple and as profound as that.

The Pure in Heart, pp 208–9

The word 'kindness' is sometimes used in a wishy-washy way to mean nothing but anaemic good-will. Used in the New Testament sense (Gal 5²¹) it is a noble fruit of the Spirit. Actually, it is love in its briefer contacts.

In the fullest sense of the words, you can hardly love and serve people you meet for a moment and never see again, but you often have the chance to be kind to them. Kindness can travel on a smile, a word, a secret prayer. . . .

When the contact is more prolonged, the kindness can be more sustained. A man or woman living under the guidance of God can often 'divine' the deeper needs of people and (with God's help) meet them too.

Those who are alert to the swift leading of God find the opportunities for kindness in every day as it comes and goes. The Holy Spirit being in them, they have the Breath of God about them wheresoever they go. Though they may say or do nothing in the railway carriage or the queue, their very presence affects the mental atmosphere and makes it easier for other people to be kind as well. . . . The multiplication of men and women filled with the love of God would transform the community.

So be kind. Kindness is a language all men understand. It breaks down barriers; it helps people to hope again; it restores their faith in their fellows . . . and, perhaps, in God. But it mustn't be done '*for*' that. It is tainted the moment *for* comes in. Kindness, being love in its briefer contacts, must never be *for* anything—except for itself alone.

The Greatest of These . . ., p 14

Do you remember that vibrant verse in the first chapter of St John's Gospel 'And of his fulness have we all received, and grace for grace'? That used to puzzle me when I was a youth. . . . Grace for grace? It almost sounds like an exchange. How could I barter with the Almighty and, not merely receive grace, but offer it too?

I think I know now. I believe that it means grace *succeeding* grace. . . . Refuse God's offer of grace at this level of your spiritual life and you have incapacitated yourself from receiving it at the next. . . .

I remember when I sat for my first scholarship. On the eve of the examination I was rather worried. . . . I remember going to my form-master and saying: 'Sir, they tell me that when I get into the examination hall tomorrow, I shall find my desk by a number, and that there will be half a dozen sheets of foolscap on the desk. What will I do, sir, when I have used the paper up?'

He laughed. 'You needn't bother about that', he said. . . . 'At the end of the hall, a gentleman in an academic gown will be sitting on a dais. . . . If you use up your paper, just go and ask him for more.' . . . It turned out just as he told me. When my racing pen had covered the paper, I ran down the aisle between the desks and panted to the invigilator: 'Paper! Paper!'

He just gave it to me. All I could *use*.

God is so eager to give His grace—and there is so *much* of it.

> *Grace is flowing like a river;*
> *Millions there have been supplied.* . . .

Westminster Sermons (vol. i), pp 74–5

Don't be so foolish as to envy the men who have every advantage in life. The absence of advantage is sometimes the greatest advantage of all. In a beautiful office, at the headquarters of a great business house, sits the principal's son. It is a lovely room, and marked, 'Private'. He sits there every day from ten till four o'clock and fiddles with a few papers. Nobody is impressed by him. He has no grip of the business. Even the office boy laughs at him behind his back. Nothing has been denied that young man all through his petted life: Father had the primrose path specially trimmed . . . and yet . . . it cannot be denied . . . he is a disappointment. Why? One cannot be sure, but keen observers say this—'He has never faced the provocation of awkward circumstances. The things his father had to fight for have fallen into his lap and consequently he has developed no tough fibre in himself'.

And *you* have sometimes envied a man like that! I am tempted to address you in the words of scripture and say 'Thou fool!' Can't you see what they've done with him? They've choked him with cream.

Rouse yourselves. Drop this self-pitying talk about never having a chance. We can be courageous if we cannot make a fortune. The truest success is certainly within our reach. Go forward in hope. The world is before you. God is above you. There is a chance even for you.

Why Jesus Never Wrote a Book, pp 99–100

Christianity and Stoicism unite in contempt of self-pity, but in place of the chilly acceptance of life which Stoicism teaches, Christ would make us wise to transmute it into something transcendingly beautiful, and can instruct us how, even, to *use* our woes. Nor is it hard to quote instances of His triumph in this task. One thinks of St Teresa, in constant and cheerful conflict with ill-health, battling all the time with her terrible headaches, those 'rushing waterfalls' in the head and with bouts of chronic fever, and at least one paralytic stroke. Yet nothing could daunt her courage or quench her gaiety. . . . A smile and a jest were never far away. In 1580 she fell a victim to influenza, and under the awful depression which influenza brings even her conquering cheerfulness seemed to wilt. But not for long. When she shrank from the dreadful cold of a winter journey, the Voice said 'Do not mind the cold. I am the true warmth' and she went forth, as ever, with a cheerful courage on.

Catherine Booth was never well. . . . Yet she lived to be the glorious mother of the Salvation Army, and to do a work for God almost unparalleled in feminine biography. Two years of terrible pain completed her titanic life, pain which she would never permit to be dulled, despite her husband's pleadings, by the kindly numbness of a drug. . . . She could say on her deathbed that she could not recollect a single day when she had really been free from pain. But . . . thankfulness and courage were with her to the end. The doctor who attended her at the last was an agnostic, and she was full of concern for his conversion. He said himself: 'Her courage and anxiety for my welfare were beautiful.'

He is Able, pp 46–7

Faith is not a camp-follower of the lumbering army of science. It is the reconnaissance plane. It goes ahead. It sees in wholeness. . . . Respecting reason as highly as we may and must, we cannot allow that nothing is knowledge which does not come by logic or the laboratory bench. Not that faith is *un*reasonable. Some saints, it is true, speak of reason with sharp scorn, but that is usually when reason is overweening and lectures the whole personality on the impropriety of enjoying anything until reason has explained it first. Fancy being forbidden to enjoy a rose until a botanist has told you what it is! The saints do not deny the *place* of reason. They deny that all life is reason, and they hotly deny that it is only the door to reality. True knowledge can exist without explanations. Indeed, the explanations must sometimes wait for a flash of intuition. Hence the deep inwardness of the superficially absurd word of St Anselm: 'I believe *in order* to understand.'

[The saint] makes no claim to explain all mysteries. But, as the reader of a mystery story might peep at the happy end and take up the narrative again, cheerful of the outcome though unaware of the method of unravelling, so the saint sees life. He doesn't know how the unravelling will come, and may watch the way of science with fascinated interest, but of the end he is sure. Reason will serve him, for reason also is a servant of God. But he does not *depend* on reason. His normal road to reality is that of spiritual divination. In some strange way, he sees the inwardness of things.

The Pure in Heart, pp 213–4

Certainly—if you don't mean it. But what makes you so sure that you are not a miserable sinner? Is it the word 'miserable' that you object to, or the word 'sinner'? 'Miserable' simply means 'worthy of pity'. But let us leave the word 'miserable' aside. Some people continue to be cheerful sinners, and others, who have quite a high opinion of their moral selves, are often miserable. Let us just ask if we are '*sinners*' or not.

The word 'sin' is variously used. Some religious people use 'sin' just for sex offences, drunkenness, gambling and playing games on Sunday. Clearly, the definition is too narrow. . . the chief thing wrong with men and women is not this thing or that thing, but their awful self-centredness. It is true of all people, until deep religion does something for them. 'Nice manners' can't alter it; they are a device for covering it up. People are saved when the centre of their life moves from self to Christ. Then they receive supernatural help to live for others. . . . People with spiritual passion want that more than they want anything. . . . Without Him at the centre of their life, they honestly feel that they are sinners (even if they are neighbourly and do plenty of 'good turns') because their basic disease has not been cured. . . . 'Well—we can't help that,' some people protest. 'We are made that way. That is human nature.' True enough. But if we can't do something about human nature, we are finished. . . . One of the confident claims made for Christ is that He can change human nature; but before a man is ready to be changed, he must recognize and admit that he is a sinner and *needs* changing.

Give God a Chance, p 94

God is so eager to give His grace—and there is so much of it. But it can't be wasted! You can have all you can *use*, but to have more you must use what you have.

. . . You *graduate* in its use. A man can't walk into a university and submit himself for a Doctorate. He must be a Master first in his field of study.

He can't walk in and just submit himself for examination as a Master. He must be a Bachelor first and (in the university I know best) an Honours Bachelor too. He can't submit himself for a Bachelor without his Intermediate, nor his Intermediate without his Matriculation. So it runs. There is nothing foolish and arbitrary about it. . . . It is only as you absorb learning at one level that you are able to absorb it at another. We advance. We *graduate*.

So it is with grace, With infinite patience God is leading us on, but we can't cut out any step He knows to be necessary. This is what some of you have tried to do. This is the reason why—having begun the life of discipline with zest—you've slackened off and move so slowly now that it is almost a question whether you are moving at all. Do you remember the disappointment St Paul felt over some of the Galatians? He said to them in his letter 'Ye *did* run well'.

'Ye *did*!' . . . How keen you were once! It wasn't just your youth. You were responding to grace, and it came in like the waves of the sea—grace succeeding grace.

That is what I suspect. The time came when God led you to some new task or surrender . . . and you sheered off. . . . That's when you ran on the sandbank. People who started long after you have swept past you. . . . God needs the whole of you as much now as He ever did. What are you going to do if my words carry conviction to your mind?

Westminster Sermons (vol. i), pp 75–6

A famous river flows near my home, and it is no uncommon sight to see the banks of the river dotted with anglers. I am no angler, but I like to watch them. With extreme care they select their bait and fix it to the hook; with marked attention they examine their line and float, and only when every detail has been scrutinized do they fling out and hope for a bite. One wonders sometimes why they are so careful, why they go to all the trouble they do. It must be that they have learned by experience, or concluded from reflection, that they cannot catch fish lying on the bank and putting their hand in. Their aim is fish, and so they observe with care all the lore of the angler's art. Nothing is too much trouble—that will procure the fish. . . . What keen angler ever sat on the bank and forgot that he was there for fish?

It is God we want. Only as we know Him do we live. We meet for worship, and we meet in vain unless the sense of His nearness has been intensified. We read the Word, and we read in vain unless—'Beyond the sacred page, we *find* Thee, Lord'. We pray, and do not pray unless our panting spirits commune with His. Our aim is life. By what power can the machinery of our faith be moved to produce in us the fruits of the Spirit! . . . Spontaneous love! Passion—if you will. Why does a poet write verse? . . . Something within him could only find expression thus. Can you conceive Shelley resolving one day to be a poet, and then learning the various metres by heart, and finally striving to force his wild imagination into the mould he had learned from another? No! . . . This it is that converts dry bones into living bodies, and mere forms into channels of the Spirit—the impelling force of love.

Why Jesus Never Wrote a Book, pp 104–5

But many people protest, even while they admit the benison of forgiveness, that it is not possible for normal men to forgo revenge. They are probably right, so far as it concerns men who do not know the grace of God, but they are plainly wrong if they refer to those who do. It becomes a question of fact . . . Mahatma Gandhi is not a member of the Christian Church, though those who know him best insist that the Spirit of Christ dwells in him. He has made no secret of his indebtedness to Jesus and the Sermon on the Mount. He says: 'It was the New Testament which really awakened me to the rightness and value of passive resistance, and love towards one's enemies. . . .'

In 1908 Gandhi was attacked and nearly murdered by a fanatical Moslem, but he refused to prosecute his assailant or even give evidence against him. On the day of the crime, and when he lay at death's door, he summoned his fast-ebbing strength to issue an appeal to his followers to take no steps against the man. 'This man', he said, 'did not know what he was doing. He thought that I was doing what was wrong. He has had his redress in the only manner he knows. I, therefore, request that no steps be taken against him. I believe in him. I will love him and win him by love.'

When Barnardo was a medical student in East London, he was involved in a riot in a beerhouse. He had gone in to sell Bibles, but the drunken ruffians inside attacked him with fury. . . . It was six weeks before he could move about again. . . . The police intervened and Barnardo was pressed to prosecute the ringleaders. He refused. 'I have begun with the Gospel', he said, 'and I am determined not to end with the law.'

He is Able, pp 52–3

And so we come to Advent . . . and to this pertinent word:
'The people that walked in darkness have seen a great light.'*
What is Advent? What makes it the beginning of the Church
year? It speaks to us of both the advents of our Lord: the first
and the second—though it is with the first that I want to deal
now. It is the first gleam of Christmas; it is the promise of His
coming; it heralds the entrance of the Divine into human
history; it is heaven descending to earth; it is a great event
casting its brilliance before it.

It is as though a trumpeter had taken his stand upon the
turrets of time and announced the coming of the King. 'Get
ready', he seems to say. 'Get ready. He is coming.' What a message! Welcome at all times, it is doubly welcome now. The
King is coming!

> *Let every heart prepare a throne,*
> *And every voice a song.*

Now why do I say that this message, welcome at all times, is
doubly welcome now? Because for years men have been seeking
to organize human life without God. They have tried to thrust
Him out of the universe which He has made. For years they
have laughed at the preacher and told him to drop his silly
patter about redemption. They have said that man has no
saviour but himself. 'If we must have religion', they argue, 'it
must be a religion without revelation—a religion of humanity
and not a religion of God.' Walt Whitman was their poet . . .
W. E. Henley was another of the same breed. The vanity of it.
The master of his fate and the captain of his soul!

Westminster Sermons (vol. ii), p 2

* Isaiah 9².

Almost all men have moments of vision. Alas! they are fleeting and momentary with most men, if only because men are so utterly immersed in this world, working to the clock, crowding their moments with a multiplicity of things, and not even believing that the other world is there. Sickness and sorrow alone will bludgeon some of them into spiritual sensitivity. Or perhaps a great joy! But, ever and anon, a glimpse comes: an intuition which gives meaning and coherence to their experience: a sudden insight which takes them for a moment out of this world. . . . If only they would attend to those moments, or attend to Him Who gives them, turning their whole personality in that direction and sensitizing their nature to the unseen! Then they would not impatiently brush aside the testimony of the saints as 'mysticism' but would see that this is the very heart of religion—even what is called *practical* religion—and the only religion with which a man can walk confidently in the dark.

Faith, of course, belongs to all human life. It underlies friendship, marriage, medicine, the home, business, science. . . . Maybe a greater faith is called for in religion. We mortals are so easily intimidated by the visible. But faith, like so much else in the spiritual life, grows by using what one has. To trust God and His purposes through all the disguises, disfigurements and plain contradictions of the seen, calls, no doubt, for heroism, without which no man can aspire after sanctity. And therein lies, in part, the preciousness of the saints! They have pioneered this way for us, following the Great Author and Pioneer of our Faith, and we can mark the footsteps which they trod and find our way to heaven.

The Pure in Heart, p 216

Undoubtedly. It is a pity that Christians have not always realized and acknowledged it. Some men and women who doubted or denied the existence of God have been leaders in social reform and splendidly generous in the service of their fellow-men.

Some unbelievers have served us, also, in bravely challenging the bigotry of other days, and have had their honourable share in securing the freedom of thought we all now enjoy. The Christians who fought slavery had among their finest colleagues men who denied God's existence but who were busy on God's work.

Yet it is interesting to see how often these people came out of Christian homes. I once made a study of the lives of these men and women . . . almost without exception they had had the advantage of a Christian upbringing.

The two facts are not unconnected; their high regard for morals, their passion for social progress, their hatred of injustice and wrong, sprang from the religion they had come to reject. . . .

A traveller once came upon a tribe of people who were moon worshippers. He expressed some surprise at the preference and said that he would have expected them to worship the sun. 'But why?' they enquired. 'The sun foolishly shines in the day-time when there is plenty of light. The moon conveniently shines at night when it's dark!'

They did not know, either, that the moon was borrowing its light from the sun! Militant unbelievers sometimes multiply in their imagination the social service of those who share their views (and Christians must be careful not to *minimize* it), but even so, it is usually a borrowed light. Their moral zeal derives from the religion they have now tossed aside.

Give God a Chance, p 96

How were the slaves freed in the British Empire? Did all England wake up one morning and say 'This is wrong. We must free the slaves.' No! One man woke up one morning with the groan of God in his soul, and William Wilberforce and his friends laboured until that most splendid hour in our history, when Britain was worthy of herself and, under no pressure from anybody but the pressure of her own conscience, paid a larger sum than her national debt to free the slaves.

How was all the social trouble after the industrial revolution ameliorated? God groaned in the head of Lord Shaftesbury, and he toiled and toiled to serve and save the poor. How were the prisons cleaned up in England? Did everybody suddenly say 'These prisons are places of indescribable filth'? No! God groaned in the hearts of John Howard and Elizabeth Fry. How were the orphans rescued from the streets of London? A century ago (as recently as that!) God groaned in the heart of Thomas Barnardo. Progress is *not* mechanical. There is no ethical evolution in man alone. Progress is by the echo of the groan of God in the hearts of men and women. And you need never despair for our wayward race while 'the Spirit Himself maketh intercession for us with groanings which cannot be uttered'.

Westminster Sermons (vol. i), p 84

The Pharisees present the most terrible illustration in all history of how good people can go wrong. You can be an upholder of the law; you can be a close student of the Book; you can be forward in all things that make for the moral well-being of our race, and yet you can go as terribly wrong as the Pharisees went. . . .

It is usually spiritual pride which ensnares men of this quality. They reach the dizzy heights of moral achievement and they forget that one can only live at those heights upon one's knees. They begin to think that they themselves are the architect of their own virtues. . . . Most people who would have any interest in this book are probably regarded as 'good' people in their locality. . . . Let us remember . . . that unless our lives are controlled by the Holy Spirit, we also may go tragically wrong. It is a particular danger of the good at any time. . . .

. . . It is a sad thing when the warm life of God in Jesus is chilled by the rigour and coldness of our moral codes. . . . I have known good men, whose word was their bond, who were honest in all their business dealings, just and above reproach in the commerce of the nation, and yet strangely lacking in tenderness and in that melting love we look for in a follower of Christ. We stand for strict moral principles, but . . . when an unmarried girl comes in penitence to confess that she is to be a mother, let us not spurn her . . . but stretch out loving hands and help her back to God. . . . When a man, disregarding our counsel, finds himself in the grip of alcoholism, let us . . . keep the fellowship unbroken. . . . The Pharisees had lost tenderness. If we lose tenderness, we shall be more guilty than they because we have a Nobler Example.

They Met at Calvary, pp 21–3

No machinery runs without motive power: it is heavy and cumbrous until the current is supplied; but then everything performs its function and nothing is found to be superfluous. When our lives are dominated by love for Him—love that begets an utter determination to be like Him—the machinery of our faith throbs with a new-found power and reveals itself as efficient for its task. Christian fellowship becomes a real joy: the New Testament is an irresistible book: prayer cannot lose its wonder and charm: the Holy Communion is a boon never to be missed. . . .

To the poet and musician the love seems to come first, and they learn the rules or make new ones as they go along. Many of us learned the rules first. We were brought to Church: told to read the Bible: taught to pray—and it's all very proper and very dull until the love of Christ grips the heart. Then dullness and monotony fly: it all becomes amazingly rich and new: existence has flowered into life.

Religious observance was the most utterly boring thing I knew until I felt the touch of God's reality and the swelling Christ-ward heart. That is why the average congregation moves me to a mingled admiration and pity. I see so many people who are splendidly dutiful but painfully bored. . . . I have a friend who was one of the first men to take a B.Sc. degree in Aeronautics at London University. He designs aeroplanes, superintends their building, repairs them and improves them . . . but he cannot fly. He knows all about it—and nothing.

You may know all about the machinery of the faith. Have you ever flown into His burning presence? Did the mists roll away? Could you say in simple spiritual truth, 'Here, O my Lord, I see Thee face to face'?

Why Jesus Never Wrote a Book, pp 105–6

Perhaps no instance of sublime forgiveness comes quite so near the spirit of Calvary as that of Edmund Campion the English Jesuit. . . . He has been praised by Protestants and Roman Catholics alike. In the days when his co-religionists were persecuted in this country, he perilously moved from place to place, nourishing their spiritual life and narrowly avoiding arrest. But he was caught at last. Betrayed by one of his own people turned apostate, he was thrown into the Tower of London and thrice tortured on the rack. But nothing could shake either his constancy or serenity, and he heard his sentence to be hanged, drawn and quartered at Tyburn, with the calmness of a man whose life was stayed on God. He actually broke into the Te Deum. A day or two before his execution, he had an amazing visitor. The spy who had betrayed him, and knew his own life to be in hourly peril from the rage of old friends who had learned of his part in the arrest, staggered into Campion's cell, behind a jailer, and begged to be forgiven. The condemned man was weak from torture, and anticipating Tyburn, but he did not hesitate. He fully and freely forgave him. Still the traitor lingered. Would the gracious father do more? Would he help him escape the fury of his pursuers? Even this the betrayed man was ready to do. . . . He promised him a letter of introduction to a German nobleman who would accept his service, and on a rainy December morning he was tied to a hurdle and dragged from the Tower to Tyburn, through the filth and garbage of the London gutters. No hate, no bitterness, no lust for revenge. He went up the cart at the place of execution as though he were going to a wedding.

He is Able, pp 54–5

Meditation more than syllogistic reasoning is the common and natural activity of the saints. It is the way they enter that other world. Wrapt from earth, abstracted from time and sense, disciplined in concentration on spiritual things, masters of a technique fully known only to themselves, they slip through the veil—and see.

Small wonder that they come to hold loosely, and even to despise, earthly possessions, positions, honours, dignities, reputations, and even their own physical life. We see in a mirror darkly. They see face to face. Other men, seeking to understand the experience of the saints . . . have come to understanding by considering the human experience of falling in love. What is the strange movement of the human heart that can select one person from the thousand known members of the other sex, and put a supreme worth on the one? The mind is involved certainly, but it is not a judgement of mind only. (There is always something mildly amusing about a wife selected merely on a basis of reasoned thought. One remembers the tales that circulated concerning Kant who is said twice to have projected marriage but on both occasions lost the lady by protracted weighings of the pros and cons, and by calculating whether or not he could afford it.) The heart and the will are most certainly involved. The whole personality moves out in desire and self-giving, but who can 'explain' it? A man, trying to explain why he loves a certain girl, mentions half a dozen ordinary virtues, found in many other women who excite in him only the mildest admiration, and then he lamely leaves off, aware that the tenth has not been told. . . . To write off the piercing perceptions of the saints because they cannot explain them is not less foolish than to deny the reality of love because it will not go into a syllogism.

The Pure in Heart, pp 217–18

A man must settle this question for himself. It comes out of the very inside of him. It doesn't depend on how much science he knows . . . and in some senses it doesn't depend on how much he knows *about* God. I say *about* God. There are at least two ways of knowing. We can know by hearsay, and we can know by personal experience. . . . People with a personal experience of God don't know *about* God; they know *God.* Yet . . . these private reasons can't be given away, and a man without that experience may feel that he knows only *about* God. What answer has he to [this statement]?

He must go . . . inside himself. Uninfluenced, at the moment, by those who argue for a creator or against Him, let him look at the world. He sees purposefulness everywhere—in the lower forms of life and in the higher, in birds, beasts, fish, and men. . . . There is purpose everywhere. In man, it flowers. His amazing mind is now probing outer space, and he plans to land on the moon.

If there is a recognized purpose in the parts, is there none in the *whole?* Is it credible to suppose that all this came by blind chance? Is it fully rational to suppose that the mind of man is the highest mind in the universe? Did unreason produce reason?

This is what a man must settle for himself. I am with those who say 'It *couldn't* have just happened'.

Give God a Chance, p 98

So impressed are some people with the evil character of fear that they are disposed to make it the arch-demon of all life and they say 'There is nothing to fear but fear'. It is an exaggeration, but the exaggeration is pardonable. Many of our fears have no basis in reality. They are the home-made products of over-anxious hearts and as unsubstantial as the Spectre on the Brocken. The Brocken is the highest point of the Harz Mountains in Germany. For centuries it was a place of dread because of the giant who lived upon its top. Many times had the giant been seen. Credible witnesses solemnly swore that they had watched him, and people avoided the mountain as a place too dangerous to approach. But, with the advance of learning, thoughtful men grew sceptical about the giant and made investigations. And this is what they found. They found that reliable witnesses had seen the giant only at sunrise or sunset— i.e. when the sun's rays were horizontal. They found also that he appeared only when the Brocken was free of cloud and when its neighbours were covered with the mist, and they guessed the truth at once. The ghostly and terrifying spectre which the traveller sees upon the sky is nothing but a magnified and distorted image of himself. He trembles at his own reflection. He flies at his own shadow. He thinks he is being pursued by monstrous and uncanny fiends, but he is being dogged by nothing but a diseased imagination. *Some* of our terrors are like that. They are simply not real. . . . Jesus sweeps that litter from our minds. . . . These unsubstantial fears vanish when the wind of the Spirit blows through them and the Sun of Righteousness appears.

He is Able, p 23

Modern life and thought have their substitutes for Christ. A host of teachers would instruct us how to dispense with Him. . . . Let us shut the Bible and put it from us. Let us wipe the thought of Jesus from our mind and face a few of our practical problems without Him and let us see how we fare. Take, for instance, temptation. . . . Does modern life provide us a helper in this time of need? Yes! . . . Advertisements assure us that our whole case can be dealt with. . . . You know how the advertisements run, . . . 'We will kill your fears. A postcard brings our prospectus!' 'How to have a will of iron. Send three penny stamps' . . . I do not deny that there is some slight merit in these proffers of help. It is a little tabloid psychology, useful in a narrow sphere for a man already grimly determined . . . but utterly powerless in itself to succour a man faced with great temptation. . . . 'Sir, what can you do for me? I seem incapable of concentration. . . . I am bound by bad habit . . . and I have lost hope. Only some power outside myself can save me. Sir, can you mediate such power to me?' What answer have the adverts to this? They have no answer. . . . They cannot salvage the man of palsied will tossed on humanity's scrap-heap. Where shall we direct these needy souls? . . . I do not know . . . unless . . . we open this book again and direct them to Christ. To whom else can they go? But if I open this book I have amazing hope for them. . . . There are reserves of power in Christ that can be marvellously effective in their succour. I do not know how He does it . . . but I am in no doubt as to the fact. . . . I know no modern or ancient substitute for Christ. From my own knowledge of temptations I would not care to face them without Him. Men and women, there is no sure substitute for Christ in the hour of your tempting!

Why Jesus Never Wrote a Book, pp 108–110

. . . The most dangerous thing about money. It seduces the heart from God, and men look upon it as the ground of their security, and the spring of their confidence. When some dark fear of the future crosses their mind, their thoughts dart off to their money instead of to their God. 'I will be all right,' they think. 'I've got that.' Yet that simple movement of the mind has perilous consequences. In the passing of the years it builds a false faith on something which cannot sustain them in the darkest hours of life, and filches trust from the One who is alone sufficient for their need. Anything which weakens the conviction that our security is only in God is dangerous, and nothing weakens that conviction more than the love of money. A high sense of stewardship is the antidote. . . . Faithfulness in stewardship has another glorious fruit too. It saves a man from cursing his children with a fortune. It is serious enough . . . to live for money and go to face the Great Audit with a record of jealous hoarding and niggardly giving, but it is not less serious to pass on the awful responsibility to a child. What splendid lives have been spoilt in this way. How few can carry the responsibility well. Of what fine service has the world been robbed in those who never needed to extend themselves because their fathers made them 'independent' and who never displayed their best because they never faced the provocation of awkward circumstances. . . . Wesley foresaw this awful danger among the men who followed him, and . . . he warned them against the peril of leaving fortunes to their children. . . . His own use of money was plainer than his words. He made tens of thousands of pounds out of his publications, and died leaving little more than his silver spoons.

He is Able, pp 61–2

Here is the place for the will to believe!—not the conversion of desire into credulity and persuading yourself into what you know to be untrue, but the openness of the whole personality to God...a readiness to think *with* God: to wait unhurriedly upon Him for the insights He can give: the meek teachableness which is meet in mortals dealing with the Divine. . . .

The will to believe must be present, not as a superior form of self-deception and a device for hiding honest doubt, but as giving opportunity to the divine aid by which alone we can expect to come to truth. Hence the gravity with which the New Testament regards unbelief. 'They could not enter in because of unbelief.'* In this sense, unbelief becomes . . . the root of all sins, because it makes deliverance from all other sins impossible. The man who hesitates to embrace Christianity because its very attractiveness may trap him into self-deception, and who fears that he is accepting things as true because he would greatly like them to be so, should comfort himself with this; that God would have been unable to reveal those objective spiritual truths unless he had wished to believe them. The divine law is that those who seek shall find—and they alone. The failure of many to find God is not because God had hidden Himself. They have not hungered and thirsted. They have not asked and sought. . . .

Faith . . . is always something that acts. . . . It does not merely survey the unseen world and find God: it obeys Him. . . . The belief of the devout soul that the real is the spiritual has to be tested and proven in the way [a man] lives—and the saints stand out because, more than most men, they have proved their faith by their life.

The Pure in Heart, pp 220–1

* Hebrews 3¹⁹.

By no means. . . . We have *insight*. Some light falls for us on the dark road, but we cannot clear up the problems of cancer, or why one type of animal feeds on another, or why there are 'faults' in the earth's surface . . . or many other things either.

. . . The most devout Christians have areas of reverent agnosticism in their minds, and to suggest that we have 'all the answers' is foolish and vain. The Bible never claims to answer every question any man might ask. It claims to be a 'lamp to our feet'—that is, to give enough light to show a path through this dim world.

What Christians claim in 'Christian experience' is not to pick up a body of wrought-out knowledge on the cheap, and to have a pat reply to all the mysteries of the universe, but to be aware of a Presence. . . . As the Christian responds to the Presence and ventures forward, he becomes acquainted with a Person—holy, loving and merciful, and One who proves His personal care over all who turn to Him in trust. It is being sure of God and His nature which enables Christians to be sanguine in the face of ugly problems which they cannot solve. If God is there and God is love, all must ultimately be well; there *must* be an answer to these mysteries, even though it eludes us at present. To be sure of God is *not* to have the answer to all things, but to be sure that we *shall* have it some day, and that, when we have it, we shall see that it was woven with wisdom and with love.

Give God a Chance, p 104

... the window [in Liverpool Cathedral] near the entrance to the Lady Chapel, dedicated to some of the wonderful women of our race. It would interest you to see that window! Florence Nightingale, the noble nurse, is there, and Susanna Wesley, the mother of John and Charles; Josephine Butler, who fought the white-slave traffic, is there, and Grace Darling—in popular esteem the heroine of the Farne Islands. Those noble women are crowded together in one window, and I think, if you are a well-informed person, you would know them all . . . except perhaps one! Let me try her name out on you now to see how many of you know it. In that window of wonderful women, Kitty Wilkinson finds place. Kitty Wilkinson!

'And who was Kitty Wilkinson?' you ask.

Ah! I feared you would not know. She was the saint of char-women. I have a picture of her in my study. Her lovely life is little known beyond Liverpool, but they know it there and she has a place in that wonderful window. When the cholera came to Merseyside and everybody who could do so fled, she stayed and fought the cholera, becoming the foster-mother to forty-five orphaned children and earning their keep by washing and scrubbing in other people's homes.

She was the pioneer of the public washing-house. The first one that was ever opened in the country was opened by the authorities as a result of her influence. In my picture of Kitty Wilkinson it shows her hands. They are gnarled and shapeless. Forgive the word—they are 'knobbly' and swollen at the joints. . . . But what tender hands! These are the hands of the woman who mothered the motherless; these are the hands of our Blessed Lord Himself used in the slums of Liverpool more than a century ago.

Westminster Sermons (vol. i), pp 92–3

Epaphras was . . . ready to notice and to praise the virtues of his people. He wasn't obsessed only with their faults. They had them! . . . The little church at Colossae . . . was like most other churches; it had its imperfections. Nobody was more aware of his people's faults than Epaphras . . . I can imagine him going over them in his mind at the hour of his private devotions. There's Claudius, who prides himself on his modern ideas and is drawn to this gnostic heresy. . . . There's Fulvius, who is so hard to get into . . . regular work for the Master. There's Flavia, who is in danger of thinking more of her beautiful home than of her soul . . . and Mundanus, whose spiritual life is rather shallow; who never seems to get above the spirit of the counting-house. . . . But when he made the journey from Colossae to Paul in Rome, he didn't greet the Apostle with the list of his people's imperfections. He said, 'Paul, let me tell you of their love in the Spirit. There's Claudius—he has a big heart. I have only to tell him of somebody's need and he is asking me "What can I do to help?" And there's Fulvius, so free from criticism . . . so willing to believe the best. And there's Flavia; she is given to hospitality. . . . And there's Mundanus, who is so conscientious in the business affairs of the church, so . . . attentive to detail and wise in administration. They have their faults of course, and I do not minimize them, but they are God's people with all their faults and His grace will sanctify them yet.'

And Paul listened gladly, and when he settled down to write to the Colossians he spoke of their dear-fellow-servant Epaphras, 'your faithful minister of Christ, who declared unto us your love in the Spirit'.

Why Jesus Never Wrote a Book, pp 116–18

Knowing both the worth and worthlessness of money, and knowing also how ridiculous is its claim to be the chief aim of life, the steward can never fawn on wealth in others. It amazes and saddens him to see the strange adulation which men offer to others merely because they possess much money, and he gazes in bewilderment on a world where values are so strangely mixed that money is pressed on pugilists and those who amuse us, and denied to poets and master musicians, and men engaged in medical research. Milton received £5 for Paradise Lost, and another £5 when the first edition was exhausted: £10 in all for the greatest work of the second greatest figure in English letters. Tunney received $200,000 for his first fight with Dempsey. Beethoven lost £20 in producing the immortal Ninth Symphony, and Sir Ronald Ross, who discovered the secret of malaria, had to sell his papers in the eventide of life to provide himself and his wife with modest comfort; but a star baseball player earns (or receives) $30,000 a year for knocking a ball with a bat. There are fortunes for fisticuffs, but poverty for poetry and research. Yet, with all these absurd examples before their eyes, men still fawn upon wealth, and treat its possession as a ground for praise. Not so the steward. He cannot despise money because he knows the precious things that it can do, but he cannot praise it. It is a 'thing', it is meant to serve life. . . . He waits quietly on God for guidance, and seeks to use his substance in accordance with the Divine will. At the last, he hopes to hear His Master say 'Well done, good and faithful servant, enter thou into the joy of thy Lord.'

He is Able, p 62

Hartley Coleridge said:

> *Think not the faith by which the just shall live*
> *Is a dead creed, a map correct of heaven . . .*
> *It is an affirmation and an act*
> *That bids eternal truth be present fact.*

The saints live like that. Hence, at times, the imprudence of their lives judged by worldly wisdom! If one wrote an account of the 'folly' of the saints as men of the world see it, it would take many volumes. Yet it is, of course, the plain sense of things as the saints see life. Looked at in the light of eternity, what madness fortune-building is! How insane that men should scheme for a title which means little enough now, and nothing hereafter! . . . What is praise, power or position with the hearse at the door? The saint is distinctive only because he sensibly acts on what he sees. If anybody is a fool, it is not he. Moreover, the might of active faith is seen here also, in another way. We have already noticed the picture in the Gospels, of the world encompassed by the mighty power of God Who is forever seeking an entrance into human life but is so often frustrated by the unbelief of men. Faith provides, we have said, the point of entry. When it is faith of the quality of the saints, the power comes in as a flood. Miracles happen. Indeed, they are almost commonplace. Müller and Bosco have nothing but their faith, yet they feed their orphans, feed them by the thousand, and feed them for years. The Sadhu Sundar Singh crosses oceans without money. William and Catherine Booth call a great international army into being. . . . It is almost beyond the range of imagination to dream of all that God could do in this world if multitudes rose to the faith which opens our lives to power.

The Pure in Heart, pp 221–2

It isn't in religion only. Some of the most lovely things in life would be spoilt if trust were taken away and a doubting mind demanded proof where no proof could be given. Imagine a couple on the eve of their wedding. Suppose the bride picks up an evening paper and reads a report of the latest batch of broken marriages. . . . A doubt comes into her mind. . . . She turns to her bridegroom and says, 'How do I know that you will always love me? *Prove* it to me.'

What can the poor fellow do? He may say: 'We've known each other for five years. I've always been true. *Of course* I love you'. . . . Yet she persists. She says, '*Prove* it to me. Prove it to me for the future, when I'm old and grey and ill.'

What *can* he do? He will have to say: 'You must trust me. I am worthy of your trust. . . . The years will prove it.' But now a doubt intrudes into *his* mind. What is wrong with the girl, he wonders. She wouldn't keep saying 'Prove it to me' if she wasn't doubting herself. So she doubts *him*! There is hurt in that. Trust is lovelier than proof. Proof compels. Trust confides. Trust may seem less sure than proof, but it is more beautiful, because it doesn't need proof. Proof isn't better than trust in the tenderest relationships. It isn't so good.

God says 'Trust Me. I don't compel your minds and hearts. You are free to give or withhold your trust and your love. But let us live together. The passing years will bring their own experience of My constancy, and, in My own way, I will make you sure.'

Give God a Chance, p 105

The most daring thing the devout man ever says about his religion is 'I know'. Not 'I think', 'I hope', 'I trust', 'I venture', 'I believe' . . . but 'I *know*'.

He claims to know God for himself. He says (in effect) that in something of the same way by which a music-lover enters into a new realm by lovely sound, and the art-lover enters in a new world by lovely colour, so, by faith, he enters a realm where he transcends the faith he first needed, and now he can say '*I know*'.

It is, of course, an extraordinary thing to say. To know God. To glimpse the purpose of existence. To be certain that in prayer, in worship, in the Bible, at the Holy Table . . . one truly has fellowship with the Ruler of the Universe. The claim is quite staggering. Yet multitudes of rational people make it and are so sure of God that, when calamity overtakes them they are still unshaken and confidently assert that

> . . . . *One above*
> *In perfect wisdom, perfect love*
> *Is working for the best.*

Put into precise terms, the experience which is claimed is one of immediate acquaintance. It is not 'knowledge about', as I might have knowledge about, say, Bouvet Island in the South Atlantic (where I have never been and am never likely to go) but immediate experience such as I had for years with my father, at whose side I grew up, on whose strength I relied, and to whom I could turn for help in every way. The heart of religion is not an opinion about God, but a personal relationship *with* Him. Judge yourself how near you are to the heart of religion by that!

Westminster Sermons (vol. i), pp 114–15

All normal people want at times to unburden their heart and mind. They may be plagued by fears—substantial or unsubstantial. They may have business or domestic worries. There are times when the most robust Protestant feels a longing for someone strangely like a confessor.

. . . Gloriously rich is that church which includes wise, mellow, holy men and women who beget confidences and can either supplement a minister's pastoral work, or even, by their secret counsel, humbly supply an element of ministry which might be altogether lacking in him. Here is secret service of the first order. Perhaps only rare souls can reach up to the height of this. But to be in any measure a spiritual director is a vocation so high that it is hard to think higher.

What equipment is required?

First and chiefly, to be really deep in the things of God: to know Him intimately in experience; to love His book and be something of a master of prayer. And then, to know the human heart; its longings and weaknesses; its tortuous ways and self-deceits; its mingled courage and cowardice; its ineradicable ache for God.

Add to this the supernatural love which God gives His servants to make them truly pitiful to sinners and easy to talk to; the power to conceal any sign of shock at the most awful confessions, and an utterly unbreakable guard on all secrets committed to one's care . . . and one is, at least, ready to begin. The Holy Spirit and experience will do the rest.

Methodist Magazine, 1947, pp 198–9

I could put before you now the testimony of men and women who lived hundreds of years apart from one another; came from different races, and grew up in different ecclesiastical communions, but, as you read their testimony, you would see the essential coherence of it all: Blaise Pascal, the Roman Catholic; Isaac Pennington, the Quaker; John Fletcher, the Methodist; John Bunyan, the Independent; Charles Spurgeon, the Baptist; Handley Moule, the Low Churchman . . . all their testimonies harmonize. They are speaking of the same experience. They know!

What a weight of testimony! Can you resist it? Are you, my friends, to whom I am especially addressing myself this morning, content to sit there and be reminded of the weight and the quality and the coherence of this witness, and brush it all aside and say, 'There is nothing in it. *I* have never had such an experience.' Are you the final test of truth? You are too modest to think so! Things can be true enough, though so far, they have not come within your own experience.

Face this fact; it is possible to *know* God; it is possible for mortals in this shadowed world to have fellowship with the All-Highest. If you shut yourself out from that experience, you are (as I say) like some poor, blind fellow stumbling through life with his eyes closed to the wonder and rapture of the world of light.

Westminster Sermons (vol. i), pp 119–20

The saints know that they are working with Another. The unseen world is flooding by faith into the visible world. Its own laws vindicate themselves. Paradoxical on this plane, they are commonplace on that. We gain by giving. We live by dying. We win by loving. The saints see the eternal truth there, and they sense its transforming power here. By this means, this terrestrial world could be transformed into the celestial one. So by faith they press on. They cannot explain the paradoxes, but they are sure that they are true. Somehow this certitude of inner spiritual truth takes the fear and challenge from this sneering visible world of contradiction. The unravelling—as in the mystery story—is still not clear, but the consummation will be sweet. Doubt disappears from the mind of the saint, and he enjoys that certitude which is one of the conditions of his sanctity.

Those who follow the saints—even though it be a great way off—can take encouragement from their example. Nor are they left even in the foothills without confirmations of the way. Conscience lifts its warning voice at all turning from the track. Ideals of goodness beckon them from above. Their inmost nature, as spiritual, yearns for satisfaction in the spiritual world. And their ears hear a word behind them, saying, 'This is the way, walk ye in it'.*

The Pure in Heart, p 222

* Isaiah 30[21].

358

Think on Thy pity and Thy love unswerving;
Not my deserving

There are four ways by which you can become a freeman of the City of London. First, you can become a freeman by servitude—the way my old grandfather became a freeman of the City. Any male citizen of full age, on completion of his apprenticeship to a freeman, can become a freeman himself. You work your passage!

. . . There is no way into the City of God by servitude. You cannot work your passage to Heaven. Men of rigorous morality have tried to do so in every age, but they have always failed. There is no road that way. The Pharisees tried it. John Wesley tried it before his conversion. Misguided men and women are trying it still.

People outside the Churches, and uninstructed in evangelical religion, often say 'No, I don't go to church, but I never miss the opportunity of doing someone a good turn. . . .'

They do not draw the inference in so many words, but it is there. 'My good turns will get me into Heaven, if there is a Heaven to get into. Clearly, that is the place where I belong.'

My dear friends, your good turns will not get you into Heaven. At your finest, you are an unprofitable servant. There is something to be forgiven in the best things you ever do. If you put all your service into one scale—all your good turns and all your kind thoughts—and, in the other scale, your mean thoughts, your unkind words, your shabby motives, your gross self-centredness and all your bad turns (which you have probably forgotten) can you doubt which way the scale would go down? Can you not hear the righteous sentence 'Thou art weighed in the balance, and found wanting'?

Westminster Sermons (vol. i), pp 125–6

Stars are lovely to look at—but they can't *love*. Flowers are beautiful—but they have no heart. It says in the florist's window: 'Bouquets and Wreaths.' Either! The flowers don't mind. They will come to the wedding or the funeral. It is all the same to them. They are beautiful, but they are not personal. The mountains are majestic, but there is no comfort in their cold hearts.

Dr Stanley Jones has told a story of a little boy who stood before a picture of his absent father, and . . . said wistfully, 'I wish Father would step out of the picture'. That little boy expressed, in his own way, the deepest hope of the deepest souls who lived before Christ. They believed in God! Socrates and Plato did—the finest of the Greeks. The ancient Eastern sages did: . . . with overpowering intensity the Hebrew prophets did: Isaiah, Jeremiah, Ezekiel, and all the rest of them . . . the most daring of them rose even to believe that the great Creator of the universe might be called a Father. . . . In their heart, this longing, I fancy, could easily have taken shape: 'I wish the Father would step out of the picture'. . . .

Oh for a warm heart in the Universe. . . . Listen! Listen! He stepped out of the picture. He stepped out at Bethlehem. Here is the glorious truth of it: 'The Word became flesh and dwelt among us. . . . No man hath seen God at any time; the only begotten Son, which is in the bosom of the Father, He hath declared Him.'

Westminster Sermons (vol. ii), pp 10–11

In the saints it is total commitment. They do not pray in 'faith' for something and are then surprised (as we are) when it occurs! They believe utterly. Hence the miracles that occur through them. God can do His mighty works because of their belief.

How did their faith grow to these heroic dimensions? Largely because they acted on it. Picture a fledgling peering over the nest into the empty air. Is it possible that the air can hold him up? Is it not plain madness to push out into space? Does not death clearly await him as he goes? But some instinct stirs within him and he spreads his wings. Or his mother destroys the nest and snatches his snug security away. Over the edge he goes and proves that the empty air is the element devised in order to hold him, and not only to hold him, but to lift him to the upper skies.

The saint has spread his wings, lives now in the element, and soars to the skies. The great winds of the Holy Ghost bear him aloft. All his dependence is on the Divine Spirit for power and for perfecting, and to the Third Person of the Blessed Trinity he says:

> *Inspire the living faith. . . .*

By the saint's faith, God not only works miracles *through* him but the greatest miracle *in* him. . . . The Lord lives again in His servant and the great longing of these servants is that He might live in us all. . . . The Christ was who born *for* us can be born *in* us.

The Pure in Heart, p 223

I often speak a defensive word for the Puritans. I hope to do so many times again. I think that one of the things which is wrong with our country is that the Puritan contribution has been scorned of recent years. The iron that these men put into the blood of our nation is a necessary element in our corporate health.

But I admit quite plainly that they had one chief fault. Too many of them left joy out of religion. They made life grey— almost literally so. John Milton's grey cloak was symbolic! Not even his friends would have said that there was much joy in his life, and its absence was not altogether due to his blindness.

. . . Some of that influence survives still in the Church. There are still folk among us who frown on mirth; to whom the most wholesome joke is irreverent; who filter all pleasures in all anxious ways, and who regard a visit to any entertainment as a lapse from grace; who never impress people on their first contact as being full of the joy of the Lord. I say deliberately that their depression and joylessness is a hindrance to many; so far from raising an ensign on the road to righteousness they put another stone in the way. . . . It is not true to the genius of our faith.

Christianity, whenever it breaks as living water fresh from the rock, bubbles out ebulliently. The early Franciscans, the early Methodists, the early Salvationists—all were exuberantly happy. . . . So let us meet the world with joy!—a joy that can survive even our sufferings and sorrows.

Westminster Sermons (vol. i), pp 141–2

People whose ideas of saints are gathered, not from the record, but from common ignorance concerning them, suppose that they were 'born good', and had no battle to fight with a wild and passionate nature. What can they know of St Francis de Sales, or Fletcher of Madeley, or Margaret of Cortona?— who came through conflict to wholeness of personality, to poise in turmoil, and to power over temptation. It is part of the service of the saints . . . to point and prove the path to the conquest of self.

The problems of the self appear to have become more complicated of recent years. It was no news to the saints . . . that there was 'a different law' in their members warring against the law of the mind; but, since the modern psychologist has uncovered the subconscious and traced the hidden motive through the corridors of our mental underworld, the last shreds of our self-respect seem torn away. All life seems self, self, self. So chronic can egotism and selfishness become that many men are honestly unaware that they are there. Tennyson can write a dedicatory poem to his devoted wife ('Dear, near and true . . .') and eight of its thirteen lines are all about himself! A French valet, devoted to communism, bewildered his employer by leaving the party. . . . He said 'At the last meeting . . . it was proved that if all the wealth of the country were equally divided the share of each person would be two thousand francs.' 'So what?' asked his employer. 'Well,' replied the valet, 'I have five thousand francs.' Rank selfishness is not new. . . . We know that we are of the earth earthy, and feel again the greatness of those souls to whom real sanctity has come. 'There was a day', said George Müller, 'when I died, utterly died. . . .' Is this the secret? Have we to learn to die to self?

The Pure in Heart, pp 225–7

A man, with no interest in religion and something of a martyr to self-pity, read an article in a paper one day so gay and confident that he tossed it down in sheer annoyance and said something bitter about the cheap optimism of people who had never suffered as he had done. Somebody picked up the paper and recognized the author's name.

'You can't say *that* man hasn't suffered,' he said. 'I heard him once on "The Silver Lining" Programme. . . .' The story came out. While still a youngish man, the author had been forced to retire from his profession by a disease (incurable to medical science) which robbed him of his power to walk. Six years later, his devoted wife, on whom he so completely depended, died of cancer at thirty-nine. He was left with a very limited income to fend for himself and his two children. Neither his faith nor his courage flagged. . . .

Bewildered, the whiner said 'But how can a man with all that to endure, write in *this* way?' 'Well,' said his companion, 'he has religion. He *really* has it. I've heard him talk of Christ in a way which left me in no doubt that he knows Him personally; quite friends in fact. . . .'

That is how to nail it home. Don't let people think your joy arises from easy circumstances, good health and no troubles. If there is anything in you really to admire, it comes from Christ. Gently but quite firmly get them to recognize that.

Let them know that it was real *religion* that did this for you. Overcome your shyness to tell them that the explanation of it all is . . . Christ.

Westminster Sermons (vol. i), pp 143–4

. . . Before the eye of our imagination, the saints pass in all their noble pageantry. We see in them what God has done in human nature even on this earth, and we ask again what has happened to the 'self' within them so biased to evil. . . . What does their witness prove beyond a peradventure? That man *need not sin!* That it is possible, even in this evil world and with our infected nature, to act always with a perfect motive. Clearly it cannot be *non posse peccare.* Just as clearly, it *can* be *posse non peccare.**

Possible not to sin! There is the hope with which aspiring humanity faces the divine admonition, 'Be ye holy, for I am holy'. God lays no hopeless task upon us. We turn our eyes to the heights, and far above us we see the shining figures of the saints, and, in our hearts, we know that this is the way.

If self, then, cannot die in this life—in the sense that I can never hope to be beyond the *possibility* of a carnal thought, a stab of pride, a trace of envy—may I not justly hope that enticements to evil can all be kept within the confines of temptation, and that the Holy Ghost can give me constant victory over them as sins? May I not justly hope also that *self-centredness* can die? It has died in the saints. . . . Surely I need not be the centre of my own world? We have learned nothing of sanctity if we have not learned that the saints do not loom large to themselves. . . . Self-centredness can die! *Must* die! *Has* died in those elect souls. . . .

The Pure in Heart, pp 228–9

* 'not able to sin' . . . 'able not to sin'.

The Passing Years . . .

How long is it since I first became a Christian?
Have I grown steadily with the years?
Was I ever further forward than I am now?
Can I measure my progress in the last ten years?

five years?

twelve months?

I wonder how much of life remains?
What can I do now that I could not do five years ago?

Lead another man to Christ?
Distinguish guidance from my own desires?
Forgive those who wrong me?
Look death in the face and be un-afraid?
Really *enjoy* an hour of prayer?

When I think of 'getting on' in life, do I think of
worldly honours?
a larger income?
a bigger car?
a better job?
or more of grace?
and more of God?

Tell me, Father, am I really getting on?

A Spiritual Check-up

A Prayer

Lord Jesus,

Draw near in pity to us.

The nearer we come to Thee the further we feel away. Each upward step we take shows us greater distances still to tread.

Forgive us if we have sought our own sanctification and ignored the needs of the world.

Forgive us if the love we had for others and which we fancied so pure was tainted with self-concern; if we loved them because we wanted them to think what we think, do what we do . . . and not for themselves alone.

Enlarge our narrow hearts. Give us to yearn with Thee over our lost race. Help us, even when we feel the pain of the world's sin, not to feel superior to it or forget that so much of it is done in ignorance.

Change our nature into Thine, and so save us in every part of our being, that wherever we go Thy mighty heart may be beating in us, and Thy purposes shaping themselves in our eager minds, and Thy holy will directing us into wider fields of service.

> 'And we will ask for no reward
> Except to serve Thee still'
>
> for Thy name's sake.   Amen.

How Much are you Saved?, p 16

Slow Me Down, Lord

Give me, amidst the confusion of my day,
the calmness of the everlasting hills.
Break the tension of my nerves and muscles
with the soothing music of the singing streams
that live in my memory.
Help me to know
the magical restorative power of sleep.
Teach me the art of taking minute vacations . . .
of slowing down to look at a flower,
to chat with a friend,
to pat a dog,
to read a few lines from a good book.
Slow me down, Lord,
and inspire me to send my roots deep
into the soil of life's enduring values,
that I may grow
toward the stars of my greater destiny.

Amen.